MW01054230

WHILE I WAS PRAYING

Smyth & Helwys Publishing, Inc.
6316 Peake Road
Macon, Georgia 31210-3960
1-800-747-3016
©2006 by Smyth & Helwys Publishing

*Library of Congress Cataloging-in-Publication Data*

Hawkins, Ralph K.
While I was praying : finding insights about God in Old Testament
prayers / Ralph K. Hawkins.
p. cm.
Includes bibliographical references
ISBN 1-57312-463-X (pbk. : alk. paper)
1. God—Biblical teaching.
2. Bible. O.T.—Prayers.
I. Title.
BS1192.6.H39 2006
231—dc22

2005036838

# WHILE I WAS PRAYING

*Finding Insights about God
in Old Testament Prayers*

RALPH K. HAWKINS

## Dedication

To Cathy, who has prayed for me these last fifteen years

# CONTENTS

I have written *While I Was Praying* for a general readership. Few popular religious books expose readers to the ideas being discussed in the academy. One of my primary goals here has been to produce a book that can easily be understood by the non-specialist, but that includes discussion of archaeological and theological ideas. I have tried to accomplish my goal in a non-technical way and with a minimum of footnotes. This is not intended to be an exhaustive study of any of the topics introduced in the course of the discussion. The footnotes included, however, will often refer those interested in further reading to works that ill include more extensive annotation.

Throughout *While I Was Praying*, although I sometimes use the terms "God" and "Lord," I usually refer to Israel's God as "Yahweh." This term is used in academic circles, and it is the English equivalent of the divine name revealed to Moses in Exodus 3:14. It means something like "I am," "I am who I am," or possibly even "He who causes things to be." Yahweh was probably the name by which the ancient Jews knew their Lord.

# INTRODUCTION

Following the publication of Charles Darwin's *Origin of Species*, every field of inquiry began to remold itself in harmony with evolutionary theory. The study of religion was no exception, and in the latter part of the nineteenth century and the first half of the twentieth, the study of religion began to cast aside old ideas and assimilate new ones. Classic works like E. B. Tyler's *Primitive Culture*, Sir J. G. Frazer's many-volumed *The Golden Bough*, his three-volumed *The Folklore of the Old Testament*, and many other works by other authors all proclaimed that religion began with animism, evolved to polytheism, and then, only much later, developed into more advanced forms of religion, such as monotheism. It was thought that the religion of the Old Testament simply evolved out of prior systems of thought and many suggest that it is certainly not superior to other religions that developed in other times and places. If that is true, any distinctiveness of the Old Testament faith is thereby drastically reduced or even eliminated.

Despite the passage of time, these positions have not changed much—in fact, they have more or less become commonplace in seminaries and departments of religion.[1] The concept that monotheism developed out of prior polytheistic religious milieu has, in fact, dominated Old Testament studies. Most scholars have looked to a Canaanite background for the origins of Yahwism. Even as late as the time of the Judges, some scholars argue, Israel remained fully polytheistic.[2] Some of the more radical Old Testament scholars have even argued that "the statement that Yahweh is the God of Israel and Israel is the people of Yahweh was not formed until relatively late, perhaps barely in the pre-exilic period."[3] Baruch Levine, ordained rabbi and professor of Old Testament at New York University, has explained "the prevalent view" as follows:

> The period of the First Temple is seen as one of religious diversity and growing confrontations, as a time when most Israelites and their leaders had not yet accepted in practice the full force of exclusive monotheism and continued to worship the deities of the traditional, regional pantheon alongside the God of Israel, if not at times in place of him. In this view, the advocates of exclusive monotheism did not prevail until the eve of the Babylonian Exile, in the late seventh century BCE., at the earliest.[4]

The implications of these ideas are serious in that they eliminate any and all distinctiveness from ancient Israel. As one extreme minimalist has concluded, "Everything that we know about the culture of pre-exilic Israel confirms that there were no structural or ideological differences between the Israelites and the neighboring peoples."[5] A professor of Old Testament at Harvard has argued that Israel was really not that different from its neighbors and that Old Testament passages that *claim* distinctiveness for Israel were simply the nation's later efforts to *create* something like a "counter-identity."[6] According to this system of thought, the Old Testament was compiled over many years as "traditions circulated relatively freely, underwent changes, and [only] gradually became grouped together."[7] Douglas Knight, professor of Old Testament at Vanderbilt University, explains that, as a product of evolution, the theological message of the Old Testament "was always growing, in flux, adapting to new situations—and [is] not the expression of timeless, absolutistic revelation."[8]

If these assertions are true—if the differences between the Old Testament religion and those of Israel's neighbors are omitted—then one religion is as valid as another. It is true that Israel did have many items of belief and practice in common with other ancient peoples. But it is also true that the Old Testament and its theology contain many distinctive ideas that set the people of Israel apart from their neighbors. *While I Was Praying* will seek to explore a number of these distinctive ideas by looking at a number of prayers of Old Testament believers.

What better way to gain an idea of what the ancient Israelites thought about their God than to read their most intimate conversations with God? For in them they expressed what they believed to be the nature, characteristics, and attributes of God. Often, it was while they were praying or in answer to their praying that they received profound insight into the nature of

God. From Abraham's prayer of protest to Habakkuk's struggle to understand terrorism, we will seek to glean insights into how the ancient Hebrews understood their God and will address the kinds of questions raised in this introduction.

While the book focuses on Old Testament prayers, I have included the Lord's Prayer as my final chapter. In studying the Old Testament prayers and seeking to understand how the ancient Israelites perceived their God, I decided that Jesus' prayer was a vital piece of the tradition—considering that he was a devout Jew—and therefore it must be included. I believe this prayer will serve well as the final chapter in *While I Was Praying* because it includes a number of important ideas about God that will not be discussed in the other prayers.

One of the ways this book highlights the distinctive ideas of the Old Testament is by comparing and contrasting them with the ideas of Israel's neighbors. We are not necessarily interested in the habits, thoughts, and customs of the other ancient Middle Eastern peoples for their own sake but, as Norman Snaith wrote in the 1940s:

> We are concerned with them only in so far as the study of them throws into greater and clearer relief the essential differences. . . . The Bible certainly is literature, some of it comparable in excellence by any tests with any other literature in the world, but its value for us does not lie here. It is the Word of God . . . . If the Old Testament has . . . a value which no other book has, then it is essential for us to know and to be very sure what that value is, where it is different from other sacred books, and particularly where it is incomparable.[9]

Let us now embark on our journey together and see what the Old Testament believers learned about the nature of God while *they* were praying.

C H A P T E R   1

# A God Who Invites Bargaining

*Genesis 18:22-33*

When we turn to the prayer of Abraham, we are taken back almost four thousand years from our own day. Abraham likely lived early in the second millennium BC,[1] at the earliest stage of the history of God's people—almost one thousand years before the construction of the Jerusalem temple, before the development of any of Israel's religious institutions, and even before God's delivery of the Law at Mount Sinai. Abraham even preceded the disclosing of the divine name, which would not be revealed to Moses until more than four hundred years later.[2]

The period of Abraham's life described in Genesis 18–19 ends with the destruction of Sodom and Gomorrah, an event that is important for the writer of Genesis. All of Scripture affirms the significance of this story, "for the fate of Sodom and Gomorrah becomes a byword in the prophets and the New Testament and still lingers in popular religious consciousness."[3]

These cities were destroyed by fire and brimstone, a fact "viewed by some as characteristic of the vicious and brutal God of the [Old Testament]."[4] Some critics have alleged that the story is proof of God's injustice and indifference to human suffering,[5] arguing that God was willing to kill innocent people when destroying the cities. They see the story as a primitive myth about a primitive understanding of God. But when we examine the story and the prayer, we find the exact opposite. We find within Abraham's prayer and God's response a powerful revelation of the nature of God that becomes a first in the history of religious thought.

## GOD ANNOUNCES PLANS TO JUDGE SODOM

Our story begins toward the end of the occasion when "the Lord appeared to Abraham near the great trees of Mamre while he was sitting at the entrance to his tent in the heat of the day" (Gen 18:1). God had appeared to Abraham in the form of three travelers for whom he provided shade and a meal (18:1-8). During the meal, the travelers inquired after Abraham's wife, Sarah, and promised that within a year she would bear a son (v. 10). This was, of course, to be the beginning of the fulfillment of the promises God made to Abraham in Genesis 12:2-3: "I will make you into a great nation and I will bless you; I will make your name great, and you will be a blessing. I will bless those who bless you, and whoever curses you I will curse: and all peoples on earth will be blessed through you."

The story starts as the three travelers finish their meal and prepare to depart. Genesis 18:16-22 reads:

> When the men got up to leave, they looked down toward Sodom, and Abraham walked along with them to see them on their way. Then the Lord said, "Shall I hide from Abraham what I am about to do? Abraham will surely become a great and powerful nation, and all nations will be blessed through him. For I have chosen him . . . ."
>
> Then the Lord said, "The outcry against Sodom and Gomorrah is so great and their sin so grievous that I will go down and see if what they have done is as bad as the outcry that has reached me. If not, I will know."
>
> The men turned away and went toward Sodom, but Abraham remained standing before the Lord.

As the three men got up to leave, Abraham went with them to send them off. And all of a sudden, in v. 16, the reader's attention is directed to a seemingly insignificant gesture on the part of the three men as they got up to leave: "They looked down toward Sodom." As the men's heads turned to look down over the doomed city, so also the reader's attention is directed toward that city in anticipation of its coming destruction in the ext chapter.

In vv. 17-19 it appears that the Lord is speaking to Himself, considering whether to take Abraham into His confidence and relate His plans to him.[6] Abraham will certainly become a great and mighty nation. But God decides to relate His intentions to Abraham primarily because God has "chosen him" or, as it simply says in the Hebrew, God has "known him" (v. 19). And so the Lord informs His servant that He intends to determine whether Sodom should be destroyed due to its surpassing wickedness. Then the travelers start down from the hills near Hebron toward the city of Sodom.

## ABRAHAM'S INTERCESSION

What happens next is fascinating. The traditional text states that as the travelers departed, beginning their descent toward Sodom, "Abraham remained standing before the Lord" (v. 22b). But, as Bill Arnold suggests, "there [may be] good reason to think that 18:22b contains a rare intentional change in the text."[7] Arnold explains, "there is evidence that early Jewish scribes made an intentional change, and that the text originally read, 'The Lord remained standing before Abraham.' It seemed inappropriate to have the Sovereign Lord stand patiently waiting before his servant."[8] It may be that while the travelers headed down the hill to asses the situation in Sodom and to determine whether or not it warranted destructive judgment, "the Lord remained standing before Abraham" to see how he would respond to this news. If this is the correct reading, then the text is clearly suggesting that the Lord was instigating the prayer.[9] Arnold concludes,

> Either way, the phrase paints a striking picture. Whether Yahweh waits for Abraham to speak, or whether he waits while Abraham speaks, the passage portrays God patiently, even longingly, waiting for his servant to come to the rescue of potential victims of the crisis. The account teaches as much about God's view of intercessory prayer as it does about the nature of prayer itself.[10]

Abraham does indeed respond, and his extensive intercessory prayer and God's responses are found in Genesis 18:23-33:

> Then Abraham approached him and said: "Will you sweep away the righteous with the wicked? What if there are fifty righteous people in the city? Will you really sweep it away and not spare the place for the sake of the fifty righteous people in it? Far be it from you to do such a thing—to kill

the innocent with the wicked, treating the righteous and the wicked alike. Far be it from you! Will not the judge of all the earth do what is right?"

The Lord said, "If I find fifty righteous people in the city of Sodom, I will spare the whole place for their sake."

Then Abraham spoke up again: "Now that I have been so bold as to speak to the Lord, though I am nothing but dust and ashes, what if the number of the righteous is less than fifty? Will you destroy the whole city because of five people?"

"If I find forty-five there," he said, "I will not destroy it."

Once again he spoke to him, "What if only forty are found there?"

He said, "For the sake of forty, I will not do it."

Then he said, "May the Lord not be angry, but let me speak. What if only thirty can be found there?"

He answered, "I will not do it if I find thirty there."

Abraham said, "Now that I have been so bold as to speak to the Lord, what if only twenty can be found there?"

He said, "For the sake of twenty, I will not destroy it."

Then he said, "May the Lord not be angry, but let me speak just once more. What if only ten can be found there?"

He answered, "For the sake of ten, I will not destroy it."

When the Lord had finished speaking with Abraham, he left, and Abraham returned home.

This passage is not trying to show that God must be pushed and coerced before he will respond to his people. Rather, Abraham is trying to learn about this God whom he has only recently come to know.

As suggested above, these events had taken place long before any of the religious machinery was established for Israel. It's almost a thousand years before the temple will be built and at least four centuries before either the divine name or the Law will be revealed. Abraham knows nothing of the religion that will be revealed for Israel. In fact, Abraham himself was not even an Israelite! Before Abraham was called by God to travel from Haran to Canaan, he had lived with his family in Ur, which was located in southern Mesopotamia, in Babylon.[11] Remember the tower of Babel incident? This is where that would have taken place. Abraham was seventy-five years old when God called him to leave Mesopotamia. We would assume that he had spent his whole life up to this point worshiping the gods associated with these areas (Josh 24:2).

The point is that Abraham was steeped in the religion of Mesopotamia before God called him to leave the gods of Babylon behind and travel to a land God would show him. Even when Abraham responded to the call of God, we can assume he knew virtually nothing of the nature and character of God.

This is an amazing passage of Scripture because Abraham is arguing that God must abide by a standard, that God's very nature is just, and that God is the Judge of all the earth who must therefore do what is right. Never before in the ancient Middle East had anyone argued that the behavior of the gods, or a god, had to be held in check by standards of right and wrong. In fact, the opposite was true.

In the mythology of Mesopotamia, the gods were created in the image of people. It was thought that the gods created human beings because they were lazy and wanted slaves to do their work for them. They were capricious and unpredictable, flying into rages and going to war. The gods were not bound by any moral constraints, and they chased after women and engaged in all kinds of licentious behavior. The gods depended on people to feed them. The behavior of the gods was not influenced by what men and women did, and if the gods were to respond to humankind, humans would first have to beg, prod, and cajole the gods.

But you see here that God has revealed enough about Himself to Abraham that somehow Abraham knows this God is different. For this reason, Abraham seeks to test the limits of God's mercy. Bill Arnold concludes,

> The point of Abraham's hesitant bargaining is not that God needs us to cajole and bicker with him. Rather, this is a bold exploration of God's mind and heart. This was new territory for Abraham. He knew of God's intentions to destroy the city [of Sodom], but he was not sure of the limits to God's mercy. For Lot's sake, he was willing to find out.[12]

In the end, there were not even ten righteous people to be found in the city, and God did destroy it because of its wickedness. But when God did, He remembered Abraham's prayer and therefore saved Lot (19:29).

## PRAYING WHEN GOD DOESN'T MAKE SENSE

For modern readers of this account of Abraham's intercession, there are three significant lessons to be learned about prayer from this tale. First, this is the story of how God invites one to prayer. Once the Lord takes Abraham into His confidence and informs Abraham that God intends to determine whether Sodom should be destroyed because of its wickedness, the travelers then head down the hills toward the city. At this point, the Lord "remained standing before Abraham" (v. 22b). It is as if the Lord is waiting to see whether Abraham will pray on their behalf or is perhaps inviting him to pray. The text seems to suggest that the Lord Himself was instigating Abraham's prayer. For modern believers, this provides a significant teaching: God invites us to pray in the confusions and quandaries of life. When life does not make sense, God invites us to pray. When the meaning of our circumstances is not clear, God invites us to pray. And, maybe more than at any other time, when we do not understand what God is doing, God invites us to pray.

When our lives do not make sense, we often run into what James Dobson has called the "betrayal barrier."[13] We feel that God has betrayed us and we turn away from God. Rather than turning *away* from God in the midst of crisis, we should do as Abraham did and turn *to* God. Perhaps during the pause between the time when the strangers began heading down the hill toward Sodom and the time Abraham spoke, Abraham was considering how to respond to what God had said. Once the Lord had announced His plans to weigh Sodom, and possibly destroy the city, maybe Abraham was struggling with how to respond. Could he have been trying to make sense of God's plans? Was he trying to contain his anger or sense of betrayal, since the town God was considering whether to destroy was the town in which his nephew lived? Could it be that Abraham was struggling with the "betrayal barrier"? One thing is clear: Abraham did not understand how God could maintain the justness of His character and destroy a city in which there might be even just a few righteous people. It is certain that Abraham struggled with these issues.

This is why Abraham is a model of faith. While he was clearly struggling with what he knew God was about to do—struggling with whether his God was about to act unjustly—he turned *to* God in prayer instead of *away* from God. The fact that he prayed does not mean he felt good about or comfortable with God at that moment. Again, it is clear that he did not. His prayer with God is more a haggling or bargaining session than anything else, which implies that he was frustrated with God or unsure about the justice of God's approach to the matter at hand. We learn from Abraham's prayer that we should approach God not only in times of joy and gladness, but also in times of anger and bitterness. I have heard pious people shocked by the very suggestion that we might ever express disillusionment or anger with God *to* God. How could a believer address God in such a way? The implication seems to be that we should only address God in pious platitudes, using "Thee" and "Thou" and other such acknowledgments of God's otherworldly grandeur. However, we must understand that mature relationships require honest expressions of emotion. If a married person, for example, were to perpetually hide some frustration with his or her spouse, it could spell disaster for their relationship. Instead of hiding their feelings, the successful married couple understands that they must be willing to address problem areas in their relationships in order that they might work through them. When the husband asks the wife, "What's wrong?" she will not be taking steps toward improving the relationship if she responds, "Nothing." If she has something she needs to talk about, then she would be less than honest with this reply. Human relationships do not improve when we are not honest with one another. In the same way, our relationship with God will not be improved when we are less than honest with God. Only when we feel we can pray to God about anything—no matter how "unchristian" it might appear—will our relationship with God survive and flourish through the hard times.

## BARGAINING WITH GOD

A second significant element of Abraham's prayer is his effort to bargain with God. After God reveals His plans to Abraham, the patriarch then challenges God, saying,

> Will you sweep away the righteous with the wicked? What if there are fifty righteous people in the city? Will you really sweep it way and not spare the place for the sake of the fifty righteous people in it? Far be it from you to do such a thing—to kill the innocent with the wicked, treating the righteous and the wicked alike. Far be it from you! Will not the judge of all the earth do what is right? (Gen 18:23-25)

The Lord then relents from His plans to destroy the city, agreeing that if He were to find fifty righteous people in the city He would not destroy it (v. 26). Abraham reduces the number to forty-five, forty, thirty, twenty, and, finally, ten (vv. 27-33). Again, the most significant aspect of this passage is that the father of Israel is learning about this God whom he has only recently come to know.

Yet, we also see a model for a kind of prayer that has been almost completely absent from the Christian tradition—the prayer of bargaining. Like the idea of expressing anger toward God, the concept of bargaining with God has been unwelcome in Christian tradition. The prayer of bargaining has, however, been an accepted practice within Judaism for many years. The psalmist, for example, argues that God should rescue him because, if he were to die, he would not be able to praise him from the grave:

> Turn, O Lord, save my life;
>> Deliver me for the sake of your steadfast love.
> For in death there is no remembrance of you;
>> In Sheol who can give you praise? (Ps 6:4-5)

In another passage, Jonah prays a prayer of bargaining to God as he sinks through the water after having been thrown overboard in the Mediterranean Sea:

> As my life was ebbing away,
>> I remembered the Lord;
> And my prayer came to you, into your holy temple.
> Those who worship vain idols
>> Forsake their true loyalty.
> But I with the voice of thanksgiving
>> Will sacrifice to you;
> What I have vowed I will pay.
>> Deliverance belongs to the Lord! (Jonah 2:7-9)

Apparently, as Jonah was sinking, he "vowed" that if the Lord were to rescue him, he would make a sacrifice of thanksgiving to the Lord at the Jerusalem temple.

A friend who had struggled with alcohol for many years shared with me how he was unable to become sober until his sponsor urged him to use a "prayer of bargaining." He explained that he would begin the day by getting on his knees and praying the following prayer: "O Lord, if you will protect me from the desire to drink today, then I won't drink." I must admit I had a great deal of difficulty understanding this prayer when my friend first shared it with me. It seemed to me to be nothing more than a convenient way of shifting the blame for a binge. If he "fell off the wagon" on that particular day, he could simply say, "Oh well, the Lord didn't protect me from the desire to drink today. So the fact that I got drunk was God's fault." On the contrary, my friend explained, the prayer served as a powerful tool for self-analysis. If he prayed this prayer and got drunk anyway, he could know for sure that he had not really turned his desire to drink over to the Lord. He would know that he had not been honest in praying for the Lord to protect him from the desire to drink on that day. He would have learned that his continued drinking stemmed from a refusal truly to depend on the Lord for sobriety.

It began to dawn on me what my friend was trying to explain to me: the prayer of bargaining had been, for him, a way to discern what his true intentions were. After making the bargain with God, he could discover whether or not he was truly committed to giving up his drinking by whether he kept his part of the bargain. God would uphold God's side of the bargain, so binges would reveal that my friend had made the bargain in insincerity. The prayer of bargaining might prove helpful to people struggling with substance abuse or possibly to those attempting to cope with other destructive behaviors. Someone who is grappling with repeatedly "blowing up" at his spouse, for example, might pray, "O Lord, if you will keep me from rage today, I won't blow up at my spouse." While a "prayer of bargaining" would certainly not be a substitute for counseling in the case of people struggling with destructive behaviors, it could function as an important spiritual tool in terms of shedding light on the problem and helping that person depend on God.

## PRAYING FOR OUR ENEMIES

A third dimension of Abraham's prayer that deserves attention is the fact that, while other prophets—such as Moses, Samuel, and Jeremiah—made intercession for Israel, here Abraham is actually praying *for* the Canaanites. Abraham prays for unbelievers because he was once an unbeliever. As we discussed earlier in the chapter, Abraham came from Mesopotamia. He was not an Israelite; he was a precursor of the Israelites. He had an affinity with the Canaanites into whose land he had migrated.

The Hebrews had not always been in a relationship with God. Prior to the giving of the Law on Mt. Sinai, much of Israel's past was formed through the calling of non-Israelites—God made Israel out of Mesopotamians and Canaanites. The nation God made was essentially formed over a four-hundred-year period of bondage in Egypt. In fact, much of the motivation for Old Testament laws is based on remembrance of that fact in particular ways:

- Israel is to be generous with those who are indebted, because the Lord was generous with Israel in bringing them out of bondage (Deut 15:1-18).
- Israel is to free their slaves after a prescribed length of time, because "you were a slave in the land of Egypt, and the Lord your God redeemed you; for this reason I lay this command upon you today" (Deut 15:15).
- Aliens are not to be oppressed but are to be treated as citizens, with love, "for you were aliens in the land of Egypt" (Lev 19:33-34).

So, even while the Israelites would have continued conflict with non-Israelites throughout the Old Testament period, it was part of their heritage to reach out to and pray for "outsiders."

This is certainly a tradition that is carried into the New Testament. Jesus said:

> You have heard that it was said, "You shall love your neighbor and hate your enemy." But I say to you, Love your enemies and pray for those who persecute you, so that you may be children of your Father in heaven; for he makes his sun rise on the evil and the good, and sends rain on the righteous and on the unrighteous. (Matt 5:43-45)

The apostle Paul instructs Christians to "bless those who persecute you" (Rom 12:14), explaining that the natural Christian behavior toward outsiders or persecutors is that "when reviled, we bless" (1 Cor 4:12).

This is not an easy teaching to implement. But it is the case throughout the Bible that, because those whom God loves have experienced God's grace, they are to seek to spread that grace to those who remain alienated from Him.

## CONCLUSIONS

What we have encountered here is the story of a bargaining prayer by a man learning about the nature of a God just beginning to be revealed in the world. It's an amazing prayer because it reveals characteristics that had never been encountered in any of the gods of the nations. Through it we learn that God is just and righteous, that God is the Judge of all the earth, and that when God acts He will always do what is right.

### CONNECTIONS: DO YOU HAVE A CHRISTIAN WORLDVIEW?

In the prayer of Genesis 18, one of the things Abraham was struggling with was his "worldview." Our "worldview" "is simply the sum total of our beliefs about the world, the "'big picture' that directs our daily decisions and actions."[14]

According to pollster George Barna, only about 7 percent of all Protestants have a "biblical" worldview. Those who would call themselves "born again" don't fare much better—only 9 percent of them have a biblical worldview.[15] Our culture as a whole seems to be more biblically illiterate than ever before. Among the culture at large:

• 48 percent believe that, after he was crucified and died, Jesus did not experience a physical resurrection;
• 35 percent believe morality is relative;
• 65 percent do not believe in Satan;
• 65 percent believe people can earn a place in heaven by being good;
• 50 percent believe all people experience the same outcome after death, regardless of their spiritual beliefs;
• 26 percent believe that, after death, some people are reincarnated in another life form; and
• 55 percent believe one can lead a full and satisfying life without pursuing spirituality at all.[16]

The statistics are not much different for those who are "born again."[17] Biblical truth and the way it shapes our worldviews has suffered a serious blow in today's postmodern culture, where all viewpoints, all lifestyles, all beliefs, and all behaviors are seen as equally valid.

Christianity claims, however, to be "a way of seeing and comprehending all reality."[18] Colson and Pearcey explain:

> The scriptural basis for this understanding is the creation account, where we are told that God spoke everything into being out of nothing (see Gen 1 and John 1:1-14). Everything that exists came into being at his command and is therefore subject to him, finding its purpose and meaning in him. The implication is that in every topic we investigate, from ethics to economics to ecology, the truth is found only in relationship to God and his revelation.[19]

Christianity claims to give us the roadmap for living. Do we believe it? Do we live it? Each day you and I make decisions that contribute toward constructing one kind of world or another. Are we caught up in faddish worldviews? Or are we helping to build a new world characterized by the truths of the Bible and the message of Christ?

## Discussion Questions

1. Have you ever felt that the Lord was inviting you or prompting you to pray? If so, in what ways?

2. Have you ever "bargained with God"? Is so, how? What did you learn from the experience?

3. What does Abraham's prayer teach about welcoming outsiders? About loving our enemies?

## CHAPTER 2

# A God Who Salvages Suffering

*Genesis 32:22-31*

Jacob was a man for whom all of life seemed a struggle. His relationship with his family was a struggle. His relationship with God was a struggle. And seeking to understand a mysterious event in Jacob's life has been a struggle for generations of Bible readers. However, when we take the time to study Jacob's life, we can begin to make some sense out of the Jabbok event described in Genesis 32, even if we don't fully understand all the details.

The Jabbok event is basically the culmination of a lifetime of struggle. True to the meaning of his name, Jacob is a man who essentially spends his life trying to get ahead, to overcome others, "to supplant." He spends his life grasping for advantage. Like Jacob, many of us spend our lives running after something only to discover that whatever we were chasing is right behind us, bearing down on us. It may only be while we are sitting in the dark by our own Jabbok, trying to sort out our worst fears, that the "something" ambushes us.

## SETTING THE STAGE

Jacob's story begins at Genesis 25, where his birth becomes a preview of his character throughout much of his life. Even as Jacob and his twin brother,

Esau, emerged from their mother's womb, Jacob was grasping his older brother's heel. He was therefore given the name "Jacob," which means something like "he takes by the heel" or "he supplants." Jacob's name did not portend an optimistic future, and most of the remainder of the book of Genesis is consumed with Jacob's struggles with his family and with God. In chapter 25, Jacob manipulates his brother out of his birthright. In chapter 27, through trickery that deceives his father as well, Jacob steals Esau's blessing. Esau was so angry that he planned to kill Jacob as soon as their father died (Gen 27:41), so their mother urged Jacob to flee the promised land and find refuge with an uncle, Laban, who lived in Haran, from which Abraham had been called earlier.

This is a story full of suspense and tension. Jacob has inherited the threefold blessing of Abraham, which his father pronounced on him, saying,

> May God Almighty bless you and make you fruitful and numerous, that you may become a company of peoples. May he give to you the blessings of Abraham, to you and to your offspring with you, so that you may take possession of the land where you now live as an alien—land that God gave to Abraham. (Gen 28:3-4)

Yet, following his receipt of the promise, we find Jacob, the promised son, running for his life *away* from the promised land. In fact, although Jacob's mother thought she was sending him away only for "a few days" (27:44, NKJV), she would actually never see him again. It would be twenty years before Jacob returned to the promised land.

Jacob's story grows worse following his settlement in Haran. His uncle Laban exercised the same kind of trickery Jacob had used on his father earlier in order to secure Jacob's labor for more than fourteen years (Gen 29:1-30). Although Jacob secured two wives through his labor, his favoritism for one of them eventually resulted in a great deal of conflict that plagued him for the rest of his life (Gen 29:31–30:24). Jacob eventually became embroiled in controversy with Laban, and he began to suspect that it might be time to return to Canaan (Gen 31).

After Jacob and his family fled Laban's estate in the night (31:1-21) and were pursued by him through part of their journey toward Canaan (31:22-42), Jacob began to worry how Esau would respond to his return. Apparently he feared the worst, because he sent messengers to Esau implying that his livestock were Esau's for the taking (32:4-5) and placing himself at Esau's disposal. Jacob's messengers returned with disheartening news: Esau was on his way to meet Jacob with a personal army of four hundred men in tow.

Jacob was desperate. He divided his family and property into two groups in hopes that he could save at least one. Then he prayed what is surely one of the great prayers of the book of Genesis, in which he clearly acknowledged that he had no hope of survival apart from God. He said,

> O God of my father Abraham and God of my father Isaac, O Lord who said to me, "Return to your country and to your kindred, and I will do you good." I am not worthy of the least of all the steadfast love and all the faithfulness that you have shown to your servant, for with only my staff I crossed this Jordan; and now I have become two companies. Deliver me, please, from the hand of my brother, from the hand of Esau, for I am afraid of him; he may come and kill us all, the mothers with the children. Yet you have said, "I will surely do you good, and make your offspring as the sand of the sea, which cannot be counted because of their number." (32:9-12)

Jacob was not satisfied with prayer by itself, and so he sent several substantial waves of gifts for Esau, consisting of goats, lambs, rams, camels, cows, and donkeys (vv. 13-21). Along with each set of gifts, Jacob sent a message indicating that Esau's servant, Jacob, would be following behind. All of the tension that has been building in the text finally reaches a crescendo when Jacob wrestles with God at the Jabbok River. Bill Arnold writes that "Jacob's bizarre encounter with God at Peniel is the central episode in the description of Jacob's return to Canaan. It is framed literally by his preparation to meet Esau (32:3-21) and the meeting with Esau itself (33:1-20)."[1]

## THE DANGEROUS NIGHT CROSSING OF THE JABBOK

It appears that Jacob had intended that he and his family encamp beside the Jabbok River, their last barrier to Canaan, before crossing back into the promised land (32:21). But apparently Jacob was unable to sleep in the face of his pending encounter with Esau, for "that night Jacob got up and took his two wives, his two maidservants, and his eleven sons and crossed the ford of the Jabbok" (32:22). It appears that, once Jacob's family had safely completed this dangerous night crossing, for some unknown reason he returned to the northern bank of the Jabbok. The Talmud suggests that Jacob had forgotten some "small earthenware pitchers" and went back to get them.[2]

Speculating about Jacob's puzzling actions, Gordan Wenham writes that "it is not clear why Jacob should have brought his family across the Jabbok and then returned to the northern side alone. Was it duty, or anxiety, or simply to inform us that there was none of his party with him when he was attacked?"[3] Joyce Baldwin has suggested that Jacob crossed the Jabbok in order to spend the night alone in prayer.[4] In any case, Jacob was alone when his mysterious confrontation occurred.

## JACOB'S MYSTERIOUS CONFRONTATION

After he had sent them across the stream, he sent over all his possessions. So Jacob was left alone, and a man wrestled with him till daybreak. When the man saw that he could not overpower him, he touched the socket of Jacob's hip so that his hip was wrenched as he wrestled with the man. Then the man said, "Let me go, for it is daybreak."

But Jacob replied, "I will not let you go unless you bless me."

The man asked him, "What is your name?"

"Jacob," he answered.

Then the man said, "Your name will no longer be Jacob, but Israel, because you have struggled with God and with men and have overcome."

Jacob said, "Please tell me your name."

But he replied, "Why do you ask my name?" Then he blessed him there.

So Jacob called the place Peniel, saying, "It is because I saw God face to face, and yet my life was spared."

The sun rose above him as he passed Peniel, and he was limping because of his hip. (Gen 32:23-31)

The nature of Jacob's experience has puzzled readers for generations. The ancient rabbis explained that this "man" was the guardian angel of Esau in the form of a man.[5] Some modern commentators have suggested that the nameless wrestler must be some sort of river demon,[6] while others have suggested that "he is the embodiment of portentous antagonism in Jacob's dark night of the soul."[7] In the latter case, this would mean Jacob's grappling was only with himself, or possibly a grappling in prayer.

The Genesis account simply says Jacob's adversary was a man (v. 25). Hosea 12:4 states that Jacob's struggle was with an angel. At the end of the account, however, we are told that Jacob believed it was God whom he had seen face to face (v. 31). In the Old Testament era, it seems that the titles

"God" and "angel" may have been "somewhat interchangeable."[8] Gordon Wenham concludes that:

> the nature of Jacob's experience [is not] very clear. It does not seem to have been just a dream, nor can it be spiritualized into wrestling in prayer; it does appear that a real fight was involved, for Jacob went on his way limping (32:32). But having said that, the nature of the experience still remains mysterious, as all encounters with God must necessarily be.[9]

Nevertheless, the man "struggled with him" (v. 25), and Jacob had to fight for his life. The Hebrew verb translated "he struggled" rhymes with the name "Jacob" and is probably a play on the patriarch's name. The stranger's attack on Jacob might be paraphrased to read "he Jacobed him."[10] In other words, Jacob's duplicity backfired on him. Jacob, who had been the victorious manipulator, was now overpowered by God.

The struggle continued throughout the night, and dawn began to approach. At that point, the man, realizing "that he could not win, touched his hip socket, and Jacob's hip was dislocated as he struggled with him" (v. 26). While it may seem amazing that the stranger "could not win," "for Jacob . . . it was amazing that his opponent merely by touching his hip could dislocate it."[11] While some translations read that the stranger "struck" Jacob's hip, the Hebrew verb used here always means "to touch" or even to "barely touch." It's almost as if the stranger maimed Jacob with "a magic touch."[12]

At this point, Jacob's assailant demanded to be let go. But this duplicitous patriarch—whose "life has been characterized by struggle, particularly by a struggle to obtain a blessing from God"[13]—refused to let his assailant go without a blessing (v. 27). Maybe Jacob suspected that this was no mere human attacker. In any case, in order to bestow the blessing, the stranger asked the patriarch's name. Jacob's answer has traditionally been interpreted as an admission of guilt, as Arnold explains, "Jacob's answer is a confession, since he is admitting, as Esau observed years before, that he is rightly named (27:36). He has been a deceiving trickster from birth, and his current predicament with Esau is the result."[14]

Jacob's reputation as someone with a "grasping" nature, or as a "supplanter," was so well known that Hosea described him as one who had spent his life striving (Hos 12:2-4). Jeremiah even used the name in what may have been a common saying when he said that "Every brother Jacobs," which the RSV renders "Every brother is a supplanter." As Jacob wrestled in the dark, dreading his encounter with his brother Esau, the mumbling of his name to his assailant may have been an admission that he had cheated his brother. As Esau said, "Is he not rightly called Jacob? He has tricked me [Jacobed me] these two times" (27:36).

What happened next was incredibly significant in Jacob's life. Instead of simply bestowing a blessing upon Jacob, his opponent changed his name to "Israel," which forms a wordplay with his explanation: "for you have striven with God and with men, and have prevailed" (v. 28). The name "Israel" could be translated "God fights" or "God rules." As in many other passages in the Bible, a midlife name change represented a change in character. Abram,[15] Gideon,[16] and Simon[17] all underwent name changes, which symbolized a new standing for each of them. For Jacob, "the new name would attest his new standing: it was both a mark of grace, wiping out an old reproach (27:36), and an accolade to live up to."[18] Arnold summarizes, "This was God's answer to the problem of Jacob's duplicitous and grasping tendencies. God was in the circumstances and affairs of Jacob's life, working to transform his character. The transformation was accompanied by [this] important blessing of God."[19] The patriarch's old name—Jacob—brought to mind his past manipulative, underhanded dealings. This new name, Israel, was the blessing he had asked for. It would bring to mind this occasion in which he wrestled with God and prevailed.

Jacob revealed what, for him, had been the most important aspect of the encounter when he said, "I saw God face to face, and yet I was spared" (v. 30). Moses had been expressly told that no one could look on God's face and live (Exod 33:20). Jacob's statement here reveals that, despite the harrowing nature of his encounter, it had been an encounter that revealed God's grace. His life had been "rescued." And if he had survived meeting God, then surely he would survive his upcoming meeting with Esau.

## JACOB'S TRANSFORMATION

There are a number of powerful lessons the contemporary reader can learn from Jacob's encounter at the Jabbok River. The first lesson has to do with the *nature* of Jacob's transformation. As we have seen, the Old Testament seems to suggest that Jacob's mysterious encounter transformed him. The implication is that his duplicity will stop and that he will no longer be always "grasping."

However, Jacob's duplicity seems to continue when he does encounter Esau (33:13). Then, although he sends Esau ahead and claims he will meet him at a particular location, we find Jacob traveling in the opposite direction

(33:16-17). How can this be? Was Jacob's encounter with God not effica-
cious? Could Jacob have encountered God and remained unchanged? Rabbi
Burton Visotzky has argued that there is no change in Jacob at all following
this encounter with God. Visotzky says,

> You think, "Oh, now he's going to change." Indeed, his name changes. But
> then he faces Esau and lies to him again and again, not just about where
> he's going but also about his children—"Well, the children are a little frail,
> and if we keep pushing on, all these cattle will die." Nothing about Jacob
> changes. In a way . . . [it's] depressing.[20]

But Visotzky is too harsh in his criticism of Jacob. Roberta Hestenes
responds to Visotzky's negative assessment of Jacob, saying,

> Somehow, because Jacob has an encounter with God, which does change
> him, we expect him to be a perfect person all of a sudden. I think the story
> tells us that the encounter with God changes us, but not to perfection. We
> are still human. We still bear the marks of everything we are. But Jacob is a
> different man after that encounter.[21]

The truth of the matter is that Jacob *is* changed, even if only gradually.
Although his subsequent performance with Esau leaves something to be
desired, we begin to see significant changes by the end of his life. E. A.
Speiser has noted that "[t]he man who could be a party to the cruel hoax
that was played on his father and brother, and who fought Laban's treachery
with crafty schemes of his own, will soon condemn the vengeful deed by
Simeon and Levi (xxxiv) by invoking a higher concept of morality" (xlix).[22]
Jacob's change was gradual and long term. The effects of the Jabbok event
continued throughout Jacob's life. The writer of Genesis did not clean up the
story for us, and we are allowed to see Jacob's continued foibles—even after
his theophany! In commenting further on the story, Hestenes also says,

> For me, it's very important that Jacob not be whitewashed, because if the
> hidden assumption here is that God should work only with people who are
> perfect, or that God is somehow immoral, then I'm doomed. All of us are
> out of it. But God doesn't work only with perfect people. The fact that
> God works with this person, with all of his conflicting pushes and drives
> and struggles, is a sign of hope that God actually works with human
> beings.[23]

Indeed, the story of Jacob's encounter with God at the Jabbok River is not the story of how God magically transforms people. Transformation seldom occurs suddenly and completely but rather comes about only gradually, over the course of a lifetime. John Kselman, a Roman Catholic priest, points out that Jacob's imperfection and God's blessing of him despite that imperfection is exactly the point of the story: "The story isn't about morality . . . . It's about grace—the unexpected and unearned. To me, that's the wonder of this story. It's about free gifts given to the most undeserving people. I still think Jacob is duplicitous. But that encourages me."[24] Indeed, noting that Jacob did not triumph over his duplicity immediately, rabbinic commentators have suggested that his name change was not intended to be effective immediately. Assuming it was an angel with whom Jacob struggled, they suggest that the divine messenger was "merely revealing to Jacob what God himself would do later."[25] And, in fact, the patriarch continues to be referred to by the name Jacob until Genesis 35:9-10, where we are told that "[a]fter Jacob returned from Paddan Aram, God appeared to him again and blessed him. God said to him, 'Your name is Jacob, but you will no longer be called Jacob; your name will be Israel. So he named him Israel.'"

Regardless of the exact timing of the name change, the point is the same: the transformation of one's character occurs over extended periods of time. God may confer His blessing in one encounter, but those blessings are cultivated and realized over the course of a lifetime.

Another powerful lesson for modern readers has to do with the *means* of Jacob's transformation. Jacob receives his blessing, and is transformed, through suffering. At the end of his encounter with God, we find Jacob "limping because of his hip" (Gen 32:31). This idea, "that God, in blessing Jacob, also appeared to oppose him, and caused him pain,"[26] was difficult for early biblical commentators to accept. However, as David Pennant explains,

This turns out to be a recurring pattern in Scripture. Abraham, called the friend of God (Isa 41:8), suffered much anguish in waiting years for the promised son, only to find himself driving off Hagar and Ishmael twice . . . and then discovering he was commanded to kill Isaac (Gen 16; 21; 22). Moses was not only in danger of death from God . . . but in accepting God's call, ran danger of death from Pharaoh (Exod 10:28), and even from the people of God (17:4). Job, one of God's special favorites, actually had Satan's attention drawn to him by God himself, which resulted in great suffering and harassment (Job 1:8). Jeremiah, spokesman for God, was bitterly opposed by his generation (Jer 20:7-8), as was Jesus himself in his turn (Matt 27:41-4). Paul, outstanding missionary, was made aware at his call of how it would mean suffering for him (Acts 9:16; see 2 Cor 1:5; ch. 12).[27]

Father Kselman suggests the applicability of these traditions for modern believers:

> We often talk, and I think quite properly, of God as Father and of God as Protector. But what about God as Adversary? There's a long biblical tradition in the Book of Job and other places of God taking an adversarial position. But the mystery is that even the Adversary continues to love the one with whom the Adversary struggles.[28]

Many believers are uncomfortable with the revelation that God may not protect us from undergoing great personal difficulties, much less that God would force us to undergo severe struggles. How can it be that God would do these things? Why would God ever force His children into a position in which they may not be content with His leading?

## THE TRANSFORMATIVE POWER OF CRISIS

The answer is that when you and I spend our lives trying to pull ourselves up by our own bootstraps, those straps will eventually become threadbare, stretch, and break. It is often only at that point that we will truly turn to God. Many times crises have a transformative power unavailable to those who have lived the sheltered, protected life. Sometimes only when we become weak in and of ourselves are we willing to turn to God. When we are no longer in a position to depend on ourselves, we can learn to depend on God.

The apostle Paul certainly knew this. Paul had apparently grown up in an influential family, since Jewish families weren't ordinarily granted Roman citizenship. He was a Hebrew of Hebrews, blameless according to the Law. He was a member of the strictest Jewish sect—the Pharisees. He had been educated under one of the most renowned rabbis of his day—Gamaliel. It would have been easy for Paul to live independently, self-sufficiently, relying on no one but himself. It would have been easy for Paul to blind himself to his real need for God. With such status and credentials, it would have been difficult for Paul to learn to depend on God. And apparently that was exactly what happened, because Paul writes that he was given "a thorn in the flesh, a messenger of Satan, to harass me, to keep me from being too elated" (2 Cor 12:7). He pleaded with the Lord three times to remove it, but the Lord answered, "My grace is sufficient for you, for my power is made perfect in weakness" (12:9a). Paul concluded, "I will all the more gladly boast of my weaknesses, that the power of Christ may rest upon me. For the sake of Christ, then, I am content with weaknesses, insults, hardships, persecutions, and calamities; for when I am weak, then I am strong" (12:9b-10). It was through struggle with his thorn that Paul learned to find his true strength: dependence on the Lord Himself.

This truth is difficult for modern Americans to grasp. The merits of rugged individualism have been a hallmark of the American psyche for generations. All of us have been urged at one time or another to "pull yourself up by your own bootstraps," the implication being that if we will only force ourselves to be strong enough, then we can "make it" in life. But this is not the way of the gospel. In recent years, many social scientists, psychologists, and theologians have begun to figure out what the Bible has taught all along: real, substantive strength comes through weakness. Psychotherapist Robert M. Alter, for example, has written a book titled *The Transformative Power of Crisis: Our Journey to Psychological Healing and Spiritual Awakening*, attempting to elucidate this concept.[29] In it, he writes,

> To be strong, you will need to be "weak" sometimes. You'd better make sure to fall apart now and then. Falling apart allows you to keep it together. So you might have to periodically break down and cry and be scared and feel sorry for yourself. . . . Cry your eyes out—give yourself permission to be "weak"—so that you can turn around and be strong.[30]

While Alter's instructions fall short of the apostle Paul's understanding of finding strength in weakness, he illustrates the principle powerfully. It is, indeed, only through "weakness" that we can become humble enough to rely fully on our Lord.

## CONCLUSIONS

After a lifetime of duplicity, Jacob was ambushed by God. He struggled with God, and he walked away wounded. But Jacob's wound was a gift. It symbolizes for us that when we wrestle with God, we will not emerge from that encounter unchanged. The change can be painful. However, being unwounded or invulnerable does not bring about blessing in our lives. It is not out of perfect strength or infinite wisdom that we find blessing. Rather, modern people, just like Jacob, will find blessing only in our vulnerability, suffering, and brokenness. It is through these dimensions of our journey that we learn to depend on Christ.

## CONNECTIONS: CAN YOU BE A WOUNDED HEALER?

Discovering the power of weakness is not only conducive to our personal spiritual growth, but it may be that we could go so far as to say that it is *necessary* for effective Christian service or ministry. As explored in the chapter, this goes against our natural inclinations to hide our weaknesses and instead put forward an exterior image of strength and confidence. When someone who has never grown at their greatest point of weakness is placed in a leadership position, they will sometimes attempt to project a supreme confidence in that area where they have the greatest deficiency. And just as a chain is only as strong as its weakest link, it will be at this point that their leadership will snap.

Many years ago, a friend of mine was pastor of a church where the vestry (church board) chairperson—Miriam—was emotionally unhealthy. It seemed clear to everyone involved that her tyrannical style of leadership was a way of trying to cover up the feelings of inadequacy, fear, and weakness she felt inside. After repeated attempts to break through the shell of authoritarianism Miriam had constructed, her colleagues resorted to calling in a denominational officer to assist them in a forced intervention. As the members of the vestry explained the ways in which her leadership had been abusive both to them and to the rest of the congregation, Miriam began to cry. The denominational official said, "Miriam, the members of your vestry love you. Why won't you let them help you?" With her head in her hands, Miriam sobbed, "But I don't *need* help!" Miriam refused to let God into the broken places in her life and, therefore, was unable to receive His transforming and empowering grace. Consequently, she was also unable truly to be a servant leader.

Thornton Wilder wrote a play based on John 5 called *The Angel that Troubled the Waters*. In this dramatic reenactment of the healings that occurred when an angel stirred the waters of the pool at Bethesda, an elderly physician is barred by an angel from entering the healing waters when he seeks help to do so. The angel asks the despairing physician, "Without your wounds where would your power be? . . . In Love's service, only wounded soldiers can serve."[31] Wilder understood that we can never truly reach out to others until we have been ministered to in our own brokenness.

Henri Nouwen developed this idea at length in his classic work, *The Wounded Healer*, in which he explains, "the paradox of Christian leadership [is] that the way out is the way in, that only by entering into communion with human suffering can relief be found."[32] He later explained,

> A theology of weakness challenges us to look at weakness not as a worldly weakness that allows us to be manipulated by the powerful in society and church, but as a total and unconditional dependence on God that opens us up to be true channels of the divine power that heals the wounds of humanity and renews the face of the earth. The theology of weakness claims power, God's power, the all-transforming power of love.[33]

When we realize our own wounds, then we become aware of our inner poverty. This creates an emptiness—an open place—into which Christ can pour his healing power.

## DISCUSSION QUESTIONS

1. Have you ever been ambushed by God? If so, in what way? How did you respond?

2. Have the changes God has wrought in your life been sudden and overnight or more gradual and long term?

3. Have you ever felt that God has opposed you? Looking back now, do you have any insight about what God was doing in your life?

## CHAPTER 3

# A God Who Relents

*Exodus 32:1-14*

The story of Moses' prayer of protest finds its beginnings in Genesis 12, with the call of Abraham. God had called Abraham out of Babylon in order to create a people through whom He could bless the world. God called Abraham to migrate from Mesopotamia "to the land that I will show you" (Gen 12:1). With the call of Abraham came incredible promises: "I will make of you a great nation, and I will bless you, and make your name great, so that you will be a blessing. I will bless those who bless you, and the one who curses you I will curse; and in you all the families of the earth shall be blessed" (Gen 12:2-3). Abraham's wife, Sarah, gave birth to Isaac, with whom God renewed His promises. Through one of Isaac's grandsons, Joseph, the way was paved for Israel to migrate to Egypt during a famine. In Egypt, over a period of four hundred years, Israel grew into a great nation, albeit in bondage.

Moses was raised up in order to deliver Israel out of Egypt, after which God would "bring them up out of that land to a good and broad land, a land flowing with milk and honey" (Exod 3:8), in accordance with the promises to the patriarchs (Exod 3:15). Moses confronted the pharaoh and, through a series of ten plagues, he persuaded the pharaoh to release the Hebrews. The text of Exodus presents the confrontation between Moses and Pharaoh as a cosmic struggle between the true God, Yahweh, and the false gods of the Egyptian religion.[1] If Yahweh could blot out the sun in Egypt and permit light in Goshen (where the Hebrews dwelt), then obviously Yahweh was superior to Ra, the Egyptian sun-god, manifested in Pharaoh. So, after ten magnificent displays of Yahweh's omnipotence, Moses led the Hebrews out of Egypt.

Following the exodus event, God miraculously provided for Israel in the wilderness (Exod 16–17:7). He defeated Israel's enemies (17:8-16). God then appeared to Moses on Mount Sinai (ch. 19), revealed the Ten Commandments (ch. 20) as well as other legislation (20:22–23:19), and reiterated His promise to lead Israel into the promised land (23:20-33). Next, the covenant was ratified in two ceremonies: a divine appearance and sacred meal for a chosen few and a ritual of blood for all Israel (24:1-11).

Now that the covenant had been established between God and the people of Israel, Moses went up the mountain to meet God in order to learn what must be done so that both parties could leave the mountain and travel together to the promised land. The building of a portable shrine was required, along with the establishment of a priesthood to officiate within it. Moses received detailed instructions regarding these institutions (chs. 24–31), during which he was absent from the Israelite camp for "forty days and forty nights." During his prolonged absence, Aaron was left in charge (vv. 14, 18), setting the stage for the episode of the golden calf in chapter 32.

## APOSTASY AT THE FOOT OF MOUNT SINAI

When the people saw that Moses delayed to come down from the mountain, the people gathered around Aaron, and said to him, "Come, make gods for us, who shall go before us; as for this Moses, the man who brought us up out of the land of Egypt, we do not know what has become of him." Aaron said to them, "Take off the gold rings that are on the ears of your wives, your sons, and your daughters, and bring them to me." So all the people took off the gold rings from their ears, and brought them to Aaron. He took the gold from them, formed it in a mold, and cast an image of a calf; and they said, "These are your gods, O Israel, who brought you up out of the land of Egypt!" When Aaron saw this, he built an altar before it; and Aaron made proclamation and said, "Tomorrow shall be a festival to the Lord." They rose early the next day, and offered burnt offerings and brought sacrifices of well-being; and the people sat down to eat and drink, and rose up to revel.

> The Lord said to Moses, "Go down at once! Your people, whom you
> brought up out of the land of Egypt, have acted perversely; they have been
> quick to turn aside from the way that I commanded them; they have cast
> for themselves an image of a calf, and have worshiped it and sacrificed to it,
> and said, 'These are your gods, O Israel, who brought you up out of the
> land of Egypt!'" The Lord said to Moses, "I have seen this people, how
> stiff-necked they are. Now let me alone, so that my wrath may burn hot
> against them and I may consume them; and of you I will make a great
> nation." (Exod 32:1-10)

At the beginning of our text, the Israelites have become fearful because it
has been more than a month since Moses began climbing Mount Sinai, dis-
appearing into its rocky heights. He had been gone for "forty days and forty
nights" (24:18), Hebrew's colloquial way of saying "a really long time." So,
when the people surged against Aaron, urging him to make an idol, they
were not rebelling against Moses' leadership. They were trying to cope with
Moses' absence. Moses had been their representative to God since he
returned to them in Egypt, and now he had disappeared!

While English translations typically read that the people gathered
"around" Aaron, the Hebrew literally says they gathered "against" him. Their
call to him to fashion idols for them was actually a command or a threat—
"come, make" are both imperatives, punctuated with an exclamation point.
John Durham summarizes,

> [Moses'] absence in such a place, with so much yet to be done by way of
> provision and guidance, would have been problematic if even only a few
> days were involved. With the passage of a long period of time, the people
> are represented as nearly in a frenzy, some perhaps assuming Moses had
> deserted them, others more charitably fearing some tragedy had befallen
> their leader.[2]

And so this frenzied, fearful people swarmed against Aaron, he acquiesced,
and Israel lapsed into idol worship.

## THE BULL CULT

The particular image into which Aaron molded the people's gold was that of
"a calf" or a "bull" (v. 4). To modern readers, it might seem bizarre that any
ancient people would worship a statue of an animal. However, in ancient

times, bull cults were extremely popular. John Oswalt elaborates on the popularity and the reasons for it:

> All over the ancient world, wherever cattle were raised, the bull was the symbol of potency, fecundity, and power. This was true in Mesopotamia, Persia, Egypt, Canaan, Anatolia, Greece, and Rome. Whatever other natural principle the great god of the time might be identified with, he was also understood as a bull. So Amon-Re, the Egyptian sun-god, was a bull; so were Baal, the Canaanite storm god, and Asshur, the Assyrian storm god. In this environment it would be remarkable if some part of this concept did not creep into Israelite thinking. That it did so recurrently is an established fact.[3]

During the later period of the monarchy, "the biblical writers depict the worship of Yahweh with bull iconography as the standard error of the form of worship of the Northern Kingdom."[4] The sanctuaries at Dan and Bethel contained golden bulls (1 Kgs 12:26-28) and later, when Samaria became the northern capital, its primary icon seems to have been a young bull (Hos 8:5-6).

It must be understood, however, that the Israelites were not worshiping a bull in and of itself. Instead, *God* was being worshiped *in the form of* a strong and virile young bull.[5] Several factors substantiate this. First, rather than representing some new deity, the calf represented the God who had brought the people out of Egypt (v. 4). Secondly, the festival celebrated on the day following the construction of the calf was "to the Lord" (v. 6). Thirdly, "the festal activities resemble those recorded in chapter 24 regarding the ratification of the covenant between God and the Israelites."[6] If the bull only represented the Lord and served as a visual aid to the Israelites, then what was the big deal? Yahweh surely shared certain characteristics of the bull, particularly its might.

## THE SECOND COMMANDMENT

The second commandment's prohibition against representing God in any form (Exod 20:4) was not merely arbitrary. There was a reason for it. Here again, John Oswalt explains:

> The answer lies in Israel's concept of the divine transcendence. Whereas Israel's neighboring religions stressed the continuity of all things with each other, even those that were superficially alike, Hebrew religion stressed that

God was distinct from his creation and discontinuous with it. Whereas the gods of the nations were understood to be an integral part of the psycho-socio-physical world, such identification was specifically forbidden to the Hebrews. In many ways this is the profoundest insight of Hebrew religion. Whatever God is, he is not the world around us.[7]

The prevalent worldview was that the deities were immanent. The roles of the gods and humans were different, but they were not thought of as different in their essential natures. The gods corresponded with, or were continuous with, everything else that existed. Ancient peoples believed the gods "could be known directly, through immediate participation in the natural order."[8] This correspondence between the gods and humanity can be seen in the ancient Near Eastern creation accounts, in which the deities behave very much like people: they live in families, they lash out in anger, they become fearful, hungry, and envious. Like humanity, the gods are capricious. Israel, however, had a totally different understanding of its God. "In contrast to everyone around her, Israel believed in a God who stands outside the created order. He has easy access to all of the universe's parts, since he created all that is. But he is not bound by its structures or contained in its cycles. He transcends the world, standing above and beyond our present reality."[9] The Israelite God was transcendent, and it was for that reason that the second commandment prohibited representation of Him in any form. This was why the casting of a golden calf, so early in their spiritual development, was grievous. Oswalt writes,

> For the Hebrew people, fresh from Egypt with its inclusivist theology, it was not a problem to conceive of Moses worshiping a nonvisible YHWH on the mountain while they worshiped a visible YHWH in the valley. But Moses understood fully that unless the link between Creator and creation was broken, it would become impossible in any ultimate sense to maintain God's unity and exclusiveness . . . which [was] central to the new faith.[10]

Yahweh is a God who is invisible in mystery. "The calf is to be the representative of that same God, whose invisibility and mystery is compromised by an image he has forbidden."[11]

What happens in this passage is terribly ironic. Because of the disappearance of Moses, who represents the palpable assurance of God's presence among the people, the people now demand "gods . . . who shall go before us."

This, however, is precisely what the tabernacle will provide. Thus the irony in the situation is that the thing the people are demanding is exactly what is being prepared for them on the mountain. Seen in this light, the manufacture of the golden calf is a travesty of the construction of the tabernacle just authorized.[12]

As when Abraham turned from Sarah to Hagar in trying to conceive the promised son, failing to trust God's promise, so the Israelites too made recourse to other "gods."

Following Israel's worship of the golden calf and their sacrifices and communion meal the following day, they then "rose up to revel" (v. 6). The verb used here has to do with drunken, immoral orgies and sexual play.[13] Once Israel has committed to violating God's laws concerning interaction with Himself, it is not surprising that they then are less concerned about violating the laws regulating their conduct with one another. What begins as idolatry becomes a full-blown "orgy of the desertion of responsibility."[14]

Herein lies the importance of the first four commandments, all of which have to do with our understanding and honoring of God. It is only when we understand God correctly and honor God appropriately that we are able to live by the rest of the commands, all of which have to do with interpersonal relationships. Ethical demands on our lives are only valid, in other words, in light of who God is.[15] This is why the commands about monotheism, idolatry, and graven images precede commands regarding human ethics—human ethics find their basis in the person and character of God. When the church no longer understands who God is, then it is only natural for it to define itself according to current cultural norms.

Verses 7-10 record the outburst of God against His traitorous people. God speaks to Moses, saying, "Your people whom you have brought up . . . have become corrupt." Normally, God refers to Israel as "my people"; here, He refers to them as "your people." Walter Kaiser observes that "God deliberately changed the possessive pronoun, thereby indicating that he was disowning Israel."[16] Israel had become "corrupt" (v. 7), or totally depraved, just as Noah's contemporaries had (Gen 6:12). The fact that they were "stiffnecked," as v. 9 relates, suggests that they would not bow to God's authority, despite the fact that they had already bowed themselves in worship before the golden bull (v. 8). God concludes His tirade in v. 10 by commanding Moses to leave His presence, "in order that my wrath may burn hot against them and I may consume them."

## GOD TESTING MOSES?

Following God's words in 32:10 that He wants Moses to "Let me alone, that my wrath may burn hot against them," Moses begins what we might call a "prayer of protest." As we will see, God accepted his arguments, despite the fact that they were a protest. And, as we discussed in regard to Abraham in chapter 1, one almost gets the impression that God was inviting Moses to pray on behalf of Israel. Some of the rabbinical interpreters made this assumption—that God was testing Moses—suggesting that if God's decision had been final He would not have ordered Moses to leave Him alone "*in order that* my wrath may burn hot against them." As one commentator wrote, "Can we not see in these words an invitation to Moses indeed not to leave God alone with his wrath?"[17]

Indeed, at the end of v. 10, God suggests that, if He "consumes" Israel, He will still have Moses out of whom He can "make a great nation." Whether God was intending to test Moses or not, Moses could not "leave God alone" and thereby abandon his people to destruction. Drawing on the work of Everett Fox, Swedish Old Testament scholar Goran Larsson explains what this reveals about Moses:

> As never before, Moses proves what it means to be a true servant of the Lord. Behind Moses' intercession, we indeed hear the voice of the good shepherd. "What we learn from this section is not only God's forgiving nature but something significant about [Moses]: faced with a dictator's dream—the cloning of an entire nation from himself—he opts for staunchly defending the very people who have already caused him grief through their rebelling, and who will continually do so in the ensuing wanderings."[18]

Indeed, like the good shepherd, Moses takes grave risks for his sheep, whom he loves. He is willing to protest God's plans, and he daringly challenges the morality of those plans. Moses' prayer, however, cannot be called a "defense" of the people, for there was nothing defensible about what they had done. Instead, Moses' prayer appealed solely to God's own character and mercy.

## MOSES' PRAYER

Moses makes his petition on behalf of the people in vv. 11-13. The text reads:

But Moses implored the Lord his God, and said, "O Lord, why does your
wrath burn hot against your people, whom you brought out of the land of
Egypt with great power and with a mighty hand? Why should the
Egyptians say, 'It was with evil intent that he brought them out to kill
them in the mountains, and to consume them from the face of the earth'?
Turn from your fierce wrath; change your mind and do not bring disaster
on your people. Remember Abraham, Isaac, and Israel, your servants, how
you swore to them by your own self, saying to them, 'I will multiply your
descendants, and they shall inherit it forever.'"

Within Moses' prayer, the great patriarch gives a series of reasons why God
should not go through with His intended destruction of Israel. Firstly, Moses
says, God has gone to a lot of trouble to liberate them from the Egyptians
and bring them this far (v. 11).

Secondly, the Egyptians will misinterpret God's destruction of Israel as
an act of evil. Moses says, "Why should the Egyptians say, 'It was with evil
intent that he brought them out to kill them in the mountains, and to consume them from the face of the earth'?" (v. 12). The Egyptians had no
knowledge of God's covenant with Israel and, therefore, would not understand Israel's destruction as punishment for violations of that covenant. They
would simply conclude that Israel's God was capricious, wicked, and not to
be trusted. Moses urges God to protect God's own reputation.

Moses appeals, thirdly, to God's own mercy (v. 12b). Mercy is a fundamental characteristic of God. Edward Myers explains,

This is the quality (*hesed*, "covenant love"), demonstrated throughout their
history (cf. Deut 30:1-6; Isa 14:1; Ezek 39:25-29), by which God faithfully
keeps his promises and maintains his covenant relationship with his chosen
people despite their unfaithfulness (Gk. *Eleos*; Rom 9:15-16, 23; Eph
2:4).[19]

Here, Moses is urging God to be true to His own character. By not destroying Israel, God would be true to Himself.

A fourth reason God should not destroy Israel is the promise God made
to the fathers (v. 13). Here, Moses is referring to the "covenant" God made
with Abraham and renewed with the successive generations. "Covenant" may
be an unfamiliar word to us, referring to a relationship regulated by a legal
agreement. God's relationship with the Israelites was not like the relationships
of the pagans to their gods, and so it took an unusual word to describe it.

When God established a covenant with Abraham, God "did not show him an isolated kindness which he might withdraw from at his pleasure. He entered into a lasting and regulated relationship that could be understood only in legal terms because it was founded on God's own justice."[20] What God did in establishing the covenant was enter into a relationship from which He could not withdraw—He was legally bound to it.[21]

There is something unique about the covenant originally made between God and Abraham. Covenant models can be found in ancient Hittite treaties, in which powerful Hittite kings would make agreements with lesser kings and their peoples. The lesser king would swear allegiance to the high king, promising to respect the rights of the high king and other vassals. The lesser king and his people would receive, in return, the protection of the powerful Hittite king.[22] The striking difference between the biblical covenant and the Hittite covenant is that the biblical covenant is turned upside down.

> It is God, not Abraham, who binds himself with an oath (Gen 24:7; 26:3; 50:24), and he makes no specific demands upon Abraham but grants a favor to which his partner is in no way entitled. Comparison with the political covenants simply shows how strange and wonderful the covenant with Abraham truly is.[23]

What does this tell us about the covenant? It tells us that the covenant of God, even after He reveals the covenantal law to Moses, is a covenant of grace. While Israel had done nothing to merit God's favor, God had bound Himself to Israel in a covenant relationship. He had legally obligated Himself to be faithful to that covenant. And here, when God is on the brink of destroying Israel, Moses protests God's decision by reminding God of that covenant.

We must stress here that God was not somehow "trapped" by the covenant and literally *had* to refrain from destroying Israel. Certainly not! It's clear that the Lord could cut off the covenant in the case of insubordination. In 1 Samuel 2:30, for example, an oracle of condemnation is pronounced against the priestly house of Eli, which had become corrupt. In the oracle, the Lord says, "I promised that your family and the family of your ancestor should go in and out before me forever"; but now the Lord declares, "Far be it from me; for those who honor me I will honor, and those who despise me shall be treated with contempt" (1 Sam 2:30). Eli's house was to have been established "forever," but the Lord cut him off because of its continued corruption. The Hebrew words traditionally rendered "everlasting covenant" or "eternal covenant" may be better translated "open-ended" or "indefinite" rather than "eternal."[24] The covenant was conditional[25]—it would last as long as the faithfulness of those with whom it was made, or their descendants. The point here is that, despite Moses' reminding God of the covenant to which God had bound Himself, God would still have been fully justified in carrying out His plans to destroy the Israelites. In their insubordination, they had nullified the covenant.

How did God respond to Moses' prayerful effort to sway the course of action God had chosen? Verse 14 says that "the Lord *repented* of the evil which he thought to do to his people." Other translations say God "changed his mind." This and other passages like it have troubled Bible readers for many years because they seem to contradict the doctrine of God's unchangeability, as taught in Malachi 3:6: "For I the Lord do not change." A more full statement about God's consistency is found in 1 Samuel 15:29: "the Glory of Israel will not lie or change his mind; for he is not a man that he should change his mind." How can we understand this seeming contradiction?

We can say from the start that God's essence and character are unchanging. God's determination to punish sin and reward virtue is unchanging. Scripture teaches some absolute and unconditional affirmations throughout its pages. However, this does not mean all of God's promises and warnings are unconditional. Many of God's promises and warnings hinge on either an expressed or implied condition. The classic example of this is found in Jeremiah 18:7-10, which says,

> If at any time I announce that a nation or kingdom is to be uprooted, torn down and destroyed, and if that nation I warned repents of its evil, then I will relent and not inflict on it the disaster I had planned. And if at another time I announce that a nation or kingdom is to be built up and planted, and if it does evil in my sight and does not obey me, then I will reconsider the good I had intended to do for it.

This principle clearly states the condition that underlies most of God's promises and threats, even when it is not made explicit. So, whenever God does not fulfill a promise or carry out a threat He has made, the explanation is obvious: in all of these cases, the change hasn't come about in God but in the individual or nation.

In 1 Samuel, for example, God sanctioned Saul's anointing as king over Israel (1 Sam 10), but later He rejects him (1 Sam 15). In 1 Samuel 15:11a, the Lord says, "I regret that I have made Saul king, for he has turned back from following me, and has not carried out my commands." While this may seem bewildering on the surface, it is clear from the text that God does not change His approach to Saul out of indecisiveness on His own part. Rather, God changes His approach to Saul *in order to stay true to His own righteousness*. In other words, as Saul departs from the path of righteousness, God must abandon him in order to remain righteous. Walter Kaiser explains it this way: "God changed his actions toward Saul in order to remain true to his own character or essence. Repentance in God is not, as it is in us, an evidence of indecisiveness. It is rather a change in his method of responding to another person based on some change in the other individual."[26] The difficulty with understanding the aforementioned passages arises, in part, from the traditional translations. First Samuel 15:11 could be better translated, "I relent from having made Saul king." In other words, God could no longer support Saul *because Saul had changed*, having abandoned the path of righteousness.[27] In the same way, Exodus 32:14 could be better rendered, "And the Lord relented about the disaster that he planned to bring on his people."

## THE RADICAL NATURE OF MOSES' PRAYER

Moses' prayer is radical. The radical nature of Moses prayer is thrown into bold relief when it is contrasted to Abraham's prayer of intercession from our last chapter. Goran Larsson points out three differences between the prayers of the two patriarchs.[28] First, Abraham appeals to God's justice or righteousness, while Moses appeals to God's mercy. Secondly, while Abraham stopped bargaining at ten righteous people, Moses bargained "down to zero." And thirdly, in Larsson's own words:

> Moses not only bargains down to no righteous people at all, but he actually takes a great step further, which makes him unique among all the prophets of Israel (cf. Deut 18:18; 34:10). He is ready to include even himself among the sinners and to unite his own destiny with theirs: "So Moses returned to the Lord and said, 'Alas, this people has sinned a great sin; they have made for themselves gods of gold. But now, if you will only forgive their sin—but if not, blot me out of the book that you have written.'"[29]

I would add that Moses' prayer is radical for one more reason. It is radical because of the very fact that Moses thought God would relent. This is an essential truth—we worship *a God who relents*. When the wicked repent,

God pronounces them righteous. I have heard it taught in some churches that we must not allow sinners within our walls. Nonbelievers must first "clean up their act," as it were, before they qualify for salvation. God forbid that we teach this in our churches! The truth is exactly the opposite: *God saves us in the midst of our sin.* Paul argues that "while we were [God's] enemies, we were reconciled to God through the death of his Son" (Rom 5:10). Indeed, it is grace that enables us to abandon a sinful lifestyle. This principle is made clear in a passage in which Paul discusses sin in the Corinthian church. He writes,

> Do you not know that wrongdoers will not inherit the kingdom of God? Do not be deceived! Fornicators, idolaters, adulterers, male prostitutes, sodomites, thieves, the greedy, drunkards, revilers, robbers—none of these will inherit the kingdom of God. And this is what some of you used to be. But you were washed, you were sanctified, you were justified in the name of the Lord Jesus Christ and in the Spirit of our God. (1 Cor 6:9-11)

These sinners did not "clean up their act" before God allowed them to become Christians. Rather, they were only able to abandon their sinful lifestyles *because* of the grace they had received. It is only when one is touched by the radical love of Jesus Christ, when one experiences the Lordship of Jesus Christ in his or her life, and when one is infused with the transformative power of the Holy Spirit that one can begin to be freed from bondage to a sinful lifestyle.

This is the good news of Moses' prayer of protest: God loves His people, and He wants to relent from punishing them. The fact that Christ has not returned in judgment is evidence of God's longing to relent. "The Lord is not slow about his promise [to return in judgment], as some think of slowness, but is patient with you, not wanting any to perish, but all to come to repentance" (2 Pet 3:9).

## CONNECTIONS: VARIETIES OF CHRISTIAN IDOLATRY

Certainly the original prohibitions against idolatry call to mind the worship of constructed images, but it is also true that idolatry is not limited to the worship of material objects. The New Testament clearly understands that God alone is the only proper focus of obedience and worship, and it defines anything we might put in that place as idolatry. The apostle Paul defines "greed" as "idolatry" (Col 3:5) and "one who is greedy" as "an idolator" (Eph

5:5). Elsewhere, Paul makes reference to certain "enemies of the cross of Christ," and he states that "their god is the belly" (Phil 3:18-19), apparently referring to certain people within the churches who put their own concerns above those of their Lord. Though it is not clear who these "enemies of the cross of Christ" are here, he often levels some of his harshest criticisms against those who would bring division into the church as a whole or into a given congregation (e.g., 1 Cor 3:1-23). From these few New Testament passages we discover a range of attitudes that qualify as idolatry—from the way we relate to money and possessions to the way we relate to the church.

We tend to think of idols as only the bad things in our lives—things that are easy to spot, such as greed, rejection of the church for a more worldly philosophy, and so on. There is a danger here, though, and it is that this approach can lull us into a false sense of security about the true condition of our hearts. While we may be in complete obedience to the First Commandment in respect to the "bad" things, we can actually make idols out of many of the "good" things. I believe it is possible for a pastor to make an idol out of his ordination or a volunteer church worker to idolize his or her position in the congregation. C. Leonard Allen notes that

> even the Bible itself or our own religious tradition can become idols. The Bible becomes an idol to the extent that we lose a sense of Scripture as mediating a divine reality which always transcends Scripture itself. It becomes an idol when our faith becomes focused on Scripture rather than in the God Scripture reveals to us. Our religious tradition can become an idol to the extent that we absolutize it or make it identical in every respect to the Kingdom of God.[30]

We do not worship a pastor. We do not worship our role as a church committee chair, and neither do others in the church. We do not even worship the Bible. These are all good things, but when they become the *end* rather than the *means* to an end, then they have become idols.

Jesus asked those who followed him to imitate his unreserved commitment to the Kingdom of God. He asked for nothing less than the surrender of their total selves to righteousness. If we listen for him today, we will hear the same challenge.

## DISCUSSION QUESTIONS

1. How is understanding God correctly and honoring God appropriately the key to our ability to live by the rest of His commands?

2. What does the biblical covenant reveal about God's character?

3. What does Exodus 32:14 mean when it says God "repented"? Do you believe that God changes?

4. What does it mean to say we worship a God who "relents"? How is this good news?

## CHAPTER 4

# A God Who Sides with the Powerless

*1 Samuel 2:1-10*

The early chapters of 1 Samuel trace the emergence of Samuel as Yahweh's authorized leader in the land of Israel. At the center of these early chapters stands the "Song of Hannah" (2:1-10), which not only celebrates the gift of Samuel, but also clarifies that Israel's future, as well as its future king, are gifts of Yahweh to be looked forward to. Chapters 1–3 record the gracious birth of Samuel (1:3-28), the dream-appearance of God to Samuel as a child (3:1-10), and God's final statement of Samuel's authorization (3:19-21). All of these events witness to the decisive role of Yahweh in Israel's new beginning.[1] This is exactly the hope Hannah is expressing in her prayer—the hope for a new beginning for Israel.

## ISRAEL'S LONGING FOR A NEW BEGINNING

At the beginning of the story 1 Samuel records, we find Israel troubled and waiting. Israel is under threat of the Philistines, politically weak, economically disadvantaged, and spiritually bereft. As the Samuel story unfolds, we discover that Israel is waiting for a king who will protect, defend, gather, and liberate the community. What Israel is really waiting for—unbeknownst to them—is David. With the appearance of David, Israel's fortunes will begin to change, and the change will be known in Israel to be the work of God.

The story of 1 Samuel, however, does not rush to David. Instead, the triumph of David begins with other, less formidable figures who move Israel along toward the monarchy only gradually. Before presenting David, the writer presents readers with several "great men"—first Samuel and then Saul. And, in a daring move, back behind these "great men," the writer finds the origin of Israel's future and the source of its "great leaders" in the story of a bereft, barren woman named Hannah (1:2).

The story of Israel's waiting does not begin in a luxurious palace. It does not begin with Israel vanquishing its enemies. In fact, it does not begin with triumph of any kind. Instead, it begins with a single Ephraimite family in which the father has a solid pedigree (1:1) but the mother is barren—without children and without any prospect of children. Israel's story of waiting begins in barrenness. Israel's story begins with no hint of a future. Israel's waiting begins in the same way Hannah's waiting begins—in hopelessness.[2] The story of Elkanah, Hannah, and Samuel, therefore, is our entry point into Israel's waiting. The story of chapter 1 of 1 Samuel is the story of Israel in a nutshell. It is a story of newness out of barrenness.

## HANNAH'S STERILITY

Our story begins with the introduction of Elkanah, the husband of Hannah. "Elkanah" was a popular name in ancient Israel. At least five different Old Testament men shared the name, and two of them were ancestors of Samuel's father.[3] The meaning of the name, "God has created a son," is ironically prophetic of what will happen in Hannah's miraculous conception of Samuel.

Elkanah's two wives are introduced in v. 2: "He had two wives; one was called Hannah and the other Peninnah." Hannah is introduced first here, probably because she was Elkanah's favorite. She was barren, however, which was the ultimate tragedy for a woman in ancient times, since her husband's hopes and dreams depended on her providing him with a son to perpetuate his name and inherit his estate.[4]

Following the introduction of Elkanah's wives, the text relates the family's journey to the central sanctuary for the offering of a sacrifice. Three times a year all Israelite men were required to journey to the central sanctuary to offer sacrifices in observance of the main religious festivals.[5] Elkanah and his family therefore journeyed to Shiloh, which had been the location of

the tabernacle and the ark of the covenant for some time.[6] A man named Eli
served as the priest at Shiloh (v. 3), in addition to his functions as a judge
within Israel (4:18). His name means "God is exalted." Eli's corrupt sons,
unfortunately, also served as priests and, unusually, had Egyptian names:
Hophni, meaning "tadpole," and Phineas, meaning "the Nubian."

Elkanah brought his family to the Shiloh sanctuary for a festival celebration, which was a time of rejoicing in God's blessings, especially that of a
bountiful harvest. So Elkanah distributed portions of sacrificial meat[7] to
Peninnah and her children, since family members shared in certain sacrificial
offerings brought to the Lord.[8] Elkanah gave Hannah a double portion
because of his love for her. He may also have suspected that his wife's barrenness was by divine providence.[9]

Apparently, Hannah's sterility had prompted Elkanah to take Peninnah
as his second wife.[10] As it turned out, however, Peninnah became Hannah's
"rival."[11] She "kept provoking" Hannah (v. 6), resulting in "grief" (v. 16).
Her intention was to "irritate" Hannah. Hannah, however, was a devout
woman and, in the spirit of Deuteronomy, she was content to allow the Lord
to avenge the wrong committed against her.[12]

Elkanah was mindful of Hannah's grief, and he asked her, "Why are you
downhearted?" (v. 8). Literally, he asked, "Why is your heart bad?"[13] To do
something "with a bad heart" means to do it resentfully or grudgingly.
Elkanah is not so much asking her why her heart is sad, but why her heart is
bad; in other words, "why are you resentful?" Elkanah is asking Hannah
whether she is angry or full of spite because she does not have children, and
he concludes with this question: "Don't I, your husband, who loves you very
much, mean more to you than ten sons?"[14]

## HANNAH'S VOW

The depth of Hannah's misery is revealed when it plummets at Shiloh during
an annual pilgrimage. Her sadness and "bitterness of soul" (v. 10) led her to
pray and make a vow to the Lord. She made a special vow on behalf of the
son she hoped one day to bear—"a vow of separation to Yahweh."[15] Hannah
vowed that if the Lord would "remember" her and bless her with a son, then
out of gratitude she would give that son back to Yahweh.[16] Her vow also
included seeing that he abstained from using grapes in any form, never shaved
the hair on his head, and did not come in contact with corpses.[17] While
Hannah did not specifically use the term "Nazirite," it seems to be presup-
posed,[18] for the same language is used to describe Samson's Nazirite vow.[19]

Hannah's prayer reveals her conscious, intimate relationship with God. Verse 12 says she prayed "to" the Lord, which, literally, could be rendered as "she prayed *in the presence* of the Lord." The next verse also says she prayed "in her heart." The sanctuary priest, Eli, saw what happened and misunderstood Hannah's actions. In the ancient world, prayer was almost always spoken aloud,[20] and wine was drunk as a part of this particular festival.[21] So Eli misunderstood, thinking Hannah's moving lips were an intoxicated mumbling. He therefore rebuked her, saying, "How long will you make a drunken spectacle of yourself?" (v. 14). But far from pouring herself too many drinks, Hannah had been "pouring out her soul to the Lord" (v. 15), a vivid expression for praying earnestly.[22] She explained to Eli that she was "deeply troubled" and that under no circumstances did she want Eli to mistake her for a "wicked woman" (v. 16). Eli, satisfied with her explanation, told her to "go in peace" with the hope that Yahweh would soon grant her request. Indeed, godly Hannah, God's willing servant (v. 18), would soon receive the desire of her heart from God's gracious hand. And, being assured by Eli's response, she broke her self-imposed fast and her face was "no longer downcast."

The next day Elkanah's family worshiped the Lord, an experience with special meaning for Hannah this time. After the family's return from Shiloh to their home, Elkanah had relations with Hannah. Yahweh, as Hannah had earnestly prayed, "remembered her" (v. 19) by enabling her to become pregnant. It was not that the Lord had forgotten Hannah; neither is Yahweh's "remembrance" simply a matter of recalling to mind. Rather, for Yahweh to "remember" someone means He is paying special attention to or lavishing special care on someone. Indeed, enabling Hannah to conceive was surely a special blessing, for, as she recognized, children are *always* a gift of God, who is Himself the Great Enabler of conception and childbirth.[23] Like the matriarchs of ancient Israel, Hannah prized the blessing of pregnancy. Difficulty in conceiving and bearing children were some of the results of the fall, the reversal of which the ancient Israelites longed for. Psalm 113:9 is of special interest here, as it seems to suggest a reversal of the curse of Genesis 3:16: God's people are to be blessed with children![24]

Once Samuel was weaned—at two to three years of age in the ancient world[25]—Hannah intended to "present him before the Lord" (v. 22). The big day finally arrived, and Hannah was ready. After the family sacrificed the bull, they brought Samuel before Eli the priest (v. 25). Eli responded to Hannah's offering of her child to the service of the Lord by worshiping the God whom they both served (v. 28).

## HANNAH'S SONG

The birth of a child to a sterile woman is not a routine occurrence at any time, and certainly not in ancient Israel. This birth was, first of all, an occasion for celebration in Hannah's life. The deepest longing of her heart had been fulfilled. This birth was also, however, perceived to be more than a personal, family event. It was an event that concerned the life of the entire community. Hannah's song became a statement that the life and future of Israel, like her womb, had been reopened. Like Hannah's dead womb, dead Israel had possibility for the future!

A newborn son is celebrated in Hannah's song, but ultimately the song does not concern the son. Instead, it is primarily concerned with Yahweh. Hannah's song focuses on the Giver, not the gift. The song lays out the theological motifs that will dominate the whole story soon to unfold in the books of Samuel. Bible readers can expect to find these motifs echoed at various points throughout the story.

Hannah sings a special song here, with reference to a specific miracle in her own life. But when she sings it, she is joining her voice to a song Israel has already been singing for a long time. Israel had always been a people of praise. The whole life of the nation was made up of praise to God for what He had done and what He continued to do. Hannah was not really singing a new song. Instead, she was appropriating a song already well known in Israel.[26] The song may have originated as a song of triumph at the Shiloh sanctuary in connection with Israel's victory over an enemy.[27] These kinds of songs would have been taught to worshipers, and maybe this one became a personal favorite of Hannah's. If this were the case, then when she brought Samuel to Shiloh to dedicate him to the Lord, she sang these words as a way of expressing her gratitude and praise to God.[28]

> Hannah prayed and said,
> "My heart exults in the Lord;
> My strength is exalted in my God.
> My mouth derides my enemies,
>     Because I rejoice in my victory.
>
> There is no Holy One like the Lord,
>     No one besides you;
>     There is no Rock like our God.
> Talk no more so very proudly,

Let not arrogance come from your
    Mouth;
For the Lord is a God of knowledge,
    And by him actions are weighed.
The bows of the mighty are broken,
    But the feeble gird on strength.
Those who were full have hired
    Themselves out for bread,
But those who were hungry are fat
    With spoil.
The barren has borne seven,
    But she who has many children is
        Forlorn.
The Lord kills and brings to life;
    He brings down to Sheol and raises
        Up.
The Lord makes poor and makes
    Rich;
He brings low, he also exalts.
He raises up the poor from the dust;
    He lifts the needy from the ash heap,
To make them sit with princes
    And inherit a seat of honor.
For the pillars of the earth are the
    Lord's,
And on them he has set the world.

He will guard the feet of his faithful
    Ones,
But the wicked shall be cut off in
    Darkness;
For not by might does one prevail.
The Lord! His adversaries shall be
    Shattered;
The Most High will thunder in
    Heaven.
The Lord will judge the ends of the
    Earth;
He will give strength to his king,
    And exalt the power of his anointed." (1 Sam 2:1-10)

Hannah's song begins with gratefulness. Her heart, strength, and mouth—all she thinks and does—are centered in the great acts of God!

## "MY HORN IS RAISED"

In the second phrase of the song, Hannah uses a Hebrew expression that is often lost in the English translations: "my horn is raised." NRSV renders it "my strength is exalted." The raising of the horn is a common metaphor in Hebrew poetry, and it is used to make us think of a horned animal. The horn itself is a sign of strength: to "raise a horn" is to show power and dignity. Many Bible translations, therefore, simply render the word as "strength," because readers will understand this much more readily than the image of a horned animal. In the Bible, the image of the horn appears as a sign of victory or success,[29] and it is sometimes used with specific reference to God's giving of children. For example, in 1 Chronicles 25:5, the text recounts that "All these were the children of Heman . . . in accordance with God's promise to raise up his horn." The image of the horn is appropriate for expressing Hannah's joy.

But why not simply drop the antiquated metaphor and render it as the more modern translations do? The reason is that there is special significance in this metaphor, which is not only used in v. 1 in reference to the raising of Hannah's horn, but also to close the song in v. 10 with the raising of the king's horn. The real thrust of the song is that "the power of Yahweh, which can make the barren woman rejoice in a child, can also transform threatened tribal Israel into a kingdom."[30]

The appearance of this expression, along with the themes of war, is significant and has led even some conservative Bible commentators to conclude that a later redactor, or editor, has expanded Hannah's original words.[31] The argument here is that if the song was early, then the reference to a king must have been a later addition. Scholars who take a more liberal approach to the inspiration of Scripture argue that Hannah's entire song was invented many years later, long after the founding of the monarchy, and inserted in the text of Samuel at a later date.[32] The famous Hebraicist and archaeologist, William F. Albright, however, rebutted this kind of thinking, explaining that "some very archaic verse has been preserved as the Song of Hannah . . . It is highly probable that it does go back to the time of Samuel."[33] However, even without technical linguistic arguments, such as those made by Albright, one can accept the Song of Hannah as early when one understands the role of the monarchy in Old Testament history.

The fact is that the monarchy was a significant factor in God's plans for His people even in the earliest biblical period. When Yahweh first made promises to Abraham, He said, "I will make you exceedingly fruitful; and I will make nations of you, and kings shall come from you . . . . As for Sarai your wife . . . I will bless her, and moreover I will give you a son by her, I will bless her, and she shall give rise to nations; kings of peoples shall come from her" (Gen 17:6). Later, when God renewed His promises to Abraham's grandson, Jacob, He hinted at the establishment of a continuing dynasty:

> The scepter shall not depart from Judah,
>     nor the ruler's staff from between his
>         feet,
> until tribute comes to him;
>     and the obedience of the people is his. (Gen 49:10).

Exodus 19:6 explains that Israel was to be "a kingdom of priests and a holy nation." And, in Numbers, when a king of the Amorites summoned Balaam to prophesy against the Israelites, Balaam's prophecies indicated that Israel would produce a monarchy. He said,

> I see him, but not now;
>     I behold him, but not near—
> a star shall come out of Jacob,
>     and a scepter shall rise out of Israel;
> It shall crush the borderlands of
>     Moab,
> and the territory of all the
> Shethites.
> Edom will become a possession,
>     Seir a possession of its enemies,
>     while Israel does valiantly.
> One out of Jacob shall rule,
>     and destroy the survivors of Ir. (Num 24:17-19)

Additionally, when Moses was outlining Israel's laws in Deuteronomy, he included a section in which he gave the divine expectations Israel's kings were to meet (Deut 17:14-20).

The point here is that references to a coming monarchy within the song of Hannah do not imply that the prayer must have been composed after the establishment of that monarchy. As a faithful Hebrew, Hannah would have understood that the monarchy was a part of God's plan for Israel from the beginning. Her hope for a king was part of her confident expectation that Yahweh would ultimately turn His threatened people into a kingdom.[34]

## THE UNIQUENESS OF YAHWEH

For Hannah, Yahweh is holy, unique, and mighty. She celebrates God's holiness, His otherness, in righteous victory.[35] She then connects God's uniqueness with the metaphor of the Rock, exactly as David later does when he says, "For who is God, but the Lord? And who is a rock, except our God?" (2 Sam 22:32). However "rocklike" others might be or consider themselves to be—human or divine—"their rock is not like our Rock" (Deut 32:31).

This image of God as the Rock is one of the most recognizable and familiar images of divine refuge and strength. And this is not only the case in the Old Testament,[36] but also in Christian hymns like "Rock of Ages" and "O Safe to the Rock that is Higher than I."

## GOD SEES THE POWERLESS

After she describes Yahweh in His majesty and power, Hannah warns anyone who would puff themselves up in their pride, including, of course, Peninnah, who has ridiculed her for her sterility. In the light of all that God is and does, Hannah sings in vv. 3-5, arrogance is both foolish and futile.[37]

> Talk no more so very proudly,
>     Let not arrogance come from your mouth;
> For the Lord is a God of knowledge,
>     And by him actions are weighed.
> The bows of the mighty are broken,
>     But the feeble gird on strength.
> Those who were full have hired
>     Themselves out for bread,
> But those who were hungry are fat
> with spoil.
> The barren has borne seven,
>     But she who has many children is forlorn.

Yahweh, who knows the *heart*, judges and weighs *it* rather than external appearances. Ralph W. Klein explains, "The warning against arrogance is grounded in Yahweh's omniscience, particularly his ability to see through deeds to their true character . . . . This assertion is . . . the theological basis for the reversal of social conditions that is hailed as Yahweh's regular behavior in the following verses."[38] God is all-knowing. Because God is all-knowing, he sees the powerless and disadvantaged and consequently acts on their behalf.[39] This is a theme that will recur throughout the book of 1 Samuel, "particularly in David's victory over Goliath."[40] Jesus' teaching, therefore, that it is the "meek" who are blessed (Matt 5:5) does not originate with the New Testament. God has always had a special concern for the weak and downtrodden, for orphans and widows. God has always been a God of justice and compassion, not merely in the New Testament.

It is Yahweh's capacity in the face of human action that gives hope to the weak and the marginal. Yahweh's intervention changes the balance of power and potential in human events. In war, the mighty may not win and the feeble may be strong (v. 4).[41] This judgment about war looks forward to the triumph of Israel to come and, again, will have special application in the case of David's defeat of Goliath (1 Sam 17). Ultimately, "bow-breaking" will be part of the peaceable kingdom (Zech 9:10).

The last half of v. 5 had special meaning for Hannah: "The barren has borne seven, but she who has many children is forlorn." Like the mother of Samson, another lifelong Nazirite, the mother of Samuel had once been barren.[42] Now Hannah, the barren one, has given birth. "Seven" here simply means "many,"[43] symbolizing completion; in other words, "just the right number" of children. The formerly barren Hannah eventually had a total of six children,[44] "just the right number" for her.

## REVERSAL OF FORTUNES

Hannah's song continues with the idea that the sovereign God, according to His own good pleasure, ultimately blesses some and curses others:

> The Lord kills and brings to life;
>     He brings down to Sheol and raises up.
> The Lord makes poor and makes
>     Rich;
> He brings low, he also exalts.
> He raises up the poor from the dust;
>     He lifts the needy from the ash heap,
> To make them sit with princes

> And inherit a seat of honor.
> For the pillars of the earth are the
>     Lord's,
> And on them he has set the world. (vv. 6-8)

The meaning of v. 6 is not completely clear. Some have interpreted it as teaching a belief in resurrection, while others see it as having to do with Yahweh giving rescue from the brink of death after a serious illness, contrasting sickness with health. Professor Baldwin, subscribing to the former view, believes the passage is a remarkable affirmation of the doctrine of resurrection. She writes, "This, the most surprising couplet of all, envisages the Lord bringing people back to life from the realm of the dead. Sheol, the abode of the dead, is depicted as a huge underground cave, where judgment takes place (Deut 32:22; Ps 88:3-6), but the Lord can deliver even from Sheol (cf. v. 9)."[45] In favor of the latter view, however, is that Psalm 30:2-3 seems to refer to healing rather than resurrection:

> O Lord my God, I cried to you for help,
>     And you have healed me.
> O Lord, you brought up my soul
>     From Sheol,
> Restored me to life from among
>     Those gone down to the Pit.

These verses seem to present two sets of contrasts: death with life and sickness with health.[46] Certainly the least one could say is that the Old Testament passages teach that the Lord delivers believers from the most dire of circumstances and, in light of the New Testament, one could also affirm that God will ultimately bring people back to life from the realm of the dead. The idea of the reversal of fortunes is certainly clear.

The Lord also can and does reverse the fortunes of the poor and rich[47] and of the humble and the proud.[48] On the individual level, the song offers hope to the marginal. "A person's status in life is not to be regarded as fixed and unchangeable, for the Lord is well able to reverse it."[49] Verse 8 mentions that Yahweh "raises up the poor from the dust" or "from the ash heap." The "ash heap" probably refers to the town dump, where beggars would sleep by night and ask alms by day. God so reverses the fate of these poorest of the poor, and He does it to such an extent that they may sit with nobility! On the national level, the song points readers ahead to lowly Israel's taking a place among the kingdoms and to David as a shepherd who nevertheless will be king.[50] This great reversal would certainly be reflected in Israel's own life as a nation. Israel "had come into Canaan, with few possessions, to find relatively wealthy cities which, under the good hand of God, they had overthrown."[51] Norman Gottwald summarizes, "Those formerly ruled and deprived in all the basic areas of their existence are now self-ruled, abundantly provisioned, prolifically reproduced, and socially fulfilled."[52] All of this is possible, v. 8 says, "For the pillars of the earth are the Lord's, and on them he has set the world." The song here links the hope of the marginal with Yahweh's sovereignty over creation. This is a connection we find expressed in Deuteronomy 10:14, 17-18:

> Behold, to the Lord your God belong heaven and the heaven of heavens, the earth and all that is in it . . . . For the Lord your God is the God of gods and the Lord of lords, the great, the mighty, and the terrible God, who is not partial and takes no bribe. He executes justice for the fatherless and the widow, and loves the sojourner, giving him food and clothing.

Yahweh's cosmic power is mobilized precisely for those on the margins of society. It is no wonder that Hannah sings!

## YAHWEH'S COMING "ANOINTED ONE"

Hannah's song comes to a close with these words:

> He will guard the feet of the faithful
>     Ones,
> But the wicked shall be cut off in
>     Darkness;
> For not by might does one prevail.
> The Lord! His adversaries shall be
> shattered;
> The Most High will thunder in
> heaven.
> The Lord will judge the ends of the
>     Earth;
> He will give strength to his king,
>     And exalt the power of his anointed. (vv. 9-10)

Yahweh will distinguish between the "faithful ones" and the "wicked" (v. 9a). The faithful are the ones who trust God's promises, receive God's gifts, and keep vows to God—people like Hannah. The wicked are those who rely on their own strength—people like Peninnah and the Philistines. Arrogant human strength, however, cannot prevail against the judging, ruling power of Yahweh (v. 9b). No power, no social arrangement, no alternative claim to authority can withstand the rule of Yahweh, "For God's foolishness is wiser than human wisdom, and God's weakness is stronger than human strength" (1 Cor 1:25).

Hannah's song comes to a close with the fantastic claim that the rule of Yahweh is in the strength of the "king," or "anointed one" (v. 10). As mentioned earlier, it may seem somewhat strange that, long before Saul or David or any king appears in Israel, Hannah would assert that the coming king will be an agent for the poor, needy, hungry, and barren.[53] However, the poem—maybe prophetically—looks forward to the hope placed in kingship for time to come. In addition, the poem gives the criteria by which later kings will be evaluated. The evaluation of Jesus' ministry along these lines would lead many first-century Jews to conclude that he was their "anointed one," their Messiah, the fulfillment of all that the Israelite kings had failed to be.

## THEOLOGICAL IMPORTANCE OF HANNAH'S SONG

The song of Hannah gives us what we might call an "interpretive key" for the books of 1 and 2 Samuel.[54] The message we see is that Yahweh has the power to intervene in the life of Israel. Throughout the books of Samuel, readers will "watch while the despised ones (Israel, David) become the great ones. At the center of this startling inversion is the eighth son (16:11-12), who sits with princes and inherits a seat of honor (2:8)."[55] Bruce Birch concludes:

> The experience out of which Hannah sings offers hope to Israel and to us that a different reality is at work in the world from what we customarily acknowledge. Hannah's hope becomes hope for Israel and for us that power is not irrevocably tilted in favor of those that the world defines as powerful—definitions that leave many powerless and without hope. . . . God is heavily interested in the welfare of the weak, the powerless, the poor, the hungry, the dispossessed, the barren.[56]

Another point we should note is that it is not accidental that Israel's hope for a king—an anointed one—is voiced through the experience and the song of a barren woman. If God's transforming power for Israel takes the shape of a king, then Israel's king cannot be disinterested. The leadership of this king should reflect the priorities of a God who is interested in the poor and the powerless. As one commentator has written, "God's anointed one must serve the reversals of power about which Hannah sings."[57] When Jesus, the ultimate "anointed one," carried out his ministry, he did so while including women among his disciples, talking with them publicly, allowing them to sponsor his ministry, appearing to them first following his resurrection, and commissioning one to be the first witness to the resurrection. The early church continued to enact these and other great "reversals."

Finally, Hannah's song is echoed strongly in the song of Mary[58] and then in Jesus' own inaugural sermon. That opening sermon of Jesus consisted of a brief reading from Isaiah as follows:

> The Spirit of the Lord is upon me,
> Because he has anointed me
>         To bring good news to the poor.
> He has sent me to proclaim release to
>     The captives
> And recovery of sight to the blind,
>     To let the oppressed go free,
> To proclaim the year of the Lord's favor. (Lk 4:18-19)

Jesus then commented on the passage from Isaiah with these words: "Today this scripture has been fulfilled in your hearing" (v. 21). The prominence and the recurrence of these themes should point us to the fact that the mission of the church ought to be characterized by the same kinds of concerns.

## CONNECTIONS: WOMEN'S ROLES IN THE CHURCH

While women have been ordained in some denominations since the 1970s, the status and role of women have continued to be a subjects of intense debate in the church. The recent runaway bestseller, Dan Brown's *The DaVinci Code*, claims that "patriarchal Christianity" has suppressed the supposedly pristine faith of matriarchal paganism. In Brown's view, there should be room within Christianity—or in some alternative, New Age form of it—for the worship of a goddess.[59] In response, some feminist theologians are calling for a reappraisal of Sophia, the goddess of second-century Gnosticism. Collections of various Gnostic writings have begun to be republished and purchased by women who apparently presume that they will find affirmation within those materials.

However, women looking for affirmation will not find it in the Gnostic gospels, which are patently patriarchal and ascetic. In the *Gospel of Thomas*, Simon Peter asks Jesus to make Mary leave the group of disciples, explaining that "females are not worthy of life." Jesus answers, "Look, I shall guide her to make her male, so that she too may become a living spirit resembling you males. For every female who makes herself male will enter the Kingdom of Heaven" (saying 114). The *Dialogue of the Savior* counsels that the disciples should only pray when no women are present, and that "the works of femaleness" must be "destroyed" (144:16-20).

The truth of the matter is that no religion has ever placed women on a higher plane than Christianity. Jesus' attitude toward women was revolutionary in its implications. He ate with women publicly, included women among those who traveled in his entourage, and called women to be his "disciples," a term never used of women in ancient rabbinic writings. In his list of personal greetings at the end of the letter to the Roman church, nine out of the twenty-six people Paul personally greeted were women.[60] Paul singled out four as having "worked hard," and he says they are "outstanding among the apostles." Women clearly held a prominent place among Paul's friends and associates. While the interpretation of passages like 1 Corinthians 14:33b-36 and 1 Timothy 2:8-15 continues to be debated,[61] they must be interpreted in light of Galatians 3:28—"there is no longer male or female" in Christ. This passage reveals God's ideal as expressed prior to the fall and that should now begin to be implemented in Christ.[62] The church should serve as a catalyst for moving toward the ideal held out by Paul.

## DISCUSSION QUESTIONS

1. Why was having a child so important to Hannah? Are there differences in the perceptions of the ancient Israelites and ours toward having children? What might these differences teach us?

2. How does Hannah's song express a confident expectation that Yahweh would eventually turn His threatened people into a kingdom?

3. Jesus, as a man, apparently found the song particularly relevant for his own self-understanding. Why do you believe this was so? How is Hannah's prayer relevant for the whole church, as well as for women, today?

CHAPTER 5

# A God Who Justifies

*Psalm 51*

Psalm 51 was inspired by the events recorded in 2 Samuel 11–12—David's adultery with Bathsheba, the lies that grew out of the affair, and how the events grew ever more tangled, eventually resulting in murder.

The story begins "in the spring of the year, the time when kings go out to battle" (2 Kgs 11:1). In the previous year, David's armies had secured victories against the Ammonites and the Arameans (10:1-19). But, for whatever reason, when the armies went out during this spring, King David remained behind. While it is possible that his army insisted he remain behind to avoid danger to himself,[1] the reasons for his failure to accompany his army are unknown.

In any case, David was apparently napping on the palace roof, which would have been breezy and cool in the late afternoon, an ideal place for a nap. What happened next would begin to weave a web of darkness in the king's heart that would only be broken by the harsh confrontation of a prophet: "It happened, late one afternoon, when David rose from his couch and was walking about on the roof of the king's house, that he saw from the roof a woman bathing; the woman was very beautiful" (2 Kgs 11:2). David then inquired about the woman, probably to find out whether she was married. If she was unmarried, then the king could add her to his harem. The woman's name was Bathsheba and, as it turned out, she was well married. Her husband was Uriah, one of David's "thirty" best soldiers.[2] Bathsheba was from a distinguished family.

Despite the fact that she was married, David sent for her. She came to him, and he had sexual relations with her. The writer tells us in a parenthetical note that Bathsheba "was purifying herself after her period" (v. 4). This information might clue readers in to the coming pregnancy, since she was at the most fertile time of her cycle when David slept with her. It is therefore no surprise when we are told that a child has been conceived as a result of this adulterous union (v. 5). David attempted to handle the problem by sending for Uriah and giving him a month's leave, expecting him, after having been away at war, immediately to sleep with his wife and therefore consider himself responsible for the pregnancy (vv. 6-8). However, "Uriah slept at the entrance of the king's house with all the servants of his lord, and did not go down to his house" (v. 9). Even after getting drunk, Uriah still refused to sleep with his wife (v. 13). Interpreters have typically understood Uriah's refusal as having been motivated by loyalty to his fellow soldiers, who were unable to share the same joy of being close with their wives. However, it is more likely that this was intentional contrast between an adulterous David and a pious Uriah, who, having been consecrated for battle, refused to violate his oath of sexual abstinence.[3]

David solved this problem by sending Uriah back to the battle with a letter to the general, Joab, instructing him to place Uriah "in the forefront of the hardest fighting, and then draw back from him, so that he may be struck down and die" (v. 15). Joab unhesitatingly carried out the instructions, and Uriah was killed in the next day's battle (vv. 16-17). A messenger was dispatched to relay these occurrences to King David, who callously responded, "Do not let this matter trouble you, for the sword devours now one and now another" (v. 25). David then waited for the time of mourning to elapse, and then he sent for Bathsheba and married her.

In his devotional study of the life of David, Eugene Peterson reflects on David's shocking behavior, exclaiming that, "We aren't prepared for such a David. What begins as a lustful whim develops into an enormous sex-and-murder crime. How does such sin happen? As with most sins, gradually and unobtrusively."[4] Peterson seeks to understand David's sin by comparing it with the original sin of gradually attempting to become autonomous, to push God to the periphery, and not only to function without God, but to put oneself in God's place. Peterson writes,

> The subtlety of sin is that it doesn't feel like sin when we're doing it; it feels godlike, it feels religious, it feels fulfilling and satisfying—a replay of the episode in Eden when the tempter said, "Ye shall not die . . . ye shall be as gods" (Gen 3:4-5, KJV). David didn't feel like a sinner when he sent for Bathsheba; he felt like a lover—and what can be better than that? David didn't feel like a sinner when he sent for Uriah; he felt like a king—and what can be better than that? Somewhere along the line he had withdrawn from the life of worship: adoration of God had receded, and obsession with self had moved in.[5]

David had become so self-centered at that point, in fact, that even after having committed adultery and murder, he blinded himself to any culpability. Even when confronted by the court prophet, Nathan, with a story analogous to his own sin, David refused to see the parallel.

Nathan went to David and told him the following parable:

> There were two men in a certain city, the one rich and the other poor. The rich man had very many flocks and herds; but the poor man had nothing but one little ewe lamb, which he had bought. He brought it up, and it grew up with him and with his children; it used to eat of his meager fare, and drink from his cup, and lie in his bosom, and it was like a daughter to him. Now there came a traveler to the rich man, and he was loath to take one of his own flock or herd to prepare for the wayfarer who had come to him, but he took the poor man's lamb, and prepared that for the guest who had come to him. (2 Sam 12:1-4)

David, having become drawn into the story, indignantly replied, "As the Lord lives, the man who has done this deserves to die; he shall restore the lamb fourfold, because he did this thing, and because he had no pity" (vv. 5-6). It is at this point that Nathan delivered his sucker punch: "You are the man!" (v. 7). And then, in a "thus saith the Lord," Nathan launched into a lengthy rebuke of David, recalling how the Lord had raised him up from obscurity to kingship and asking why he had "despised the word of the Lord, to do what is evil in his sight" (v. 9). Indeed, David had descended from love and obedience into calculation and cruelty.

## DAVID'S LAMENTATION AND PRAYER FOR FORGIVENESS

According to the superscription of Psalm 51, David composed one of the most powerful prayers of confession, repentance, and requests for forgiveness in the Old Testament, in relation to his sin with Bathsheba and the murder of her husband, Uriah.

Have mercy on me, O God,
    According to your steadfast love;
According to your abundant mercy
    Blot out my transgressions.
Wash me thoroughly from my iniquity,
    And cleanse me from my sin.

For I know my transgressions,
    And my sin is ever before me.
Against you, you alone, have I sinned,
    And done what is evil in your sight,
So that you are justified in your sentence
    And blameless when you pass judgment.
Indeed, I was born guilty,
    A sinner when my mother conceived me.

You desire truth in the inward being;
    Therefore teach me wisdom in my secret heart.
Purge me with hyssop, and I shall be clean;
    Wash me, and I shall be whiter than snow.
Let me hear joy and gladness;
    Let the bones that you have crushed rejoice.
Hide your face from my sins,
    And blot out all my iniquities.

Create in me a clean heart, O God,
    And put a new and right spirit within me.
Do not cast me away from your presence,
    And do not take your holy spirit from me.
Restore to me the joy of your salvation, and sustain in me a willing spirit.

Then I will teach transgressors your ways,
    And sinners will return to you.
Deliver me from bloodshed, O God,

O God of my salvation,
> And my tongue will sing aloud of your deliverance.

O Lord, open my lips,
> And my mouth will declare your praise.
For you have no delight in sacrifice;
> If I were to give you a burnt offering,
> > You would not be pleased.
The sacrifice acceptable to God is a broken spirit;
> A broken and contrite heart,
> > O God, you will not despise.[6]

This psalm is one of the most beautiful laments in the Psalter and has been described as a literal "storehouse of Hebrew vocabulary for sin and forgiveness."[7] Christians have turned to it repeatedly over the centuries in order to ponder the forgiveness of God. Yet, there is a problem. The problem is that, throughout a large part of the history of the church, commentators have argued that there was no forgiveness available in the period of the Old Testament.

## NO FORGIVENESS FOR THE OLD TESTAMENT SAINTS?

It was a widely held belief in the early church that between his crucifixion and resurrection Jesus descended into Hell in order to release the Old Testament saints, who had died without forgiveness.[8] The early church seems to have believed that righteous people who died before the coming of Christ were consigned to Sheol, Hades, or Hell because there was no means of grace prior to Jesus' coming. Despite the faith of the Old Testament saints, they were unable to be saved because they lived prior to the saving work of Christ. The idea of Christ's preaching to the dead is found from the beginning of the second century onward. Apparently drawing on 1 Peter 3:19-20, the church believed Christ descended into Hell following his death, preached to the Old Testament saints, and then brought them out of Hell and into Paradise at his resurrection. For example, Origen, a third-century theologian, said, "I believe that, when our Lord the Savior came, Abraham, Isaac, and Jacob were blessed with God's mercy,"[9] which they had not experienced before. Other immanent theologians and church leaders such as Justin, Clement of Alexandria, Irenaeus, and Hippolytus shared this understanding.[10] This became so much a part of the early church's belief that it eventually became an article of the Apostle's Creed.[11]

While many modern Christians would argue that Old Testament saints *were* saved, they would argue that they were saved by law rather than by grace. We could consider history to have been divided into various ages, during each of which God dealt with humankind differently. During the Old Testament, men and women lived in an "age of Law," when God saved people based on whether or not they were able successfully to abide by Law. The New Testament period ushered in an "age of grace" wherein, because of Christ's atoning sacrifice, men and women can be saved by grace. According to this system, therefore, God has dealt with men and women differently in different ages.

## JUSTIFICATION BY GRACE THROUGH FAITH—IN THE OLD TESTAMENT!

Both of the aforementioned views are the result of a failure to understand how God deals with humankind in the Old Testament. Certainly the Old Testament believers all fell short of the glory of God and were therefore worthy of condemnation (Rom 3:23). But I would suggest that God saved them by grace, through faith, for two reasons. First, if God saves believers by grace through faith today, then He must have saved them by grace through faith yesterday, because God never changes. Moses revealed that

> God is not a human being,
>     That he should lie,
> Or a mortal,
>     That he should change his mind. (Num 23:19)

When Samuel reported God's rejection of Saul, he adapted the Numbers passage, saying, "The Glory of Israel will not recant or change his mind; for he is not a mortal, that he should change his mind" (1 Sam 15:29). The Old Testament records God Himself as saying, "I the Lord do not change" (Mal 3:6). Ever since the fall of humankind, men and women have remained inadequate and unable to save themselves. They have always had to depend on God's grace to save them, even during the Old Testament period.

The second reason I believe God saved Old Testament believers by grace through faith has to do with properly understanding the Law. Israel was commanded to "consecrate [themselves] and be holy, for I am holy" (Lev

11:44-45). The book of Leviticus gives instruction for how the Hebrew community was to engage in "holy worship" and "holy living," so that they might enjoy the blessing of Yahweh's presence.

For the ancient Hebrews, everything in life was either clean or unclean. Clean things could become holy through sanctification or unclean through pollution. Holy things could be profaned and become common or even unclean. Uncleanness could be caused by disease, contamination, infection, or sin. And something or someone could only be cleansed by ritual washing and sacrifice. This is why the instructions about sacrifices in the book of Leviticus were so important. The presence of the Holy God dwelled in the Israelite camp, within the tabernacle, and therefore it was extremely important to prevent the unclean from coming into contact with the holy. Failure to prevent contamination resulted in death.[12]

Ritual sacrifice was one way the Hebrew people might gain access to their God. Certain of those sacrifices were necessary to atone for or "cover" sin, accomplish reconciliation with Yahweh, and restore the penitent sinner to fellowship with other people and with God. According to Leviticus 17:11, the principle of life is represented in the blood. Consequently, blood on the altar was necessary for the symbolic cleansing of sinful human beings.[13] Through the sacrificial system, provision was therefore made for "atonement," which has to do with appeasement of and reconciliation with God.

However, as Andrew Hill and John Walton explain, the

> Old Testament teaching very clearly indicates that animal sacrifices were not salvific or effective in any way for individual or corporate Hebrew redemption. The believer under the old covenant was made righteous by faith in the promise of Yahweh, which he or she would demonstrate through obedience to the covenant stipulations (e.g., Gen 15:6; Hab 2:4). The external act of ritual sacrifice was symbolic and representative of the internal attitude and disposition of the heart.[14]

Indeed, all of the Hebrew Scriptures testify to the truth that God does not desire sacrifice, but repentance leading to obedience.[15] When an Old Testament believer approached God with a broken and contrite heart, God would grant forgiveness. Only by actual confession and petition could one experience the removal of guilt in the Old Testament. Hill and Walton suggest that

Ultimately the purpose of Hebrew sacrifice was didactic in that the carrying out of the ritual of atonement was designed to instruct the Israelites in the principles of God's holiness, human sinfulness, substitutionary death to cover human transgression, and the need for repentance leading to cleansing and renewed fellowship within the community and with Yahweh.[16]

I think a more accurate way to talk about the Law in the Old Testament is to use "sacramental" language. A sacrament is an outward and visible sign of an inward and invisible grace. Just as baptism, therefore, is the outward and visible sign of what God is invisibly doing inside a person, so obedience to the Law or the proper carrying out of a sacrifice was indicative of one's inward condition. In other words, it was not the sacrifice that saved a person in the Old Testament, but the inward repentance one expressed by that sacrifice.

Understanding God's unchanging nature and the real function of the Law helps us appreciate the fact that God did indeed save the patriarchs and matriarchs by grace through faith.

## DAVID'S PLEA FOR FORGIVENESS

David, the king of Israel, had committed adultery and murder. Adultery was "an offense against God, with mandatory prosecution and a sentence of death."[17] Murder, likewise, required a capital punishment, regardless of class.[18] David acknowledges that these heinous sins were not covered by sacrificial provision and, therefore, "If I were to give a burnt offering, you would not be pleased" (Ps 51:16b). David's sins were *so grievous* that there was no provision within the Law for their atonement. Herein lies the power of the psalm: David petitions God for forgiveness anyway, and he expresses an assurance of having received it. David's song consists of six components, each of which we will look at briefly.

*Prayer for forgiveness* (51:1-2). David begins by asking God for mercy and cleansing from sin using two words that appear throughout the Old Testament to express God's care for His people. The first of these is *hesed*, translated variously as "covenant love," "steadfast love," or "loving-kindness," which has to do with God's covenant faithfulness. This word is generally used in the context of covenant-making and has to do with "the obligation assumed by one person to act on behalf of another, who is usually dependent on the aid of the first and helpless to function adequately without it."[19] God had bound Himself to Israel by way of a covenant, and therefore Israel continually depended on God's "loving-kindness," or "covenant love," for its survival. Marvin Tate explains, "Thus in Ps 51 [David] appeals for mercy on the basis of God's willingly assumed and continued obligation (his "loyal-love") to act for the removal of anything, including guilt, which threatens the welfare of an individual (or people) for whom he is responsible."[20] This should not be taken to mean that God only shows *hesed* to the Israelites because He has to due to having bound Himself to them by covenant. The fact is that Israel's continued violation of the covenant had abrogated it, and therefore God would have been justified in abandoning Israel. This makes it clear that loving-kindness is, rather, "a type of loyalty that does not merely meet an obligation but goes the second mile (Jer 2:2). . . . God's demonstrated loyalty to creation has an uncoerced, gracious quality."[21] In other words, God's love is such that God continues to be faithful even when Israel is not. God's faithfulness goes way beyond any normal expectations, as demonstrated in His command to Hosea to marry "a wife of whoredom and have children of whoredom."[22] Hosea's marriage was to symbolize Yahweh's relationship with recalcitrant Israel.

Secondly, David appeals to God's "abundant mercy," which comes from the Hebrew word *raham*, meaning "womb." The word "suggests the idea of the feelings of a mother toward her baby,"[23] intending to reveal the tenderness of God's love. Just as a mother would not turn her back on her child, neither would God abandon His children, Israel.

Based on these two characteristics of God—loving-kindness and abundant mercy—David proceeds to ask God to forgive him using three verbs expressing the vigorous way in which he desires that forgiveness to be carried out. First, David asks God to "blot out his transgressions" (v. 1), a phrase that comes from a Hebrew word variously translated as "wipe off," "erase," or "obliterate."[24] Secondly, using a word derived from the mundane chore of washing clothes,[25] David asks God to "wash" him from his iniquity. Thirdly, David wants God to "cleanse" him from his sin (v. 2), a request that may express his desire for ritual purity.[26] These are requests for real forgiveness, and they are not made based on any quality of or action performed by David, but solely on qualities within God Himself.

David is fully aware of his need for real forgiveness and, corresponding to the three words for forgiveness, he uses three key words to describe his sin in vv. 1-2. The first word for sin, *pesha*, comes at the end of v. 1 and is usually translated "transgressions." This word has to do with "willful, self-assertive defiance of God,"[27] which basically means "rebellion."[28] The second word for sin David uses, *awon*, comes in the first phrase of v. 2 and is usually rendered as "iniquity." It has the basic idea of bending or twisting. The third word, *hatta*, comes in the last line of v. 2 and is often translated simply as "sin." The root idea has to do with "missing the mark," but "it is important to remember that the failure involved is the result of choice or of a clear act of will."[29] While these three words may express slightly different shades of meaning, they are basically synonyms for "sin" in the sense of a deliberate choice of a path other than that on which God would have us walk. The point is, David clearly understands the extent of his sinfulness, and he knows that nothing short of God's grace can change his condemned status before God.

*Confession of sin* (51:3-5). David is aware of his condition before God, as he confesses, "I know my transgressions" (v. 3). The grammar stresses the first person "I" with the word "know"—the same word used for sexual relations in Genesis 4:1. In Hebrew, the verb "to know" reaches beyond theoretical knowledge to an inner experience.[30] Again, David is deeply aware of his sin as he pleads with God for forgiveness.

*Prayer for forgiveness* (51:6-9). David's prayer for forgiveness draws on images of tabernacle worship: happy songs of praise; hyssop, a small bushy plant used for sprinkling to symbolize cleanliness;[31] and divine protection.[32] David particularly requests that he might experience restoration of joy (v. 8). VanGemeren explains the significance of that joy:

> Joy is the result of God's work in man (cf. Isa 65:17-18). Even as God's displeasure with sin brings judgment, metaphorically described as broken bones (v. 8, cf. 32:3; 42:10), so his pleasure brings joy of heart (vv. 8, 12). The joy is more than an emotional expression; it is a contented resting in God. The security of having been reconciled with the Lord and of having peace with him (cf. Rom 5:1) is of the greatest import. This joy is hence known as "the joy of your salvation" (v. 12).[33]

In full awareness of the seriousness of the sins he has committed, David asks God for forgiveness, believing he can be restored to this joyful condition of salvation.

*Prayer for restoration* (51:10-14). This part of the psalm probably expresses a desire to be restored to participation in the worship life of the community. Again, due to the sins of adultery and murder, which made him unclean, David was no longer in a condition to participate in the worship of

Israel. "David knows of no sacrifice that will suffice (v. 16) but he is confident that the Lord does."[34]

*Thanksgiving* (51:13-17). David vows to teach sinners the "ways" of God. While this could refer to the behavior God expects of people or the ways approved by God, in this context it probably has to do with "the ways of God in dealing with sinners."[35] In other words, having experienced God's gracious, forgiving restoration, David will share God's forgiving "ways" with other sinners. In this main part of the psalm, David concludes with celebration at having been restored to the worship life of the community. "From guilt to innocence, from death to life, the psalmist breaks into songs of praise and is restored to the . . . assembly (Ps 15:24). Yet . . . sacrifice did not achieve this transformation, only God did."[36]

*A prayer for Jerusalem* (51:18-19). David recognized that he could not sin simply as a private individual, but that his sin would have an effect on the Israelite community. He was, therefore, "as anxious for the building up of Jerusalem as for his own restoration."[37] After having learned that getting right with God was a matter of the heart (v. 17), he wanted to share his discovery with others. And so, David prayed that the Lord would "rebuild the walls of Jerusalem" (v. 18), which was a metaphorical way of praying that the Lord would make these principles "a foundational reality in the new community."[38]

## CONCLUSIONS

Psalm 51 focuses on confession of sin and restoration with God.

The second half of the psalm focuses on restoration, which naturally leads to ministry. King David made a commitment to teach transgressors and sinners the "ways" of God (v. 15). When we confess our sins and experience divine forgiveness, a powerful urge to minister will stir within us.

David's confidence was not in offerings or other sacrifices. Instead, David acknowledged that when God accepts offerings or sacrifices, it is only because they express "the sacrificial reality of the 'crushed' heart of the worshiper."[39]

This is a psalm about actual forgiveness granted in the Old Testament. Eugene Peterson summarizes the power expressed in the psalm:

> David's sin, enormous as it was, was wildly outdone by God's grace. David's sin cannot, must not, be minimized, but it's miniscule compared to God's salvation from it. It's always a mistake to concentrate attention on

our sins; it's God's work that's the main event. Our sins aren't that interesting; it's God's work that's interesting.[40]

Indeed, God's work is interesting. It's shocking. It's amazing grace.

## CONNECTIONS: EXPERIENCING THE FORGIVENESS OF GOD

Many people have tremendous difficulty experiencing the forgiveness of God. The difficulty experiencing heavenly love may stem from having experienced a deficiency of earthly love. John Powell explains, in *Why Am I Afraid to Love*, that "if the life and world of a person is marked by the absence of love, the reality of God's love will hardly evoke the response of the whole heart, soul and mind."[41]

In the novel *The Mission*, Robert Bolt tells a stirring story of two brothers—Rodrigo and Philipo Mendoza—who became orphans in 1725. As the eldest of the two brothers, Rodrigo, who was fourteen, put three-year-old Philipo in a convent school while he supported them both in the only way that he—a young, uneducated Spaniard—knew how, by joining the crew of a slave-trading ship. Mendoza lived by the sword and came to be respected by the upper classes of Spain and feared by the Guarani natives whom he hunted in the borderlands of Argentina, Paraguay, and Brazil. While Mendoza lived this life of darkness, he saw to it that Philipo was raised in comfort, received education, and was taught etiquette and culture. Over the years, Mendoza visited Philipo often and loved him deeply. At the same time, however, resentment simmered within Mendoza and, ultimately, when he discovered Philipo had a relationship with the woman whom he had his heart set upon, he killed his brother in a confrontation in the street.

To avoid arrest, Mendoza sought asylum in the church, where he was allowed to sleep in a small room. He would not eat, however, nor would he receive any ministrations from any of the clergy. A priest from a mission in the region where Mendoza had hunted the Guarani finally challenged Mendoza to seek God's forgiveness in a trek into that territory. With a huge sack of the weapons of his slave trade dragging behind him from a rope tied around his waist, Mendoza followed the priest through the jungle and, ultimately, on a dangerous climb up the side of a waterfall to a Guarani mission. The tribespeople—who had been elated when they saw the priests arriving— fell silent when they saw Mendoza crawl into view, exhausted from dragging his burden and battered by repeated falls. The tribal chieftain ran to him, grabbed him by the hair, and put a knife to his throat. The priests and tribespeople watched in silence. Then, in one deft movement, the chief moved the knife from Mendoza's throat to the rope that held his burden, cut it, and rolled it off the side of the waterfall, where it plummeted into the mists. Mendoza began to tremble, crying softly, and the chief and his tribespeople gathered around him, hugging him and tugging at his beard. His cries became sobs of joy as the Guarani he had once hunted embraced him, loved him, and forgave him.[42]

Mendoza's life was a hard one marked by rejection, abandonment, and a requirement that he adopt a posture of independence and self-reliance. Consequently, despite the lengths to which his sins had taken him, he had terrible difficulty experiencing forgiveness cognitively. He actually had to *experience* it. And he finally did experience forgiveness when the tribal chieftain extended it to him. Powell concludes that "there is no human being who will not eventually respond to love if only he can *realize* that he is loved."[43]

The human struggle with accepting and receiving forgiveness makes it difficult for us to accept the idea that it is offered to us freely in Christ. But this is a concept inherent within Christianity, and it is one of our faith's distinctive features. No other book of religion except the Bible teaches that God completely forgives sin. This truth is taught throughout the pages of the Old and New Testaments.

## DISCUSSION QUESTIONS

1. What are the points the author uses to make the case that the Old Testament believers were justified by grace through faith? Do you agree with these points? Why or why not?

2. How is "sacramental" language helpful in understanding the concept of Law in the Old Testament?

3. Discuss the words *hesed* and *raham*. What insights do these words bring to your understanding of God's care for His people?

4. What new insights does the study of Psalm 51 reveal to you about the nature and character of God in the Old Testament?

## CHAPTER 6

# A God Who Dwells among His People

*1 Kings 8:22-53*

Solomon, son of David and Bathsheba and third king of Israel, was one of the major figures of biblical history, famous for his wisdom, wealth, and construction of the temple. The writer of Kings paints a picture of Solomon as having comprehensive wisdom that spans juridical, administrative, and natural subjects.[1] His wisdom was so extensive that he developed a unique reputation both within Israel and internationally.[2] Solomon's wisdom was significant not because of the celebrity status it earned him, but because it brought about the fulfillment of two divine promises made to David. First, Solomon's wisdom made it possible for Israel to enjoy "rest from all your enemies" (2 Sam 7:10-11).[3] The royal wisdom of the king contributed to the well-being of society, resulting in Solomon ruling over a vast empire. The land was secure, and the people lived in prosperity (1 Kgs 4:20, 25).

This period of rest created the necessary conditions for the fulfillment of the second divine promise to David, which was the building of the temple. The construction of the Jerusalem temple was a major achievement in Israelite history, and the writer of Kings devotes four chapters to recounting its glorious construction, furnishings, and dedication (1 Kgs 6–9). At the center of these four chapters is Solomon's dedicatory prayer, which has been called "one of the major speeches in the Deuteronomistic history."[4] Solomon's prayer is important because of the way it articulates the role the temple is to have in the life of the nation of Israel. The speech, Gary Knoppers explains,

> presents the temple as a unifying symbol in Israelite life, a place to which people can turn to God in all kinds of predicaments (1 Kgs 8:22-53). Not only does the author link the temple's completion to the Davidic promises, but also to the Law of Moses. As an inducement to piety, the temple is also an inducement toward obedience to torah (1 Kgs 8:58-60).[5]

Solomon's dedicatory prayer is also incredibly important because of the sophisticated theology he articulates within it. Liberal critics of the Bible have long argued that early Israel's theology was simple and it only arrived at its more sophisticated views over many years of evolution. Howard Vos writes,

> An analysis of Solomon's prayer demonstrates the maturity of his theology and that of Israel at the time and argues against the critical view that Israel's theology was not highly developed until about 500 BC. Critics are so obsessed with the evolutionary view of Israel's religion that they find it hard to take anything in the early history of Israel at face value, even though archaeological and historical evidence continues to mount in support of the authenticity of the Old Testament.[6]

Indeed, when one examines Solomon's prayer of dedication, one will discover a highly sophisticated theological understanding of God that sets ancient Israel apart from the nations.

## THE JERUSALEM TEMPLE AND TEMPLES IN THE ANCIENT NEAR EAST

The Jerusalem temple was one of the wonders of the ancient world and, having been completed in 953 BC, stood for more than a thousand years before its destruction in AD 70.[7] Archaeologist Carol Meyers describes the amazing endurance of the temple's influence in the Western world:

> The Jerusalem Temple holds a place of great prominence in the architectural history of the Western world. No other building of the ancient world, either while it stood in Jerusalem or in the millennia since its final destruc-

tion, has been the focus of so much attention throughout the ages. Such attention has taken the form of the prayers and pilgrimages of the faithful, the discussions and deliberations of the postbiblical sages, and, in recent centuries, the incessant explorations, excavations, and expositions by the scholarly community.[8]

The Jerusalem temple is mentioned in more than half of the books of the Old Testament and in eleven of those in the New Testament. Many extrabiblical books as well contain references to the temple: 1 Esdras, Ecclesiasticus, 1 Maccabees, the *Letter of Aristeas*, the Temple Scroll, the Mishnah, and the Talmud. The historians Josephus and Philo both discuss the temple.[9] The only thing left of the temple today, the Western Wall, still holds an extremely important place within the lives of many Jewish people. After the six-day war in 1967, the Jews were once again given access to the Western Wall, and they flocked to it in celebration. Even today, many Jews carry out their Sabbath prayers at the Western Wall.

Temples played significant roles in ancient Near Eastern societies. Most importantly, they were seen to be the locus of a god's existence or of his power. In Babylonia, temples were understood to unite the sky, earth, and underworld. The Egyptian temple was understood to be the mansion "where the god lived" and where his ritual worship was carried out. Inscriptions refer to the inner sanctum of a Ptolemaic period temple as the "High Seat," which refers to "the mythical mound of primordial creation, the most powerful and sacred earthly place imaginable."[10] As one commentator has written, "The peoples of the ancient Near East believed that a god's temple on earth was a reflection or incarnation of the god's heavenly residence: to approach the temple of a god was to approach the presence of the god."[11] What is so fascinating about Solomon's prayer is the way in which it contrasts theologically with these views.

## INTRODUCTION, GATHERING OF THE ASSEMBLY, AND THE INSTALLATION OF THE ARK OF THE COVENANT: 1 KINGS 8:1-13

After lengthy descriptions of the construction and furnishings of the temple (chs. 6–7), the only things lacking within the structure were the ark of the covenant and the presence of the Lord Himself. Neither had the prayers and sacrifices of dedication been offered. To proceed with the dedication, Solomon called together the "elders of Israel," the "heads of the tribes," and the "princes of the father's houses" as representatives of Israel to bring the ark

up from the city of David. When they had all arrived in the temple court-
yard, they offered numerous sacrifices of thanksgiving and rejoicing, after
which the priests carried the ark into the holy of holies, setting it beneath the
protective wings of the cherubim (1 Kgs 8:6-7). The cherubim were sphinx-
like creatures with outstretched wings that served as a royal throne upon
which Yahweh sat.[12] The ark, containing the two tablets of the Ten
Commandments, served as His footstool. Reproductions of similar thrones
have been found on a sarcophagus of King Hiram of Byblos and on a carved
ivory panel from Megiddo.[13] Wright explains, "The winged beings described
as part of the throne . . . are common features in the iconography associated
with ancient Near Eastern thrones. Like any earthly king, Yahweh, too, sits
on a winged cherubim throne."[14]

Verse 8 makes what may seem like a curious reference to the carrying
poles of the ark. Two long poles, passed through rings on either side of the
ark, were used to carry the ark without actually touching it. As the ark was
deposited in the holy of holies, the carrying poles were left in place and were
seen protruding from either side of the curtain that shielded the most holy
place from the inner sanctuary. Rather than being an incidental side note,
this detail actually gives us a foretaste of the theology we will see in
Solomon's dedicatory prayer. Princeton scholar Choon-Leong Seow explains,

> The poles indicate the mobility of the ark and, hence, also the freedom of
> the deity from the sanctuary; this was no footstool of a deity permanently
> enthroned in the building. . . . the ark was merely a reminder of God's
> [kingship] and the covenant that bound Israel to the deity.[15]

Indeed, the stress in the text is on the fact that the ark is "the ark of the
covenant of the Lord" (vv. 1, 6), and the writer specifically noted the fact
that they contained the tablets that had represented the covenant between
God and Israel since the time of Moses (v. 9).

Once the ark of the covenant had been placed inside the holy place
within the temple, the text reports,

> And when the priests came out of the holy place, a cloud filled the house of
> the Lord, so that the priests could not stand to minister because of the
> cloud; for the glory of the Lord filled the house of the Lord.
> Then Solomon said,
> "The Lord has said that he would dwell in thick darkness.

> I have built you an exalted house,
> A place for you to dwell in forever." (vv. 10-13)

Choon-Leong Seow has argued that the poetic lines of vv. 12-13 should be translated as follows: "The Lord has said he would *tabernacle* in thick darkness. I [Solomon] have, indeed, built you a royal house, An *establishment of your enthroning*."[16] The idea of God's "tabernacling" presence is certainly prominent throughout the Old Testament. Seow explains,

> It is a way of conveying the free presence of the deity, an avoidance of the language of an enthroned and entrenched deity. So Ezekiel and the Priestly tradition of the Torah speak not of God enthroned in the Temple, but of God's glory, represented by a cloud that "tabernacles" at the sanctuary, coming and going as God wills (Exod 25:8; 29:45; Ezek 10:19, 22; 43:1-2).[17]

Talking about the temple as being filled with the cloud of the Lord's "glory" (vv. 10-11) and the "tabernacling" of the Lord through thick darkness "is a way of expressing the mysterious and free presence of the deity."[18]

## SOLOMON'S PRELIMINARY REMARKS: 1 KINGS 8:14-21

In his preliminary remarks, Solomon affirms the dual election of the Davidic dynasty and of Zion. He does this through a historical summary, reviewing how God had ultimately chosen Jerusalem for His abode and David to rule there. David had wanted to build the temple, but, despite God's complimenting him for his desire to do so, God promised that his son would do it instead. God had kept His word, as Solomon now sat on the throne and had built a temple "for the name of Yahweh." Solomon again stressed this carefully nuanced idea of divine presence, stating that "the deity is not enthroned in the Temple per se, yet divine presence is somehow represented by the Name of God in the Temple."[19]

Specifically, the temple is identified here as "a place . . . for the ark, in which is the covenant of the Lord that he made with our fathers when he brought them out of Egypt" (v. 21). This is certainly a reference to the ark's containing the tablets inscribed with the Ten Commandments. So, in addition to the temple being a place for the name of Yahweh, it was also a place that was to radiate Yahweh's covenant. For "It is the salvific presence of God, culminating in the covenant with Israel, that the Temple affirms. The

Temple is not so much the *locus* of God's presence as it is a reminder of God's free presence that is made good in the covenant."[20]

In this sense, the covenant is certainly more important than the temple, for the covenant will be the means by which God's promises to Abraham will ultimately be fulfilled. The temple may be one means of bringing about that fulfillment, but it accomplishes that only to the extent to which it points to the covenant and the God of the covenant.

## SOLOMON'S DEDICATORY PRAYER: 1 KINGS 8:22-53

> Then Solomon stood before the altar of the Lord in the presence of the assembly of Israel, and spread out his hands to heaven. He said, "O Lord, God of Israel, there is no God like you in heaven above or on earth beneath, keeping covenant and steadfast love for your servants who walk before you with all their heart, the covenant that you kept for your servant my father David as you declared to him; you promised with your mouth and have this day fulfilled with your hand. Therefore, O Lord, God of Israel, keep for your servant my father David that which you promised him, saying, 'There shall never fail you a successor before me to sit on the throne of Israel, if only your children look to their way, to walk before me as you have walked before me.' Therefore, God of Israel, let your word be confirmed, which you promised to your servant my father David.
>
> "But will God indeed dwell on the earth? Even heaven and the highest heaven cannot contain you, much less this house that I have built! Regard your servant's prayer and his plea, O Lord my God, heeding the cry and the prayer that your servant prays to you today; that your eyes may be open night and day toward this house, the place of which you said, 'My name shall be there,' that you may heed the prayer that your servant prays toward this place. Hear the plea of servant and of your people Israel when they pray toward this place; O hear in heaven your dwelling place; heed and forgive." (1 Kgs 8:22-30)

This dedicatory prayer is at the heart of the entire account of the dedication ceremony. The account emphasizes a number of things, the first of which is the covenant. This is entirely appropriate if the festival coincides with the Feast of Tabernacles, which was the time when the covenant was ceremonially renewed.[21] There is no one like the Lord, neither in heaven nor on earth. Israel's God is the king who keeps covenant promises.

There is a "movement away from the notion of God's enthroned presence in the Temple," which is "especially clear in the rhetorical question posed in v. 27: 'Will God indeed sit [enthroned] on the earth?'"[22] As one commentator has written, "Solomon clearly expresses God's infinity in these verses: heaven cannot contain him, much less a temple on earth."[23] Rather than being a literal place where God dwells, the temple is a place where God "manifests" His presence.[24] Choon-Leong Seow explains,

> The Temple is a reminder of God's kingship; it is an establishment of God's eternal "enthroning." That enthroning is not limited by any place; it is certainly not limited to the Temple, for Solomon pleads that God's attention be turned toward it.[25]

Solomon begs God, who is everywhere present, to "keep his eyes open upon this Temple constantly, so as to hear the prayers directed toward it." Again, Seow helps clarify:

> The Temple is not the place where the very person of God is; rather, it is merely the place where God's presence may be known, where the authority of God is proclaimed. . . . Locality is not at issue in this talk of God's realm. God's transcendence and sovereignty are.[26]

Indeed, Solomon is under no illusion that Yahweh could somehow be contained in the temple that he has built. John J. Bimson summarizes the issues cogently:

> His prayer is, therefore, not that God will take up residence in the temple, but rather that his attention will be focused on it to hear the prayers directed towards it. God will still be in "heaven, your dwelling-place" (v. 30), but the supplications of king and people will be received in the temple. In other words, Solomon prays that the temple might be the meeting-place for human need and divine mercy.[27]

"Solomon insists on the Deuteronomistic conviction that God does not literally reside in the Temple. Instead, it is only the Lord's 'name' that dwells there."[28] The "name" of Yahweh is what is called a "hypostasis," an extension or representation of his true being.[29] The name of Yahweh dwells in the temple, but not Yahweh in all the fullness of His being.

The next section of the prayer, vv. 31-53, is made up of seven petitions, all of which envision particular circumstances in the lives of individuals or the nation. Solomon continues,

If someone sins against a neighbor and is given an oath to swear, and comes and swears before your altar in this house, then hear in heaven, and act, and judge your servants, condemning the guilty by bringing their conduct on their own head, and vindicating the righteous by rewarding them according to their righteousness.

When your people Israel, having sinned against you, are defeated before an enemy but turn again to you, confess your name, pray and plead with you in this house, then hear in heaven, forgive the sin of your people Israel, and bring them again to the land that you gave to their ancestors.

When heaven is shut up and there is no rain because they have sinned against you, and then they pray toward this place, confess your name, and turn from their sin, because you punish them, then hear in heaven, and forgive the sin of your servants, your people Israel, when you teach them the good way in which they should walk; and grant rain on your land, which you have given to your people as an inheritance.

If there is famine in the land, if there is plague, blight, mildew, locust, or caterpillar; if their enemy besieges them in any of their cities; whatever plague, whatever sickness there is; whatever prayer, whatever plea there is from any individual or from all your people Israel, all knowing the afflictions of their own hearts so that they stretch out their hands toward this house; then hear in heaven your dwelling place, forgive, act, and render to all whose hearts you know—according to all their ways, for only you know what is in every human heart—so that they may fear you all the days that they live in the land that you gave to our ancestors.

Likewise, when a foreigner, who is not of your people Israel, comes from a distant land because of your great name—for they shall hear of your great name, your mighty hand, and your outstretched arm—when a foreigner comes and prays toward this house, then hear in heaven your dwelling place, and do according to all that the foreigner calls to you, so that all the peoples of the earth may know your name and fear you, as do your people Israel, and so that they may know that your name has been invoked on this house that I have built.

If your people go out to battle against their enemy, by whatever way you shall send them, and they pray to the Lord toward the city that you have chosen and the house that I have built for your name, then hear in heaven their prayer and their plea, and maintain their cause.

If they sin against you—for there is no one who does not sin—and you are angry with them and give them to an enemy, so that they are carried away captive to the land of the enemy, far off or near; yet if they come to their senses in the land to which they have been taken captive, and repent, and plead with you in the land of their captors, saying, "We have

sinned, and have done wrong; we have acted wickedly"; if they repent with
all their heart and soul in the land of their enemies, who took them captive, and pray to you toward their land, which you gave to their ancestors,
the city that you have chose, and the house that I have built for your name;
then hear in heaven your dwelling place their prayer and their plea, maintain their cause and forgive your people who have sinned against you, and
all their transgressions that they have committed against you; and grant
them compassion in the sight of their captors, so that they may have compassion on them (for they are your people and heritage, which you brought
out of Egypt, from the midst of the iron-smelter). Let your eyes be open to
the plea of your servant, and to the plea of your people Israel, listening to
them whenever they call to you. For you have separated them from among
all the peoples of the earth, to be your heritage, just as you promised
through Moses, your servant, when you brought our ancestors out of
Egypt, O Lord God. (1 Kgs 8:31-53)

The seven petitions in this lengthy passage have to do with oaths sworn
before the altar (31-32); defeat by an enemy (33-34); drought (35-36);
famine, pestilence, and other such catastrophes (37-40); the needs of foreigners within the land (41-43); going into battle (44-45); and captivity
(46-51). The seven examples of situations in which people might pray
toward the temple are not accidental: throughout the Old Testament, the
number seven signifies completeness and perfection. "Probably, then, these
seven examples are meant to represent all possible situations which could call
forth the prayers of individuals and the nation. All contingencies are covered."[30] Solomon seems to be saying that the efficacy of praying "to you,"
"toward your land," or "toward your temple" is complete.

Another feature of Solomon's speech is of special significance—
Solomon's prayer for blessing on God-fearing foreigners in vv. 41-43. Vos
argues that "this passage is absolutely remarkable."[31] He explains,

> Solomon not only recognized that God did not live in Jerusalem alone or
> in the temple alone but was the omnipresent God of all the earth.
> Moreover, though God had a covenant relationship with the Hebrews, He
> was not their God alone but was the God of all peoples who would wor-
> ship Him by faith. Thus he was far advanced beyond the narrow
> provincialism of a Jonah and others like him who thought of Yahweh as a
> kind of personal possession of the Hebrews and therefore they should have
> no interest in proclaiming Him to the nations.[32]

These verses represent "possibly the most marvelously universalistic passage in the Old Testament; it asks that the prayer of every foreigner may be heard, so that all the peoples may fear and know Yahweh."[33] Indeed, this was the original intent of the temple, that it be a "house of prayer for all nations." The great prophet Isaiah had looked forward to a time when this dimension of the temple's purpose would be realized:

> And the foreigners who join themselves to the Lord,
>> To minister to him, to love the name of the Lord,
>> And to be his servants,
> All who keep the Sabbath, and do not profane it,
>> And hold fast my covenant—
> These I will bring to my holy mountain,
>> And make them joyful in my house of prayer;
> Their burnt offerings and their sacrifices
>> Will be accepted on my altar;
> For my house shall be called a house of prayer
>> For all peoples. (Isa 56:6-7)

When Jesus drove out the traders and moneychangers, he did so because they had perverted the use of the temple, distracting from this important function (Mark 11:17). Far from being a peripheral purpose, the internationalization of the temple's message was to be *the very culmination* of Israel's life of worship! This becomes the theme of the New Testament.

## THE "GLORY" OF GOD MANIFESTED IN JESUS

Choon-Leong Seow writes, "In the New Testament, the presence of God is made manifest most decisively through Jesus."[34] The doctrines of the incarnation, atonement, and establishment of the church particularly reveal this idea.

The incarnation is probably taught most clearly in the prologue to the Gospel of John. In this deeply theological passage, John writes that "the Word became flesh and lived among us, and we have seen his glory" (v. 14). When John says he "lived among us," that could be translated literally as "he tabernacled" among us. During the wilderness sojourn, Yahweh tabernacled among the Hebrews in the tent of meeting. During the period of the monarchy he tabernacled "in thick darkness," manifesting himself in the Jerusalem temple. And now, in Christ, Yahweh has "[become] flesh and tabernacled among us." The doctrine of the incarnation teaches that God has "pitched his tent" and "revealed his glory" in the midst of all humanity, and, in this respect, Christianity is the internationalizing of Judaism.

The doctrine of the atonement, secondly, has deep implications for the way we are to understand the temple. Jesus used the analogy of the temple to talk about his death and resurrection. After he had "cleansed" the temple (John 2:13-17) of the traders and moneychangers, certain Jewish leaders asked him what authority he had to perform such an act, which seemed to be a heinous offense against the temple (v. 18). Jesus responded to them, "Destroy this temple, and in three days I will raise it up" (v. 19). The Gospel writer goes on:

> The Jews then said, "This temple has been under construction for forty-six years, and will you raise it up in three days?" But he was speaking of the temple of his body. After he was raised from the dead, his disciples remembered that he had said this; and they believed the scripture and the word that Jesus had spoken. (vv. 20-22)

Jesus' death and resurrection abrogate the need for the temple. Jesus is, in and of himself, the new temple.

Following Jesus' ascension into heaven, his disciples became his representatives in the world. Christians are the body of Christ in the world, which means that they, therefore, are the temple. In writing to the Corinthian church, the apostle Paul challenges them to understand that they, as a community, are "God's temple" and that God's Spirit dwells within them (1 Cor 3:16-17). This, indeed, is a humbling realization. When people encounter the Christian community in a church, they will not see a cloud of thick darkness. When someone meets a Christian on the street, they will not see all the finery of Solomon's temple. They will only see you and me. We must pray, therefore, that the Lord might make us worthy witnesses, that we might make manifest the Lord's glory in the world.

Lord, prepare me
    To be a sanctuary,
Pure and holy,
    Tried and true.
With thanksgiving,
    I'll be a living,
Sanctuary . . .
For you.[35]

## CONNECTIONS: WHY SHOULD WE CARE ABOUT UNITY?

It is difficult for a congregation of people with different backgrounds and social and economic levels to live together in unity. A particular church that comes to mind was having great success. Great numbers of people were repenting, believing the gospel, and turning to the Lord. There were even many within the congregation who claimed that they had experienced a miracle. Problems began to surface, however, when the church treasurer ran off with the money. Various people within the community began to get upset with the leadership. A member of the congregation's leadership team always seemed to act impulsively and immaturely. The situation eventually became so difficult that many of the people who had been founding members of the congregation actually moved to another city to worship.

If this story sounds unfamiliar, it shouldn't—this was the first congregation in the first century, made up of men and women who had personally been with Jesus![36] Since the first century, of course, the church has divided countless times, and we have hundreds of denominations today. Many believers even ask, "With all the division that has taken place in the church in the past, why even bother trying to maintain unity?" The reason remains the same today as it was in the first century. In his last hours, Jesus offered a prayer for his disciples that has come to be known as Jesus' High Priestly Prayer—it highlights the unity of Father, Son, and the believing community. As Jesus prays for the strength of the disciples to endure the difficulties they are about to face, he prays these words:

> I ask not only on behalf of these, but also on behalf of those who will believe in me through their word, that they may all be one. As you, Father, are in me and I am in you, may they also be in us, so that the world may believe that you have sent me. The glory that you have given me I have given them, so that they may be one, as we are one, I in them and you in me, that they may become completely one, so that the world may know that you have sent me and have loved them even as you have loved me. (John 17:20-23)

Jesus indicates that unity among his followers is important in order that the world might believe. Christ claims to be the great bringer of *shalom*—peace ("He is our peace"—Eph 2:14). Therefore, if the church is truly his body but full of chaos and dissension, then it disproves Christ's claim to be the true peace of humankind.

We must give our full attention to working toward maintaining unity within our congregations and establishing positive working relationships interdenominationally.

## DISCUSSION QUESTIONS

1. What was the role of temples in the ancient Near East? In what ways might the temples be compared to churches today?

2. Discuss 1 Kings 8:41-43. Why has this been called "possibly the most marvelously universalistic passage in the Old Testament"?

3. How does Jesus relate to the temple? What are the implications of Jesus' death for the way we are to understand the temple?

CHAPTER 7

# A God Who Never Sleeps

## 1 Kings 18:19-40

The contest between Elijah and the prophets of Baal on Mt. Carmel is probably one of the most dramatic and well-known passages of the Old Testament. In it, a lone prophet faces off against a king and his 450 "yes-men." A simple prayer is spoken, and the God of Israel rains fire from heaven that consumes a soaking wet altar and sacrifice. Baal is humiliated and his 450 prophets are slain by a riverside, where their blood washes away with the current. The point of the text that seems to come across from a superficial reading reminds me of one of the old Special Forces slogans: "If you mess with the best, you'll die like the rest." However, while the contest between Elijah and the prophets of Baal certainly demonstrates the power of Yahweh, it has much more to teach us. What it teaches us provides profound insight into the heart and mind of the God of Israel.

### THE NINTH-CENTURY CONTEXT

Our story is initially about a clash between a king and a prophet. The offices of king and prophet arose contemporaneously in Israel, with the role of the prophet being to hold the king in check. When the Israelites first demanded

a king, it was so they could be like the nations around them.[1] Samuel resis-
ted, giving them many reasons why they should refrain from allowing a
monarchy to be established in Israel. He gave what has come to be known in
academic circles as the "regulations of the kingship."[2] The "regulations of the
kingship," as described by Samuel, were totally lacking in any redeeming features and only described oppressive requirements. Among them was forced
labor, including compulsory recruitment of both military recruits[3] and
laborers in the field[4] and in the foundry.[5] The palace would require large
numbers of horses, and the king's chariots would need frontrunners.[6]
Women would not be exempt from the draft into royal service.[7] Even in desperate times, the king would always get his share—a minimum of 10 percent
of the income from field and flock.[8] Samuel's "regulations of the kingship,"
which would not benefit the average Israelite, were based on contemporary
Canaanite society. Samuel was begging the people not to impose on themselves a Canaanite institution alien to their own way of life.[9] Various pieces
of these regulations were later implemented by Saul[10] and Absolom,[11]
although Solomon would become the most notable offender. In the end,
Yahweh acceded to the Israelites' request, and Saul, an unknown donkey
wrangler, became Israel's first king.

   With the beginning of the monarchy came the beginning of the
prophetic movement. The prophets were teachers of ethics, writers of apoca-
lyptic material, historians, and authors of liturgical music. "The chief
function of the prophet," however, "is . . . to promulgate the law, preach its
observance after the manner of Moses, and transmit it to posterity."[12] This
means the prophet is not only to proclaim the Law, but he is "to predict the
consequences of ignoring or contravening it."[13] Accomplishing these tasks
"most often [meant] interaction with kings or other leaders of the nation."[14]
And so we find prophets confronting kings and queens, involved in partisan
political struggles, leading coups, enthroning particular kings, and seeking to
control foreign policy. As one commentator has written, "In general, then,
prophets were religious intermediaries who functioned at the national
level."[15] Arising contemporaneously with the monarchy, it seems that they
were to function with the monarchy as a sort of "checks-and-balances"
system. The prophets were to keep the power of the government in check
and to urge the king to conduct his reign in harmony with the Law.

## AHAB—"TROUBLER OF ISRAEL"

Ahab, who ruled from about 875–854 BC, was considered to have been the most evil king in Israel's history.[16] He succeeded his father Omri, who had reigned for twelve years during a period of political turmoil.[17] Ahab married the infamous Jezebel, daughter of the Phoenician Ethbaal, king of Tyre, and, in deference to her, he promoted the worship of Baal in Israel alongside the worship of Yahweh. The author of Kings reports that Ahab built both a temple and an altar for Baal in Samaria.[18] He also erected a "sacred pole" for the Baal's consort, the goddess Asherah.[19] The Canaanite cult of Baal apparently gained equal status in Israel with the worship of Yahweh, even receiving government support through the influence of Queen Jezebel and her court.

Yet, Ahab was a complex character. Some have argued that Ahab himself was not a worshiper of Baal, but that he simply instituted a political policy "of religious compromise and coexistence" in an effort to foster domestic peace. As one commentator has written, "Ahab himself, however, was hardly a Baal worshipper (contrary to 1 Kgs 16:31); the names of his sons Ahaziah and Jehoram contain the root of Yahweh's name, and these names were Ahab's way of demonstrating his attachment to the God of Israel."[20] In addition to giving his sons Yahweh names, Ahab also battled in the name of Yahweh,[21] placed Obadiah in charge of his palace,[22] and heeded the words of the prophets Micaiah[23] and Elijah when they reprimanded or challenged him. Despite the condemnation of the biblical writers, many of the rabbinical sources hold a positive view of Ahab. "Rabbi Johanan," for example, "argues that Ahab is worthy of 22 years of power because he revered the Torah's 22 letters and supported the sages."[24]

These positive assessments, however, are not warranted by the biblical text. The biblical writers make it clear that Ahab's leadership in the worship of Baal resulted in the drought and famine that ravaged Israel and led to Elijah's prophetic activities.[25] The drought lasts three years, and when King Ahab appears in chapter 18, it has gotten so bad that the king himself, along with a servant, is out personally scouring the countryside in hopes of finding grass to keep the horses and mules alive (1 Kgs 18:5-6). When Ahab and Elijah finally meet in 18:17, Ahab angrily identifies Elijah as a "troubler of Israel." Elijah fearlessly replies, however, "I have not troubled Israel; but you have, and your father's house, because you have forsaken the commandments of the Lord and followed the Baals" (v. 18). Elijah unhesitatingly pinpoints Ahab as the true source of trouble and charges him directly with apostasy—

that of personally following Baal and of instituting Baal worship throughout the land.

## THE WORSHIP OF BAAL IN ANCIENT ISRAEL

We know that throughout much of Israel's history, the nation struggled with idolatrous worship of other gods. Baal was one of the most popular gods they worshiped. Who was this deity? Why were the Israelites so drawn to him?

Baal was the Canaanite storm and fertility god. He was one of the most significant deities in the ancient Near East, which makes sense in light of the fact that populations were dependent upon rain-fed agriculture. The Baal cult likely played "a major role" in the daily life and ritual of ancient Canaanites, "given the paramount need for rain and its continuous impact upon the population."[26] The god Baal was also thought of as governing fertility, a concept that naturally extends from that of rain. Deriving from this idea is the representation of Baal as a bull, "underscoring the fructative powers of the god."[27] In addition, Baal is also represented as a warrior with a bolt of lightning in hand, an image surely inspired by the inherent power of thunderstorms themselves. Given the arid environment in which Israel existed, it should not be surprising that the people would be tempted to worship this god who offered potency, fecundity, and power.[28]

The evidence, in fact, shows that they frequently and continually succumbed to those temptations. Many of the sites bearing on Israelite religion, founded and settled during this period, were named after Baal. In fact, sites bearing his name are more common than those named after any other god.[29] The Bible gives the names of many sites with names like Baal-Peor, Baal-hermon, Baal-meon, Baal-hazor, Baal-gad, and others. Many Israelites in this period also used "Baal" in their names or in naming their children. Mepibaal, for example, means "from the mouth of Baal." Beelliada means "Baal knows."[30] There are also two examples within the Old Testament of individuals who simply bear the name "Baal" itself.[31] It is not that the people abandoned Yahweh worship altogether, but they believed they could worship other gods—especially Baal—in addition to Yahweh.

The data from the period suggest that while the "official" religion of Israel was monotheistic Yahwism, on the popular level many people were polytheistic.[32] One Old Testament scholar writes,

> There is evidence from the OT that Yahweh and Baal could [even] be equated in syncretistic circles. One may compare the personal name

Bealiah, lit. "Yahweh is Baal" (1 Chr 12:5), and Hosea's declaration, "And in that day, says the Lord, you will call me 'My husband,' and no longer will you call me 'My Baal' (2:16)."[33]

It is clear from the Old Testament that the Baal cult provided the greatest and most enduring threat to the development of exclusive worship of God within ancient Israel. Beginning with the wilderness events at Baal-peor (Num 25), Israel began to worship Baal on a regular basis. Throughout the book of Judges, the cycles of foreign political oppression centers on the worship of Baal.[34] The degree of syncretism was extensive, and it plagued Israel well into the exile.[35]

At the point of Israel's history with which we are dealing in this chapter, Israel had an altar for Baal housed inside a temple dedicated to the god, both commissioned by Ahab and financed by the public purse.[36] Ahab was, indeed, the "troubler of Israel" in that he continued to promote and sponsor the Baal cult.

## RADICAL MONOTHEISM

The appellation "troubler of Israel" was first used by Ahab in regard to Elijah, however. Ahab was furious with Elijah because, in addition to emphasizing the religious issue of who controlled the rainfall, the drought also threatened the basis of economic life in Israel. This "would have also precipitated a political crisis, since a disaster of this magnitude would tend to raise questions about the legitimacy of the dynasty."[37] So Ahab was determined to bring the drought to an end for more than religious reasons. Thus he conceded to Elijah's suggestion that they hold a contest between Yahweh and Baal on Mt. Carmel, a mountain ridge just south of Haifa Bay and not far from Phoenician territory.

The contest was arranged, with "all Israel" called to watch as Elijah and 450 prophets of Baal carried out their "standoff." Elijah began the proceedings by confronting the people with a question: "How long will you go limping on two crutches?" (v. 21). In other words, he wanted to know how long they would attempt to depend on Yahweh and Baal at the same time, combining Yahwism and Baalism in a syncretistic approach. He advised them to make their choice: "If Yahweh is God, go after him; but if Baal, go after him" (v. 21). Many modern scholars have argued that the choice Elijah presents here is given with a syncretistic understanding. In other words, neither Elijah nor the Israelites had any conception of Yahweh as "the *only*

God." What was at issue, according to this approach, is the matter of worshiping Yahweh alone. Susan Ackerman, for example, makes this argument:

> Almost all [biblical scholars] would now suggest that what we know today as self-conscious, philosophical, or radical monotheism was a fairly late development in Israel, and a date during the exile is commonly cited. Yet this does not imply that the Israel of the pre-exilic period was radically polytheistic. Scholars tend instead to describe the nation as monolatrous or henotheistic. That is, while Israel does not deny the existence of other gods, she does reject the idea that these other gods play a significant role in her national cult. For the Israel of the first half of the first millennium, then, while Yahweh is not the only god, Yahweh is the only god who matters.[38]

Ackerman is surely wrong. The natural reading of the text implies that Elijah's contest challenges "not only the power but even the existence of Baal."[39] Battenfield has argued that "the struggle was not one of political expediency or religious preference only; it was to the death, so violently opposed were the two competing systems."[40] The whole point of the passage is that "Elijah swept away such syncretistic thinking. The people must make a decision: Yahweh or Baal."[41] "Syncretistic worship of both at the same time is impossible."[42] While modern critics argue that monotheism *evolved* from polytheism, the biblical writers insist that polytheism, in Israel, always *devolved* from monotheism. The Bible depicts ancient Israel as holding to an unadulterated form of Yahwism, even in its earliest periods. This should come as no surprise to those familiar with the monotheistic revolution in Egypt and Mesopotamia at the close of the Bronze Age. The monotheism of Moses, and even of Abraham, rather than being a fanciful retrojection of a post-exilic author, is entirely plausible,[43] as is the radical monotheism of the ninth-century Elijah.

Indirectly, the contest between Elijah and the prophets of Baal also had significant political ramifications for Israel. While the biblical prophets were not *primarily* interested in politics, their activity was usually *inherently* political in light of the fact that Israel was intended to be a theocracy. Norman Gottwald made these significant observations:

> Elijah does not appear to have had any clear concern with foreign affairs as such. Only to the extent that he contends for the Yahwistic purity of Israel does he have any strong convictions on relations with other states. By forbidding Israelite kings to recognize foreign gods and to provide reciprocal

worship, the prophet forecloses the possibility of foreign relations among equal states.[44]

While many Americans might cringe at Elijah's presumption that he could "forbid" the state to something or other on religious grounds, the prophet's radical monotheism precluded international relations if those relations would threaten the religious integrity of the nation. Gottwald even speculates, "In fact, the contest between Baal and Yahweh on Mount Carmel may have been a frontal attack upon the Israelite treaty with Tyre."[45]

## THE PRAYER CONTEST BETWEEN ELIJAH AND THE PROPHETS OF BAAL

Once the people had gathered on Mt. Carmel, Elijah proposed his criteria for the test (vv. 22-23). Two bulls would be secured, one for Baal and the other for Yahweh, and prepared for sacrifice. However, the sacrificial fires would not be ignited. Instead, the devotees of each god were to call on their deity, and whichever one responded by igniting the fire would be recognized as the true God.

Elijah let the prophets of Baal make their sacrifice first, in order that they could not claim he had left them with an inferior bull or that he had put them at a disadvantage in any other way. He probably believed they would not be able to get their sacrificial fire lit and that this would therefore leave Yahweh with an opportunity to make a dramatic intervention.

So the Baal prophets were given every advantage and the entire day. Over and over, they tried to rouse their god. Verse 26 says "they hopped about the altar they had made." Their hopping, limping step here may imply a ritual dance of some sort, meant to attract the god's attention to the people's request.[46] Elijah eventually began to mock them sarcastically, telling them to call more loudly. He said, "Maybe he's meditating, or he has wandered away, or he is on a journey, or perhaps he is asleep and must be awakened" (v.27). Elijah's taunting is deeply satirical, as evidenced by his crude suggestion that Baal has "wandered away," which is generally understood to be a euphemism for going to the bathroom. Elijah is suggesting that because Baal is attending to his own bodily needs, he is unavailable for the needs of his priests. By his caustic wit and sardonic expression, Elijah is trying to show the fallacy of believing in a god who is, in fact, not a god at all.[47]

When their day's prayers were unsuccessful, the prophets of Baal "cried aloud and, as was their custom, they cut themselves with swords and lances until the blood gushed out over them" (v. 28). In the Bible, the shedding of blood is associated with rites of mourning and was probably an expression of extreme grief. It was actually outlawed for Israelites,[48] possibly because of a connection with a cult of the dead. Finally, the prophets had worked themselves into a frenzy, and they are described in v. 29 as "raving." Ecstatic activity among prophets in Canaan and Mesopotamia often involved the use of dirt, self-infliction of wounds, and self-mutilation.[49] In any case, the Baal prophets resorted to this kind of behavior in the hope that it would move Baal to action.

All the activity of the Baal prophets, however, was to no avail. Later Jewish tradition embellished the story greatly in order to heighten the humiliation of the prophets of Baal. Talmudic scholar Louis Ginzberg summarizes the traditions thus:

> The priests sought to deceive the people. They undermined the altar, and [a prophet named] Hiel hid himself under it with the purpose of igniting a fire at the mention of the word Baal. But God sent a serpent to kill him. In vain the false priests cried and called, Baal! Baal!—the expected flame did not shoot up. To add to the confusion of the idolaters, God had imposed silence upon the whole world. The powers of the upper and the nether regions were dumb, the universe seemed deserted and desolate, as if without a living creature. If a single sound had made itself heard, the priests would have said, "It is the voice of Baal."[50]

There was, however, "no voice and no answer" (vv. 26, 29), and the silence speaks volumes. Baal does not speak. He does not act. The truth of the matter is, he does not exist.

Elijah then moved ahead with his own game plan, bringing the witnesses up close in order that they could be sure he was not tricking them. He prepared an appropriate sacrifice on a restored altar of twelve stones, a symbolic construction that probably represented "the participation of 'all Israel' in the proceedings being commemorated."[51] He then cut a deep trench around the altar, soaked the altar itself, and filled the trench with water, all to heighten the miracle. Elijah finally stepped up to where he could be seen by the assembled crowd (v. 36), and he uttered a simple prayer to Yahweh.

O Lord, God of Abraham, Isaac, and Israel, let it be known this day that
you are God in Israel, that I am your servant, and that I have done all these
things at your bidding. Answer me, O Lord, answer me, so that this people
may know that you, O Lord, are God, and that you have turned their
hearts back. (vv. 36-37)

Elijah's prayer was that the Lord Himself would demonstrate who is truly
God. His focus was on the people, "that they may know." He prayed that the
Lord Himself would prompt their repentance (v. 37). Interestingly, Elijah's
words here are the same as those prayed by the prophets of Baal (v. 26).

Then "Yahweh's fire descended and consumed the offering, the wood,
the stones, and the dust" (v. 38). The image painted here is that of Yahweh
personally answering Elijah's prayer, for "the fiery apparition often symbolizes [Yahweh's] presence."[52] Yahweh Himself, in the form of the fire,
responds from heaven, consuming Elijah's sacrifice and turning the people's
hearts back. While it is Baal who is often pictured on reliefs as the storm-god
with a lightning bolt in his hand, it is Yahweh who controls the elements.
The passage is powerful because, "in contrast to the dancing and slashing
prophets of Baal, Elijah himself does not act. The Lord does it all."[53]

As dramatic as the fire from heaven is, however, it is not the climax. The
actions and words of the people, who witnessed the contest between Baal
and Yahweh, make up the real climax. "When the people saw this, they fell
on their faces and said, 'The Lord indeed is God; the Lord indeed is God'"
(v. 39). The confession of the people echoes Elijah's initial challenge of v. 24:
"the god who answers by fire is indeed God."

## SLAUGHTER OF THE PROPHETS OF BAAL

The people's confession is immediately followed by an order to slaughter the
prophets of Baal (v. 40) in obedience to the command of Deuteronomy
13:5, which calls for the death of false prophets. The prophets are seized,
taken down to the Kishon Valley, and killed. Many readers have great difficulty understanding or accepting passages such as this. Terence Fretheim,
while praising Elijah's leadership in proposing the contest between Yahweh
and Baal, concludes that the killing of the Baal prophets is a sad example of
human corruption.

Yet human violence is in evidence here as well (v. 40). This should not be
explained away, but neither should it be considered necessarily just, even if

it is understood to obey the law (Deut 13:1-5). Once again, God does not act alone; but God works in and through that which is available, with human beings as they are, with all of their flaws and foibles. God does not perfect people before deciding to work through them.[54]

Even evangelical writer John Bimson has difficulty accepting the verdict on the false prophets and consigns Elijah's actions to a "fanatical tendency": "The writer [of Kings] relates the massacre without comment here, but Elijah is later rebuked for a train of thought that amounted to fanaticism, and his all-out slaughter of the prophets of Baal should perhaps be seen as an outcome of his fanatical tendency."[55] Cogan argues, however, that these invalid efforts to explain away the harshness of this passage is "introducing contemporary moral sensitivity foreign to the text."[56]

The fact is, the capital punishment of the prophets of Baal is not some violent appendage to this text but is, rather, at the heart of what this passage is all about. Israel was called for a specific purpose: in order that every nation might ultimately be blessed (Gen 12:3). False prophets—spiritual and intellectual leaders within Israel—could not be tolerated within the nation because "the whole call of Israel would be put in danger by such a person."[57] False prophets put God's whole program of salvation history at risk and must, therefore, be dealt with severely. "Idolatry would, and did, undermine the very purpose for which God had chosen Israel, which was in the end the salvation of the world."[58]

In putting the Baal prophets to death, Elijah is obeying the command of Deuteronomy 13:4-5, which reads as follows:

> The Lord your God you shall follow, him alone shall you fear, his commandments you shall keep, his voice you shall obey, him you shall serve, and to him you shall hold fast. But those prophets or those who divine by dreams shall be put to death for having spoken *treason* against the Lord your God—who brought you out of the land of Egypt and redeemed you from the house of slavery—to turn you from the way in which the Lord your God commanded you to walk. So you shall purge the evil from your midst.

When Yahweh brought Israel out of Egypt, He established the covenant with them. Yahweh was the suzerain, and Israel was the vassal. The covenant was a vital part of the formative period of Israel, designed to protect the identity of Israel as God worked out His plan ultimately to redeem humankind through that nation. Due to the critical nature of protecting Israel's identity during the nation's formative period, the covenant promised not only substantial blessings for those who followed it, but severe punishments for those who violated it. The covenant was a legal arrangement. You will notice the legal word I have italicized in the quote from Deuteronomy 13:5: the false prophets are to receive the capital punishment because they have committed a capital crime against the nation—*treason*. In carrying out their work as false prophets, they are attacking and subverting the fabric of Israelite society; they are betraying the divine suzerain.[59]

The seriousness of the punishment for false prophets must be seen in light of the fact that the Hebrew faith was still in its nationalist stage, and the national religious identity needed to be protected. So the contest between Elijah and the prophets of Baal was a duel to the death.

> Yahweh is the only God for Israel, and divided allegiances are as unfaithful as abandonment of Yahweh altogether. Israel's limping with two different opinions needs to be named for what it is: It is not neutrality, tolerance, apathy, indecision, indifference, or lukewarmness. It is apostasy, pure and simple.[60]

## THE RESTORATION OF AHAB?

With Yahweh's drought brought to its conclusion, Elijah instructed Ahab to "go up, eat and drink" (v. 41). He himself then withdrew in order to undertake an intense prayer ritual, in response to which God broke the drought (vv. 41-46). As Elijah prayed atop Mt. Carmel, the sky blackened and the rain came, completing the demonstration that Yahweh, not Baal, is the God of life and fertility. When it became clear that rain was on its way, Elijah sent word to Ahab to hurry and hitch up his chariot and drive to Jezreel before his chariot got mired in the muddy roads.

The account closes in vv. 45-46 with an unusual event: "Ahab rode off and went to Jezreel. But the hand of the Lord was on Elijah; he girded up his loins and ran in front of Ahab to the entrance of Jezreel." This closing detail is often seen as a final demonstration of superiority over Ahab. As Ahab headed back to the palace, Elijah raced past him as if to remind him who was who. One author also takes this approach: "Charged with superhuman vitality by the agency of the Lord's spirit, the prophet runs the 17 miles (26 kilometers) to Jezreel at chariot speed. Once again the writer uses a tale of superhuman prophetic powers to celebrate the authority of the prophetic word."[61]

Rather than showing further humiliation of Ahab, however, the writer may be intending to indicate that Ahab has returned to exclusive Yahweh worship. Howard Vos points out, "There is no record of Ahab's opposition to the execution [of the priests of Baal], nor is there any indication of how he really felt about Yahweh's miraculous demonstration of himself."[62] Ahab did not object to the contest; indeed, he obeyed Elijah's instructions to summon the people as witnesses. When the contest was over, he did not object to the killing of the Baal prophets. Mordechai Cogan interprets these factors positively, drawing the conclusion that at this point "Elijah took up the role of one of Ahab's outrunners, showing the respect due him as king after the victory over Baal and his worshipers, and Ahab's return to the national God."[63] It is true that under normal conditions in Israel "king follows prophet," and so Elijah's running ahead of Ahab's chariot to Jezreel may symbolize a return to Israelite normalcy,[64] which would indeed provide a "happy ending" to the story of the contest on Mt. Carmel.

## WHAT KIND OF GOD IS THE GOD OF ISRAEL?

This dramatic story of Elijah facing off against the prophets of Baal is usually seen as an account intended to demonstrate the power of Yahweh over against the false, Canaanite gods. God's answer to Elijah's prayer is usually perceived to be evidence of God's transcendent power. While these points are certainly a part of the theology of the biblical writer, Fretheim identifies two points within the text that have much deeper theological lessons for us than the mere demonstration of Yahweh's power. Each of these points reveals something about what kind of God this is that has responded to Elijah's prayer.

First, the God who has answered Elijah's prayer is *immanent*. Yahweh is understood to be near, both in proximity and involvement. Whereas the gods of the Canaanites were capricious, unpredictable, and unavailable, Yahweh wanted to be known, trusted, and even loved by His people. Deuteronomy 6:4-5, which became something of a creedal statement for ancient Israel, held this immanence of God at its core: "Hear O Israel: The Lord is our God, the Lord alone. You shall love the Lord your God with all your heart, and with all your soul, and with all your might." Fretheim explains this immanence in contrast to Baal's unavailability:

The problem with Baal is not that he is distant or removed, but that he does not listen or speak or feel or act or care: "There was no voice, no answer, and no response" (vv. 26, 29). The concern here is more to protect Yahweh's immanence than to demonstrate divine transcendence. Yahweh listens to Elijah's prayers and responds to them.[65]

Yahweh is immanent.

Second, the God who answered Elijah's prayer is a God who is *committed*. Again, the contest between the two gods is usually seen as a demonstration of power. It is often thought of as revealing Yahweh's freedom to act in contrast to Baal's inability to act. As one commentator has written,

> But more to the point here is the concern for God's commitment, which by definition entails a self-limitation of freedom. God has promised to send rain (v. 1); God honors the relationship with the prophet; God remembers commitments made to Abraham, Isaac, and Israel (v. 36; cf. v. 31) by responding to that particular formulation in the prophetic prayer.[66]

Yahweh answers Elijah's prayer because of His commitment to Israel. God had bound Himself to them in covenant, and this inherently meant He was limited in the ways He could respond to them. In order to be true to His promises—indeed, in order to remain just—Yahweh had to respond. Elijah has prayed that God will send fire to the sacrifice "so that His people may know" that He alone is God.

> For God to respond to a prayer with this basic motivation is for God to remember commitments made, most fundamentally to Abraham, Isaac, and Jacob. God has named this people Israel (v. 31; all twelve tribes), has called them his own, and acts in faithfulness to that relationship.[67]

In summary, the God who responds to Elijah's prayer is a God who is involved in human affairs. The Canaanite gods were unpredictable and unknowable. They could not be trusted and, if they were to be involved in human affairs, it would only be as a result of having been begged and cajoled by their subjects to do so. This is what we see in the contest on Mt. Carmel: the priests of Baal beg and cajole their god to respond, but he does not. Fretheim concludes,

> The concern of the text, then, is not simply to show that Yahweh alone is God, as important as that is. The concern here is also to reveal something

about the basic character of this God. Yahweh is one who is active in human affairs, who listens, speaks, and acts, and who honors commitments made to chosen representatives and to the people with whom a special relationship had been established. It is precisely *this kind of God* that is to be the only God for Israel. Even more, it is this kind of God who is the only God, period.[68]

So the contest at Mt. Carmel reveals much more than the might Yahweh can muster. It reveals who Yahweh is. It reveals His attributes. It reveals His love.

## "DON'T PRAY AS THE GENTILES DO"

Jesus wanted his disciples to understand these attributes of God as well. He said to them on one occasion, "When you are praying, do not heap up empty phrases as the Gentiles do; for they think that they will be heard because of their many words. Do not be like them, for your Father knows what you need before you ask him" (Matt 6:7-8). In the non-Jewish world, prayer was often characterized by magical incantations or actions. In these cases, what was considered important was saying the incantation correctly or a certain number of times. If magical actions were being performed—as on Mt. Carmel when the prophets of Baal seem to have been performing something like a rain dance—then what was important was performing it properly. The worshiper's attitude or intention was not at issue in either of these cases.

Jesus urges his disciples away from the pagan perception of prayer as something mechanical. I do not think Jesus is saying not to repeat a prayer, because we are told specifically that on at least one occasion he repeated his own prayer—and he repeated it three times (Matt 26:44). He is also clearly not arguing against set forms of prayer, because in the verses immediately following he gives his disciples a set form-prayer (Matt 6:9-13). R. T. France explains, "This is not a prohibition either of repetition in prayer or of set forms of prayer, but of thoughtless, mechanical prayer. It is not many words that God responds to, but an attitude of prayerful dependence."[69] Unlike the pagan gods, the God of Jesus does not have to be bullied into taking notice. True prayer, therefore, is not about technique but about relationship.

Early homileticians—or preachers—often associated Jesus' teaching in Matthew 6 with the approach the prophets of Baal took to their god in 1 Kings 18. In a sermon on Matthew from the patristic period, for example, an anonymous preacher said this:

Let us note carefully the gods to whom the pagans pray, that we may understand how not to pray. They pray to demons, which may hear but are not able to heed. They are not even able to supply evil things, unless God permits it. They pray to dead kings . . . and others, whose crimes are more manifest than their names. They were not able to help, even while they lived. They pray to insensate idols, which are not able to hear or to give responses. Understandably then their priests spend a long time summoning when there is no one to hear. When the priests of Baal called on their gods through immolated sacrifices, Elijah said in a mockery, "Shout, shout strongly: perhaps your gods are sleeping." In the same way the person who prolongs his prayer with a lot of talk rails at God, as if he were sleeping.[70]

## CONCLUSIONS

The encounter between Elijah and the prophets of Baal on Mount Carmel, and the short prayer Elijah prayed that brought the contest to its dramatic end, have much to teach modern believers. The prayer, first of all, revealed Elijah's radical monotheism. Rather than being a fanciful retrojection of an eighth-century writer, radical monotheism seems to have been a part of the life of Israel early in its history. Israel at its best did not conceive of Yahweh as one god among many, or as one god over many, but as the only God who really existed at all. Further thought might also be given to how seeing Elijah's actions as a possible protest of the treaty with Tyre, and therefore an acceptance of its gods, may affect how we think about the relationship between faith and politics.

Of primary interest is what this passage has to teach us about who God is. From this text, the Christian understands that God is both immanent and committed. God is near. God is involved in our world, and in the lives of those who have committed themselves to Him. God is there. And He is not sleeping.

## CONNECTIONS: ABERRANT CHRISTIANITY

Just as Old Testament believers struggled with aberrant Yahwism, the early church also struggled with a variety of aberrant forms of Christianity. In the first quarter of the second century AD, the Docetists doubted the full reality of Jesus' humanity and claimed that Jesus only appeared to be human. A bit later, the Marcionites disclaimed the Jewish roots of the new Christian movement and wanted to jettison the Old Testament entirely. The

Jewish-Christian Ebionites wanted to hold on to the food laws and other aspects of Jewish ritual, and they denied the Virgin Birth. In the latter part of the second century, the Montanists refused to accept canonical Scripture but accepted the continued revelations of their own charismatic prophets. One of the most persistent enemies of the early church was Gnosticism, whose greatest leaders flourished between about AD 135 and 165. Rejecting the Jewish tradition (like the Marcionites), they offered instead a complex mythological system with a hierarchy of numerous spiritual forces that together made up the *pleroma*, or "fullness." In Gnostic theology, Jesus was simply one spiritual force among many.[71]

While many think of these as "ancient" heresies, many of them are actually strangely modern and, through both the academy and mainline churches, have come into the mainstream. Within the church, a notorious example is the now infamous Re-Imagining conference of 1993, held in Minneapolis and sponsored in part by the United Methodist and Presbyterian Church (U.S.A.), where participants partook of a Eucharist (Lord's Supper) using milk and honey and offered prayers to Sophia, the patron of the movement. One of the speakers, Delores Williams, a seminary professor, declared, "I don't think we need a theory of the atonement . . . . I don't think we need folks hanging on crosses and blood dripping and weird stuff."[72]

More recently, retired bishop John Shelby Spong has denied every supernatural aspect of Christianity, including the incarnation, the Virgin Birth, and the resurrection. He has even denied theism and its concept of a personal God, and asks whether there are other alternatives to theism other than atheism.[73] Another notorious example in the academy is the Jesus Seminar, which has tried to fashion itself as an organizational alternative for a new, ultraliberal Christianity. Robert Funk, its founder, has proclaimed that "there is not a personal god out there external to human beings and the material world" and that "it is no longer credible to think of Jesus as divine."[74]

The early Christians carefully articulated their faith, first in the New Testament and later in the creeds, in ways that clearly refuted the heresies—both ancient and modern. One of the earliest of the creeds is the Apostles' Creed, which reads:

I believe in God the Father almighty, creator of heaven and earth. And in Jesus Christ, his only son, our Lord, who was conceived by the Holy Spirit, born of the Virgin Mary, suffered under Pontius Pilate, was crucified, died, and was buried. He descended into hell, on the third day rose again from the dead, ascended to heaven, sits at the right hand of God the Father almighty, thence he will come to judge the living and the dead.

I believe in the Holy Spirit, the holy catholic church, the communion of saints, the forgiveness of sins, the resurrection of the body, and life ever-lasting. Amen.[75]

The creeds provide a direct challenge to the work of the Jesus Seminar, which argues that the church stifles the reality of the historical figure of Jesus, and "the smothering cloud [is that of] the historic creeds."[76] For Christians who use the creed, we must recapture its power, for it "enunciates a powerful and provocative understanding of the world, one that ought to scandalize a world that runs on the accepted truths of Modernity."[77]

## DISCUSSION QUESTIONS

1. What was the relationship between the kings and the prophets intended to be? Does that relationship have implications for how Christians should relate to political leaders and/or to the government as a whole?

2. What were the differences between Israel's "official" religion and its "popular" religion? Can inferences be drawn about the existence of an "orthodox" Christianity in contrast to a "popular" Christianity? Can we identify forms of aberrant Christianity existing today?

3. What are the implications of the slaughter of the prophets of Baal? What does Elijah's prayer contest teach us about prayer?

## CHAPTER 8

# A God Who Values the Ordinary

## *1 Chronicles 4:9-10*

Jabez's prayer may be the most well-known prayer in America today. While people may not be able to recite the prayer itself, Christians and non-Christians alike are at least familiar with the title of Bruce Wilkinson's bestseller, *The Prayer of Jabez*. The account of Jabez and his prayer is found in 1 Chronicles 4:9-10:

> Jabez was honored more than his brothers; and his mother named him Jabez, saying, "Because I bore him in pain." Jabez called on the God of Israel, saying, "Oh that you would bless me and enlarge my border, and that your hand might be with me, and that you would keep me from hurt and harm!" And God granted what he asked. (NRSV)

This description of Jabez and his prayer are typical of the brevity of many of the accounts within 1 and 2 Chronicles. While there is much ambiguity in the passage, Wilkinson has developed an entire theology from Jabez's prayer, some of which we will explore in this chapter.

## Does Blessing Mean Financial Gain?

One can read the "testimonies" of many readers of *The Prayer of Jabez* at the web site dedicated to the book. Many readers report having prayed about opportunities to share their faith, coping with the loss of a loved one, or praying that a friend facing difficult times might come to know the Lord. For many other readers, however, God's blessing apparently means something material. An individual who had recently retired and was worried about money prayed the prayer and, miraculously, he received a refund check from his life-insurance company, along with his first retirement check. A young person prayed the Jabez prayer for his mother, who then got an advancement that led to financial increases of "thousands of dollars a day." One man increased his real estate sales while a woman reported that, after praying the prayer, "my clients just started calling in orders for more business." Another woman received a payment from her insurance company that had previously been denied. After praying the Jabez prayer, someone found an unexpected income tax check in the mailbox in the exact amount a creditor had recently demanded, someone else was able to get a new car, and another individual got the amount of a speeding ticket reduced.

While financial concerns are important, and the Bible certainly has a lot to say about money, it would be an anathema to suggest that the blessing of God is to be equated solely with wealth. There are surely many people around the world who have lived well below what Americans would consider "poor," yet who could testify to the richly blessed lives they have lived. Rather than requiring money to enrich one's life, the Bible teaches that it is "*the blessing of the Lord* [that] makes one rich" (Prov 10:22). In other words, it is the blessing of the Lord *itself* that enriches one's life. In this sense, experiencing the blessing of the Lord has to do with one's relationship with God[1] and all the ways in which that relationship affects one's life. Rachel Magdalene suggests, "The benefactions of God are diverse and include vitality, health, longevity, fertility, land, prosperity, honor, victory, and power."[2]

My point here is simply that any understanding of "blessing" limited to financial gain impoverishes the idea of blessing. Certainly some of the most important ways to understand blessing have to do with the process of sanctification, or seeking to conform oneself to the holiness of God, since Paul calls God "blessed" in the sense of being holy (Rom 1:25). Another significant means of receiving blessing is that of experiencing Christ through the Lord's Supper, since Paul calls the communion wine the "cup of blessing" (1 Cor 10:16).

## CAN WE LIMIT GOD?

A second area of concern I have about *The Prayer of Jabez* is its premise that believers are impeding God's ability to work in their lives by their failure to ask for blessing. Wilkinson explains that "your life will become marked by miracles . . . [when] God's power to accomplish great things suddenly finds no obstruction in you. . . . Suddenly the unhindered forces of heaven can begin to accomplish God's perfect will—through you."[3]

When it comes to God working in your life, Wilkinson explains, "there's a catch."[4] And the catch is, God can only bless you when you specifically ask God to do so. Furthermore, Wilkinson explains, God will only bless you with specifically what you ask for. He asks, "What if you found out that God had it in mind to send you twenty-three specific blessings today, but you got only one. What do you suppose the reason would be?"[5] In answer to the question, he tells a fictitious story about a Mr. Jones who, upon arriving in heaven following his death, is shown an enormous warehouse in which is housed row upon row of shelves, each stacked with "all the blessings that God wanted to give him while he was on earth . . . but Mr. Jones had never asked."[6] Wilkinson concludes, "Even though there is no limit to God's goodness, if you didn't ask Him for a blessing yesterday, you didn't get all that you were supposed to have. God's power is limited only by us, not by His resources, power, or willingness to give."[7]

Is God's ability to bless truly limited by whether or not fragile, fallen human beings remember to pray? If and when people pray, is God's power held in check by whether or not they pray for the right things? As the great apostle Paul exclaimed so often, God forbid! In fact, the Bible teaches exactly the opposite. In Exodus 33:19, God claims that He can bless whomever He desires to bless: "I will have mercy on whom I will have mercy, and I will have compassion on whom I will have compassion." Paul quotes this passage in making the argument that the fulfillment of God's plans does not "depend on man's desire or effort, but on God's mercy" (Rom 9:16).

The truth of the matter is that men and women are fallen creatures. Among the effects of the fall is what theologians call the "noetic" effect, which refers to sin's impediment of the human mind.[8] Having experienced the noetic effects of sin, men and women are now unable to engage in fully pure thought processes. Even believers will never gain the loftiest heights of creativity, love, or nobility because, along with every other dimension of creation, their minds are "subjected to futility" (Rom 8:20). This means that, even when Christians remember to pray, they will often pray wrongly, selfishly, or for things that are not in harmony with God's will. And yet, an amazing thing happens. Paul describes it with these grace-filled words:

> the Spirit helps us in our weakness; for we do not know how to pray as we ought, but the Spirit himself intercedes for us with sighs too deep for words. And he who searches the heart of men knows what is the mind of the Spirit, because the Spirit intercedes for the saints according to the will of God. (Rom 8:26-27)

This is a powerful teaching indeed. Even after coming into a saving relationship with Christ, believers remain weak. Only at the second coming will "glory" be revealed in us (Rom 8:18). Until then, we are in the "bondage to decay" (Rom 8:21), meaning we will continue to grapple with imperfection and sin. We will forget to pray, and when we do remember to pray, we will often pray for the wrong things. But the Holy Spirit will pray on our behalf. And the Spirit will pray the right things, praying "according to the will of God." Throughout Scripture we see prophets running from the call of God,[9] sometimes praying that God will leave them alone to die or even kill them Himself.[10] God works in the lives of those who believe in Him, but God also works in the lives of those who don't believe in Him.[11] God worked in the life of the Babylonian king Nebuchadnezzar in such a way that the powerful king eventually came to "praise and exalt and glorify the King of heaven" (Dan 4:37). Isaiah refers to the Persian king Cyrus as God's "shepherd" (Isa 44:28), explains that God is the source of Cyrus's extraordinary military ability (Isa 45:1-4), and even calls Cyrus God's "anointed one," or "messiah" (Isa 45:1)—even though Cyrus is not a follower of Israel's God. God's ability to work in someone's life does not depend on whether they are praying correctly, whether they are praying at all—or even whether they believe in Him!

Humankind cannot limit God. If the wicked cannot limit God through their evil deeds, then certainly the righteous cannot limit God by their failure to pray. Whether we pray or not, whether we are praying the right things or not, God is working in our lives in such a way that "everything works together for good for those who love him" (Rom 8:28).

## THE PRAYER OF JABEZ AND THE OVERALL PURPOSE OF CHRONICLES

The major shortcoming of Wilkinson's book is that it misses the way Jabez's prayer fits into the book of Chronicles as a whole. Wilkinson describes the book of Chronicles as "boring"[12] and says "a story breaks through" only when you get to the prayer of Jabez.[13]

Wilkinson sees the prayer as Jabez's private prayer, dealing with his own personal life and his private relationship with God. He believes it is a gem that just happened to be found in the boring book of Chronicles.

I want to suggest to you that when we look at how the prayer of Jabez fits into the book of Chronicles as a whole, we'll find that his prayer goes vastly beyond personal concerns and that it has a relevance for us that's much more important than our private goals.

## THE PURPOSE OF THE BOOK OF CHRONICLES

The book of Chronicles covers biblical history from Adam (1 Chr 1:1) to the Persian King Cyrus (2 Chr 36), which is basically the end of the Old Testament history.[14] St. Jerome called it "the chronicle of the whole of sacred history." By the time the Chronicler wrote this history, the nation of Israel had basically been wiped out. The Assyrians had deported and dispersed the people of Northern Israel in 722 BC, and the Babylonians had destroyed Southern Israel and the Jerusalem temple in 586 BC. The Babylonians then carried many Israelites into captivity—a period known as the exile. After the exile, what was left of Israel limped back to its homeland to try to start over.

So the Chronicler is writing during a time when religious enthusiasm is at a low point in the nation, and he's trying to encourage the people in their faith. He does it by reviewing the entire biblical history. He shows how, through all the calamities Israel had experienced in its history, through all the national disruption, God had preserved His people. God's promises had not failed. Israel had not been destroyed. Israel had not been divided. God had preserved His people, and the promises God had made to Israel were still intact.

One scholar says that, taken as a whole, the books of 1 and 2 Chronicles show us "the principle of the continuity of the people of God through a period of national disruption."[15]

Chronicles, then, is an important and patriotic piece of work for the nation, reinforcing "the indivisibility of Israel." Just like we say in our pledge of allegiance, we're pledging our loyalty to "one nation, under God, indivisible . . . ." We don't pledge allegiance to a divided nation, but an *undivided* nation, an indivisible one. When we say the Pledge of Allegiance, we're promising that we'll help maintain the indivisibility of our nation, the oneness of our nation.

That's the big picture of what the writer is trying to do with Chronicles. He's talking about how the nation had been preserved throughout its history, even when that history was very dark.

## CHRONICLES' HISTORY COMPOSED OF ORDINARY PEOPLE

But the history of a nation is built on the lives of real people. The Chronicler, in telling the story of Israel, uses genealogies of ordinary people to carry the story along. Interspersed throughout the genealogies are various speeches, sermons, and prayers.

Basically, the writer is saying, "Yes, our nation has been through hard times. We've seen times when our nation was characterized by moral depravity, and there were times when it seemed as if our nation had been all but destroyed. But it hadn't been destroyed. Here and there were faithful men and women, and through them God preserved the nation."

This is a book about national preservation through the ordinary people who worked and prayed in the land of Israel. The circumstances and prayer of one such individual are recorded in 1 Chronicles 4:9-10.

## JABEZ THE MAN

We know little about any of the people named in vv. 8-16 of this genealogy, and all we're told about Jabez is that his mother gave him his name because, she said, "I bore him in pain." His name rhymes with the Hebrew word for pain.[16] Wilkinson writes,

> All babies arrive in this world with a certain amount of pain, but there was something about Jabez's birth that went beyond the usual—so much so that his mother chose to memorialize it in her son's name. Why? The pregnancy or the delivery may have been traumatic. Perhaps the baby was born breech. Or perhaps the mother's pain was emotional—maybe the child's father abandoned her during the pregnancy; maybe he had died; maybe the family had fallen into such financial straights that the prospect of another mouth to feed brought only fear and worry.[17]

We just don't know. But we do know his mother gave him a name in commemoration of that pain. Everyone knows how burdensome a bad name can be. Many young people endure the ridiculing of one another's names on the playground. Could Jabez's playmates have made fun of the fact that his name rhymed with "pain"? When he got in trouble, did Jabez's mother ever say, "You're such a pain"?

We certainly cannot build a biography about Jabez from this one line, but we can see that he must have decided that, rather than becoming bitter, he would become better. We are told that Jabez developed a reputation in life as being more honorable than all his brothers.

His life was characterized by the prayer recorded here, where he says, "O Lord, that you would bless me indeed, and enlarge my territory."

## JABEZ'S PRAYER

Now, at first glance, that may seem like a selfish prayer. But let's remember the context. The Chronicler sees Jabez's prayer as somehow contributing to the survival of the nation, to the indivisibility of the nation.

In Israel, the physical manifestation of God's covenant with Abraham, Isaac, and Jacob was the land of Israel itself. God had promised to give it to the twelve tribes of Israel. Jabez was in the tribe of Judah. As he prays, he's not praying for himself, but he's saying, "Lord, enlarge my territory, enlarge the tribe of Judah. Be true to your covenant. Preserve and build this nation, your people."

Throughout Israel's history, the nation was constantly going after idols, worshiping other gods, and violating their covenant relationship with God. While it often seemed that the nation had gone too far, there were at all times ordinary men and women who remained faithful to God. These people prayed on behalf of the nation. This seems to be the Chronicler's whole point in writing his book: it was because of the efforts and the faithfulness of ordinary people like Jabez that God preserved the nation.

## THE JABEZ PRAYER TODAY

You and I can certainly pray the Jabez prayer today, and we should. It means praying that God will use us to enlarge His kingdom. For us to pray that God will enlarge our "territory" would essentially mean we're asking to God to enlarge our influence in ways such as these:

- If we own a business, it would be a positive thing to pray for its enlargement. This would mean the possibility of creating jobs for people, who would then come under our influence. It would mean increasing our income, which could mean an increase in our tithe.

- If we are teachers, we might pray for more students or the opportunity to more specifically influence the lives of our students.
- If Jabez had been a wife and mother, the prayer might have gone, "O Lord, bless me with children. Smile on my marriage, and increase the influence of my family in my community."
- For the church to pray the prayer would mean the same thing. "Lord, increase our territory. Increase our opportunity for ministry in this community. Increase our effect on those who live in our sphere of influence. Give us more opportunity to spread the gospel. Help us be a part of influencing and preserving this nation in which we live by making an impact on our own community and city."

As you can see, the prayer of Jabez for us today would simply challenge Christians to seek more blessing, more opportunity to glorify God, and more guidance than we have ever asked for before.

The prayer of Jabez is noteworthy because it calls us to seek to make the biggest impact possible. It calls us to pray that we will live lives that make an impact. It calls us to go after "the big prize" in terms of the difference our lives can make when we live them for Christ.

St. Paul certainly had this attitude. He said, "I press toward the goal for the prize" (Phil 3:14). He looked forward to the day when he could give an account for what he had done (2 Cor 5:9-10).

May we, too, have such ambitions. That's what the prayer of Jabez calls us to.

### CONNECTIONS: WHAT ABOUT THE POOR?

A "gospel of health and wealth" has sometimes promoted the idea that those who are truly faithful will be rewarded with increased income and material rewards. This idea implies that those who have greater incomes have had a more genuine Christian experience than those who have lower incomes. Where do the poor fit into this kind of thinking? Do people suffer in poverty because they have not believed enough? These understandings of wealth and poverty do not reflect biblical teaching.

While the book of Proverbs does generally present a principle of "cause-and-effect" by which one can be responsible for one's own poverty,[18] the Old Testament also acknowledges a variety of groups within Israelite society who experienced poverty as a result of circumstances over which they had no control. In a patriarchal society where the male was the worker, widows and

orphans struggled to survive. "Strangers,"[19] too, who had no tribal or famil-
ial connections and therefore no status in the land, often had difficulty
surviving. Old Testament legal texts regulate the treatment of the poor,
regardless of which of the three categories they were in—widows, orphans, or
strangers (Lev 19:9-10; 25:25, 35). Yahweh is said to care deeply for these
groups, and Yahweh Himself is even spoken of in the Psalms as being the
defender of the poor (Ps 22:26; 35:10).

This understanding of the poor is carried over into the New Testament.
James, the brother of the Lord, defined "true religion" as "caring for orphans
and widows in their distress" (Jas 1:27).[20] The apostle Paul spearheaded an
extensive fundraising campaign among the wider church to help the poor
believers in Jerusalem (Rom 15:25-27, 30-33; 1 Cor 16:1-4; 2 Cor 8–9; Gal
2:1-10). Jesus himself taught that when we reach out to the poor, we are
reaching out to Christ (Matt 25:37-40).

To explore ways in which you and your church might get involved further in ministering to the poor, have your Sunday school class or small group
read and discuss *The Welfare of My Neighbor: Living Out Christ's Love for the
Poor*, by Deanna Carlson (Washington, DC: Family Research Council,
1999), along with the *Workbook and Supplemental Guide: Applying the
Principles Found in The Welfare of My Neighbor*, by Amy Sherman and
Deanna Carlson.[21]

## DISCUSSION QUESTIONS

1. Can the blessing of God be equated with wealth? Why or why not?

2. Do believers impede God's ability to work in their lives by failing to ask
for blessing? Does God only interact with us in ways in which we ask Him
to? Read Romans 8:26-27 and comment on how these verses might apply.

3. Review the Old Testament cases in the chapter where God worked in the lives of those who did not even believe in God. What is your reaction to these cases? What are the implications for the life of a believer?

4. What is the purpose of the book of Chronicles? How does the brief account of Jabez fit into the overall purpose of the book of Chronicles?

## CHAPTER 9

# A God Who Never Loses Hope

*Daniel 9:1-19*

In the midst of exile, living among a pagan people, the prophet Daniel articulated a stirring prayer. Daniel made his prayer to God during the first exile
of the Israelites. The Babylonians, under the leadership of Nebuchadnezzar,
had invaded Jerusalem in 587 BC and taken back to Babylon all the people of
Judah who had not escaped to the hills. The highest officials, priests, and
most skilled artisans were particular targets of the aggressor nation.
Deportation of this educated class affected the leadership and economy of
the nation. These were tactics to demoralize Israel, weakening them so that
they would not have the strength or leadership to retaliate. The Babylonians
weakened the nation's sense of identity and nationality. The exile was a
calamitous time in Israel's history.

From the outset, however, the author of Daniel wants readers to know
that Nebuchadnezzar's success did not come about through his power alone;
rather, it was the work of the one, true God—Yahweh, Lord of Hosts. It was
the Lord who brought about the complete collapse of the Jewish monarchy.
It was Yahweh who caused the people of Judea to be deported in exile. On
the surface, it may have seemed that what had happened was a political acci-
dent. But Daniel would have us understand that God was and still is in

control. The divine purpose behind all of Israel's dreadful humiliation, suffering, and loss was redemptive. God could snatch the Israelites away from their bondage at any time, but that would only happen when they were ready to renew their covenant fellowship with Him. God's purpose in Daniel is to bring His people back to repentance through disciplinary suffering. Daniel's powerful prayer articulates and expounds upon these ideas.

## BACKGROUND TO DANIEL'S PRAYER

In Daniel 9, we find the prophet trying to understand the "seventy years" of which Jeremiah spoke concerning the restoration of Jerusalem after the Babylonians destroyed it in 587 BC. The prophet had written that seventy years would be allotted to Babylonia for their domination of Israel.[1] Speaking on behalf of God, Jeremiah had said, "Thus says the Lord: only after seventy years have elapsed for Babylon will I visit you and fulfill for you my promise to bring you back to this place [Jerusalem]" (Jer 29:10). Daniel was studying the prophecies of Jeremiah in an attempt to discover when the end of the Jewish persecution would be. As he struggled with these issues, he sought understanding in prayer. As intriguing as the angel Gabriel's response will be in the later chapters of Daniel, the focus here, as in previous chapters, will be on what Daniel's prayer can reveal to us about the nature of Israel's God as the people perceived Him in the seventh century BC.[2]

## DANIEL PRAYS FOR UNDERSTANDING

The author of the book introduces Daniel's prayer with notes regarding the historical context and then begins to record the prophet's petition. What compels Daniel to pray in this case is his desire to gain insight regarding Jeremiah's comments about the restoration of Yahweh's holy city—Jerusalem.

> In the first year of Darius son of Ahasuerus, by birth a Mede, who became king over the realm of the Chaldeans—in the first year of his reign, I, Daniel, perceived in the books the number of years that, according to the word of the Lord to the prophet Jeremiah, must be fulfilled for the devastation of Jerusalem, namely, seventy years. (9:1-2)

The setting of this chapter is the first year of the Persian king, Darius, whom readers first encounter in 6:1, in the story of Daniel in the lion's den (6:2-29). Daniel has been reading "the Scriptures," literally, "the books," containing the prophecy of Jeremiah. This is the first mention in the Bible of a special collection of sacred books, and it may refer to a collection of prophetic works that at that time was already accepted as a single portion of what would eventually become the Old Testament.

## DANIEL'S PRAYER OF LAMENT

After introducing us to the setting in which Daniel prays, the author then begins to record his actual petition, which begins with a lament: "Then I turned to the Lord God, to seek an answer by prayer and supplication with fasting and sackcloth and ashes" (9:3). Daniel's prayer is curious because it is not a personal prayer for enlightenment about the seventy weeks, as we might expect. Instead, it is a humble confession of the nation's sins and a heartfelt plea for mercy and deliverance. Daniel turns to Yahweh, "pleading in earnest prayer, with fasting, sackcloth, and ashes" (v. 3). According to Exodus 34:28 and Acts 13:2, fasting is a preparation for receiving a revelation and, at the end of his prayer, Daniel would hope to receive a divine message from the angel Gabriel. Sackcloth and ashes were used as a form of penance in biblical times.[3]

Daniel proclaims his faith in divine mercy for those who love God and keep the covenant by observing the commandments (v. 4). God is ever true to His word: God's mercy is always present to those who are faithful to Him.

## DANIEL'S CONFESSION OF THE NATION'S SINS

Following his lament, Daniel begins to confess the nation's sins.

> I prayed to the Lord my God and made confession, saying,
> "Ah, Lord, great and awesome God, keeping covenant and steadfast love with those who love you and keep your commandments, we have sinned and done wrong, acted wickedly and rebelled, turning aside from your commandments and ordinances. We have not listened to your servants the prophets, who spoke in your name to our kings, our princes, and our ancestors, and to all the people of the land.
> "Righteousness is on your side, O Lord, but open shame, as at this day, falls on us, the people of Judah, the inhabitants of Jerusalem, and all Israel, those who are near and those who are far away, in all the lands to which you have driven them, because of the treachery that they have committed against you. Open shame, O Lord, falls on us, our kings, our officials, and our ancestors, because we have sinned against you. To the

Lord our God belong mercy and forgiveness, for we have rebelled against
him, and have not obeyed the voice of the Lord our God by following his
laws, which he set before us by his servants the prophets.

"All Israel has transgressed your law and turned aside, refusing to obey
your voice. So the curse and the oath written in the Law of Moses, the servant of God, have been poured out upon us, because we have sinned
against you. He has confirmed his words, which he spoke against us and
against our rulers, by bringing upon us a calamity so great that what has
been done against Jerusalem has never before been done under the whole
heaven. Just as it is written in the Law of Moses, all this calamity has come
upon us. We did not entreat the favor of the Lord our God, turning from
our iniquities and reflecting on his fidelity. So the Lord kept watch over
this calamity until he brought it upon us. Indeed, the Lord our God is
right in all that he has done; for we have disobeyed his voice." (9:4-14)

Daniel then confessed the sins committed by the chosen people in the Holy
Land as well as "in all the countries to which [God has] scattered them" (vv.
5-14). Daniel acknowledged that it was not the Babylonians who destroyed
the kingdom of Judah, but rather it was God Himself who brought "upon us
in Jerusalem the greatest calamity that has ever occurred under heaven" (v.
12).[4]

The subject of the exile has raised issues of justice in the minds of many
readers. How could a loving God send His people into exile under the heavy
hand of an enemy? Walter Brueggemann portrays the exile as a result of
Yahweh's "inclination," an occasion in which God is "sloughing off" the
people to whom He has constrained Himself to be faithful.[5] Is the exile
indeed a "sloughing off"? An occasion in which Yahweh simply "blows off"
His people or "makes light of" His covenant commitment to them, as
Brueggemann's language implies? In the ancient Middle East, gods were
often perceived to have abandoned their people.

The concept of "divine abandonment" was well known in the ancient
world, and the Old Testament is not unfamiliar with it. Daniel Block has
recently undertaken a detailed study of ancient Near Eastern national theology, titled *The Gods of the Nations*, in which he cites a number of passages to
illustrate the concept of "divine abandonment" as understood by ancient
Israel's neighbors.[6] In Isaiah 46:1-2, the prophet sarcastically pictures
Babylon's gods as powerless to prevent their own capture:

Bel bows down, Nebo stoops,
Their idols are on beasts and cattle;

These things you carry are loaded
As burdens on weary animals.
They stoop, they bow down together;
They cannot save the burden,
But themselves go into captivity.

Likewise, Jeremiah predicts the exile of Chemosh, god of the Moabites: "And
Chemosh will go into exile, Together with his priests and his princes" (Jer
48:7). Lastly, Block points to Jeremiah 49:3, in which the exile of Milcom,
god of the Ammonites, is anticipated: "For Milcom will go into exile,
Together with his priests and his princes." And, while God's people mock-
ingly described pagan gods as abandoning their people, Israel also feared the
consequences of being abandoned by Yahweh. But is the exile simply another
case of "divine abandonment" when Yahweh is exposed as unreliable and no
different than the pagan gods?

The parallels are important for helping us understand the nature of the
exile, but Block enumerates six significant contrasts—all taken from the
account of the departure of Yahweh's glory from His temple in Ezekiel
8–11—that reveal the uniqueness of Yahweh and His relationship with
Israel.[7] They can be summarized as follows:

(1) Yahweh's abandonment of the temple is a response to sinfulness, not
    capriciousness.[8]
(2) Yahweh leaves His temple of His own accord—He is not taken into cap-
    tivity or expunged by enemy invasion.[9]
(3) Disastrous effects attend Yahweh's departure.[10]
(4) Yahweh promises to follow the exiles and become a sanctuary for them
    "in the lands where they have arrived."[11]
(5) Non-biblical, ancient Middle Eastern texts emphasize a change of heart
    within the god prior to reinhabiting the shrine. Biblical texts, in contrast,
    emphasize that Yahweh will change the hearts of Israelite men and
    women in order to make them eligible for restoration to the land.[12]
(6) Biblical texts imply that the story of Yahweh's relationship with His
    people cannot and will not end with His departure from the land.[13]

When these six contrasts are taken into account, Block concludes, it becomes
clear that "the vision [of Yahweh's abandonment of His temple] functions as
a deliberate *polemic against* the typical Mesopotamian understanding of
divine abandonments."[14] Yahweh did not "abandon" His people out of

capriciousness. The exile was not a "sloughing off." In fact, God did not abandon His people at all, but accompanied them into exile where He would work on their hearts ultimately in order to bring about their own restoration.

Israel's exile was not a sudden, flippant action on God's part. God had warned the people repeatedly that He would curse and destroy them if they did not heed His voice.[15] In both Leviticus 26 and Deuteronomy 28, the severance of the tie between Israel and its homeland is held out as the final, catastrophic consequence of prolonged, flagrant rebellion of the nation against its Lord. Daniel Block explains,

> The purpose of the exile will be to cause the nation to perish outside [their own land], among the nations, and to evoke remorse on the part of the people for their infidelity. Should the latter occur, the covenant would be renewed, as a result of which the nation's reunification with the land would ensue.[16]

Because kings and people alike refused to repent by turning back from their wickedness, "the Lord kept watch over the calamity and brought it on us." So Daniel praises God for being righteous and true to His word: "You, O Lord, our God, are just in all that you have done, for we did not listen to your voice" (9:14).[17] The psalmist expresses similar feelings in Psalm 119:75: "I know, O Lord, that your ordinances are just, and in your faithfulness you have afflicted me."

## DANIEL APPEALS FOR MERCY

Following his admission of the nation's sins, Daniel begins to make an appeal for God's mercy:

> And now, O Lord our God, who brought your people out of the land of Egypt with a mighty hand and made your name renowned even to this day—we have sinned, we have done wickedly. O Lord, in view of all your righteous acts, let your anger and wrath, we pray, turn away from your city Jerusalem, your holy mountain; because of our sins and the iniquities of our ancestors, Jerusalem and your people have become a disgrace among all our neighbors. Now therefore, O our God, listen to the prayer of your servant and to his supplication, and for your own sake, Lord, let your face shine upon your desolated sanctuary. Incline your ear, O my God, and hear. Open your eyes and look at our desolation and the city that bears your name. We do not present our supplication before you on the ground

of our righteousness, but on the ground of your great mercies. O Lord, hear; O Lord, forgive; O Lord, listen and act and do not delay! For your own sake, O my God, because your city and your people bear your name! (9:15-19)

Daniel affirmed his faith in the God "who led [His] people out of the land of Egypt with a strong hand."[18] Frankly confessing the sin and guilt of the whole people, including himself (vv. 15, 20), he appealed to God's mercy. Though the people had become "the reproach of all [their] neighbors" on account of their "sins and the crimes of [their] ancestors," Daniel begged the Lord to "allow [His] anger and wrath to turn away from [His] holy city Jerusalem, [His] Holy Mountain" (v. 16).

Speaking in his own name, Daniel finally prays,

Hear . . . O God, the prayer and petition of your servant; and for your own sake, O Lord, let your face shine upon your desolate sanctuary . . . . O Lord, pardon! O Lord, be attentive and act without delay, for your own sake, O my God, because this city and your people bear your name! (9:17, 19)

The God of Israel is a God who is close to His people, who can be addressed with openness and confidence. Daniel reminds God that coming to the rescue of His people is something Yahweh should do "for [His] own sake," a phrase Daniel repeats twice.[19] Jerusalem and the chosen people should be spared because they bear God's name—an idea adapted from Psalm 79:9, where the people, aware of their great sin, rely not on their own righteousness, as if they could earn God's grace, but rely only on God's "great mercy," saying,

Help us, O God of our salvation,
    For the glory of your name;
Deliver us, and forgive our sins,
    For your name's sake. (Ps 79:9)

Many modern people have lost a sense of sin and responsibility for the crime, poverty, and corruption facing our cities, our nations, and our world. But we have all "sinned, been wicked and done evil; we have rebelled and departed from [God's] commandments and . . . laws" (Dan 9:5). Nor have we obeyed "God's servants the prophets" (vv. 6, 10) who plead with us:

"Turn back, each of you, from evil way and from your evil deeds; then you shall remain in the land which the Lord gave you and your fathers, from of old and forever" (Jer 25:5). Instead of turning back to God in humble prayer and sincere repentance, however, we have often turned our backs on God. We have looked for solutions to our problems in social and political action alone, as if the demands of God do not matter in human affairs. However, confessing our sinfulness, turning away from our personal and institutional evil, and embracing a life of righteousness based on God's Law are essential if we are to survive as a people—indeed, if humanity is to survive.

The Bible teaches loudly and clearly that God has a stake in our world. Yahweh is not simply a God "out there," utterly removed and beyond humanity. He is, rather, a God who is "right here," totally present and involved in the lives of human people and communities. One recalls the words of Jesus here: "Jerusalem, Jerusalem, you who kill the prophets and stone those sent to you, how many times I yearned to gather your children together, as a hen gathers her young under her wings, but you were unwilling! Behold, your house will be abandoned, desolate" (Matt 23:37-38). The Lord is concerned about our towns and cities as well. He grieves over the drug and alcohol abuse, sexual promiscuity, homelessness, marital irresponsibility, lack of reverence for human life, crime, racial and sexual discrimination, and political and social corruption.

Daniel singles out kings, princes, and ancestors for special blame (9:8). These are the political and spiritual leaders responsible for promoting the welfare of the community. Although they, just like the rest of us, will have to give an account to the Lord, we should never hesitate to tell them that they are also accountable to us for what they have done or have failed to do. In addition, modern believers must keep in mind that we may have been part of the problem, too. Indeed, Daniel explains that "Open shame . . . falls *on us . . . and our ancestors*, because *we* have sinned against [God]" (v. 8). While Daniel singles out past leaders for special blame, somehow their sin reaches fruition in the sin of the current generation. John Goldingay explains,

> It is a common human experience that one generation will pay for the wrongdoing of the previous generation; the exile, in particular, resulted from the actions of earlier generations, as well as those of people actually alive in the sixth century BC (Lev 26:39-40; Lam 5:7). This does not mean that a generation may be punished despite being relatively innocent itself: if a generation repents, it finds mercy. It does mean that the effects of

wrongdoing accumulate over time, and that the next generation will likely walk the same way as the previous one.[20]

Old Testament confessions often acknowledge ancestral sin.[21] It is easy to allow one's thought processes—whether religious, social, political, or otherwise—to be "inherited" from the previous generation. Each generation, however, must accept responsibility for maintaining its own accountability with God. Unless all people—leaders and followers alike—are willing to repent and follow the way of the Lord, our house too will become abandoned and desolate.

Daniel longs for the restoration of Jerusalem and its temple. A major thrust of his prayer is that Yahweh reverse His abandonment and desolation of His temple (vv. 7, 16-19). Daniel 9:20, in fact, describes the entire prayer as a petition "on behalf of the holy mountain of God," which means the request for the restoration of Jerusalem—the city on Mt. Zion—was at the heart of his prayer. Goldingay explains some of the theological and political reasons for this emphasis on Jerusalem in Daniel's prayer:

> Yahweh's city, centered on Mt. Zion, is the perfection of beauty, the joy of all the earth; it is the place where Yahweh has made himself known in the history and the worship of his people (Ps 48; 50:2). It is the city Yahweh chose as the dwelling place of his name (Neh 1:9, identifying Jerusalem as the place denoted by Deut 12:5).[22]

The restoration of the city of Jerusalem—of Zion—became an extremely significant issue during the period of the exile because "the Babylonians' desolation of Jerusalem put a question mark by the theological claims that had been made for Zion."[23] Jeremiah explains the problem of the abandonment of Jerusalem in the book of Lamentations:

> All who pass along the way
>     Clap their hands at you;
> They hiss and wag their heads
>     At daughter Jerusalem;
> "Is this the city that was called
>     the perfection of beauty,
>     the joy of all the earth?" (Lam 2:15)

If Yahweh allowed His sanctuary and holy city to lie permanently in ruins and His people to remain in exile, then who among the surrounding nations would believe that the God of the Bible was the true and holy Sovereign over all the universe? Gleason Archer explains,

> That, in Daniel's mind, was the worst thing about the tragedy of Jerusalem's fall and the captivity of Judah—all the pagans would surely conclude that it was because of Yahweh's inability to protect his people against the might of Babylon's gods that Israel had fallen and been driven out of her ancestral soil.[24]

During and after the exile, therefore, the theme of Jerusalem's restoration became a significant theme for prophets and political leaders of the Jewish community. In a dramatic reversal of the abandonment of the temple in Ezekiel 10–11, the prophet drew his book to a close with a vision of the Lord's presence filling the temple once again:

> Son of man, this is the location of my throne, and the place of the soles of my feet, where I will reside in the midst of the children of Israel forever. And the house of Israel will not defile my holy name again . . . . They have defiled my holy name by their abominations that they have committed. For this reason I have consumed them in my anger. Now let them put away their harlotry and the corpses of kings far from me, and I will reside in their midst forever. (43:7-9)

The Lord would indeed dwell in their presence forever, but not in the form of the temple, which, readers discover as Gabriel responds to Daniel's prayer, will be destroyed by "the people of the prince who is to come." This seems to be a clear prophecy of the destruction of Jerusalem and its temple in AD 70. Following the tearing of the veil at the death of the Messiah,[25] the temple came to the end of its role in the divine plan, becoming abominable and unacceptable to the Lord. The writer of the book of Hebrews explains how the Law foreshadowed the death of the Messiah on the cross (Heb 10:1) and was thereby fulfilled in his death: "It is by God's will that we have been sanctified through the offering of the body of Jesus Christ once for all" (Heb 10:10). The author of Hebrews explains how this fulfillment occurred:

> Every priest stands day after day at his service, offering again and again the same sacrifices that can never take away sins. But when Christ had offered for all time a single sacrifice for sins, "he sat down at the right hand of

God," and since then has been waiting "until his enemies would be made a
footstool for his feet." For by a single offering he has perfected for all time
those who are sanctified. And the Holy Spirit also testifies to us, for after
saying,

> "This is the covenant that I will make with them
> after those days, says the Lord: I will put my laws in their hearts,
> and I will write them on their minds,"

he also adds,

> "I will remember their sins and their lawless deeds no more."

Where there is forgiveness of these there is no longer any offering for sin.
(Heb 10:11-18)

Having described the abrogation or fulfillment of the sacrificial system, the
author of Hebrews concludes by explaining that—following the cessation of
temple sacrifice—the Messiah has now become the way into the sanctuary,
or presence, of God:

> Therefore, my friends, since we have confidence to enter the sanctuary by
> the blood of Jesus, by the new and living way that he opened for us
> through the curtain (that is, through his flesh), and since we have a great
> priest over the house of God, let us approach with a true heart in full assur-
> ance of faith, with our hearts sprinkled clean from an evil conscience and
> our bodies washed with pure water. Let us hold fast to the confession of
> our hope without wavering, for he who has promised is faithful. (Heb
> 10:19-23)

## DID GOD ANSWER DANIEL'S PRAYER?

While the question of whether God answered Daniel's prayer goes beyond
the intent of this chapter, it is important to comment briefly on it because
some scholars argue that "In no way does the divine word respond to the
issues raised by the prayer."[26] Some scholars draw this conclusion because,
immediately following Daniel's prayer, the angel Gabriel appears and
addresses the issue of the ultimate end of history (v. 27), explaining, "At the
beginning of your supplication a word went out, and I have come to declare
it, for you are greatly beloved. So consider the word and understand the
vision . . ." (v. 23). The assumption may be made that Gabriel's revelation
about the end-time is the sole "answer" to Daniel's prayer and that it is,
therefore, a "non-answer." Again, one biblical scholar writes, "The text

before us would seem to disconnect the penitential prayer from the angel's announcement of the desolator's ultimate end . . . ." (v.27)[27]

However, many years later, when the Persian Empire replaced the Babylonian Empire, King Cyrus issued a decree that permitted the Jews to return to Palestine. The book of Ezra records a copy of the decree of Cyrus:

> In the first year of King Cyrus of Persia, in order that the word of the Lord by the mouth of Jeremiah might be accomplished, the Lord stirred up the spirit of King Cyrus of Persia so that he sent a herald throughout all his kingdom, and also in a written edict declared:
> "Thus says King Cyrus of Persia: The Lord, the God of heaven, has given me all the kingdoms of the earth, and he has charged me to build him a house at Jerusalem in Judah. Any of those among you who are of his people—may their God be with them!—are now permitted to go up to Jerusalem in Judah, and rebuild the house of the Lord, the God of Israel— he is the God who is in Jerusalem; and let all survivors, in whatever place they reside, be assisted by the people of their place with silver and gold, with goods and with animals, besides freewill offerings for the house of God in Jerusalem." (Ezra 1:1-4)

Earlier generations of scholars doubted the authenticity of the decree, but the decree is in line with Persian religious policy. The archaeological discovery of the "Cyrus Cylinder," a Persian period artifact on which the edict was originally published, has verified its authenticity[28] and shows Cyrus to have been, in fact, a restorer of several temples. While the Assyrians and Babylonians had policies of destroying or carrying off the religious statues of the peoples whom they conquered (to demonstrate that they had conquered the peoples' gods), "Cyrus instituted the enlightened policy of placating the gods of his subject peoples."[29] "Cyrus was not a practicing Yahwist . . . but he showed a broad toleration of local religious customs and beliefs and was more humane than previous Near Eastern rulers."[30]

Although Daniel would have been at least eighty years old by the time of the Persian conquest, the Bible claims he was retained by the new regime in what became his highest position. He was made one of three superintendents over the governors of Persia's various provinces.[31] Conservative scholar Leon Wood has suggested that in these events we may find the full answer to Daniel's prayer. He writes,

> Daniel may have had much to do with the decree that permitted Jews to return to Palestine. He held his highest position at the time of this return

and could have exerted his greatest influence. It is certain that he desired this permission to be granted, for he specifically included it as a request in prayer (Dan 9:1-19). One can imagine him broaching the idea to the Persian king and doing all that he could to encourage its realization.[32]

It is not unreasonable to conclude that the decree of Cyrus may have been the full answer to Daniel's prayer. Israel's reconstitution after the exile would have certainly been impossible without his edict. The prophet Isaiah was fascinated by the career of the Persian king and identified him as one specifically chosen by God, indeed as "his anointed" (Isa 45:1).

## SPIRITUAL INSIGHTS FROM DANIEL'S PRAYER

We have seen many important ideas emerge from our study of Daniel's prayer, but perhaps we can summarize its spiritual message with five main points.

First, Yahweh is a "great and awesome God" (9:4). We should revere and acknowledge God for what He is—the Supreme Being, maker of heaven and earth. "Fear of the Lord," an expression found scores of times in the Old Testament, involves the attitude of respect and love one should have for God as for a parent and the moral obligations following from that love: "And now, Israel, what does the Lord your God ask of you but to fear the Lord, your God, and follow his ways exactly, to love and serve the Lord, your God, with all your heart and all your soul. (Deut 10:12). The New Testament, of course, teaches that God is, *in and of Himself,* love (1 John 4:16), and certainly God's love was proved beyond question when Jesus died for humanity on the cross (John 3:16).

Secondly, God alone is the one who saves. In the Exodus, God led His people out of the land of slavery in Egypt (9:15) to the promised land of freedom.[33] In the same way, modern people find salvation and freedom only in God.[34] Television and toys may satisfy physical and emotional needs for the moment, but only God can fulfill the deepest longings of the human spirit.

Thirdly, God is righteous (9:7). This means Yahweh always does what is right and just. In turn, God also demands righteousness and holiness from His people. Leviticus 9:12 commands, "Speak to the whole Israelite community and tell them: 'Be holy, for I, the Lord your God, am holy.'" Jesus does not abrogate this teaching; in fact, he stresses the extent to which holiness is required of believers: "Be perfect, just as your heavenly Father is perfect" (Matt 5:48).

Fourthly, Yahweh is a just judge (9:11-14). He will not leave sin unpunished.[35] The wrath of God is a result of this truth. The writer of Hebrews explains, "We know the one who said: 'Vengeance is mine; I will repay,' and again: 'The Lord will judge his people.' It is a fearful thing to fall into the hands of the living God" (Heb 10:30-31).

Fifthly, Yahweh is a God of hope and mercy (9:9, 17-19). God will look with compassion and loving forgiveness on those who repent of their sins and turn back to Him. Both Testaments affirm this most important teaching. The writer of Exodus stresses that Yahweh is "merciful and gracious, slow to anger, and abounding in steadfast love and faithfulness, keeping steadfast love for the thousandth generation, forgiving iniquity and transgression and sin" (Exod 34:6-7a). In the New Testament, St. Paul writes to the believers at Ephesus, reminding them of this wonderful truth:

> You were dead through the trespasses and sins in which you once lived, following the course of this world, following the ruler of the power of the air, the spirit that is now at work among those who are disobedient. All of us once lived among them in the passions of our flesh, following the desires of flesh and sense, and we were by nature children of wrath, like everyone else. But God, who is rich in mercy, out of the great love with which he loved us even when we were dead through our trespasses, made us alive together with Christ—by grace you have been saved—and raised us up with him and seated us with him in the heavenly places in Christ Jesus. (Eph 2:1-6)

We are never beyond hope, even when we think we are hopeless.

## CONNECTIONS: FOR WHAT SHOULD WE PRAY?

For many of us, the primary model of prayer we have been taught is intercessory prayer. This means that when we have needs, we should take them to God in prayer. Teachings and sermons on intercessory prayer are often based on the parable of the persistent widow in Luke 18:1-8, in which Jesus tells the story of a widow who persistently asks a judge to hear her case and give her justice. The parable teaches certain important truths, and we should never lose sight of these. However, the emphasis on intercessory prayer has led to a common assumption in the church that prayer ought to accomplish specific results. This assumption has led many people into the habit of only praying when they need a specific result accomplished or, more often, when they have a crisis. Calvin Miller points out that "the danger of intercession is selfishness. Crisis intercession is usually offered from deep self-interest."[36] These prayers do not focus on God, but they focus on us and our needs. Miller notes, "Praying for ourselves often puts God in a box and makes him the captive of our narrow will and piety."[37]

The question is not whether intercessory prayer is wrong or whether we should ever do it. It goes much deeper than that. The question is not for what *things* should we pray, but for what *purpose* should we pray in the first place. The purpose of prayer is not primarily to ask for things but to culti-vate a *relationship* with God. The book of Hebrews has as its main theme the way Christ has completed the Law and opened full access to God. The pur-pose of this is not so that we can now ask for things, but that we can "draw near to the throne of God" (Heb 4:16). We were not redeemed so that we can have God meet our agendas, but so we can actually "draw near to Him" in His very sanctuary (Heb 10:20-22)—something that was impossible under the old covenant. The basic purpose of prayer is for us to "draw near to God." When we do this, God will draw near to us (Jas 4:8).

Prayer is primarily about building a relationship with God, and there are many ways of praying in order to do this. Make a beginning by reading Richard J. Foster, *Prayer: Finding the Heart's True Home* (New York: HarperSanFrancisco, 1992).

## DISCUSSION QUESTIONS

1. How could a loving God allow His people to be taken into exile? In what circumstances might people today feel like they are in exile?

2. How does Daniel's prayer speak to our situation today?

CHAPTER 10

# A God Who Is Evangelical
### *Jonah 4:2-3*

The book of Jonah is little known except for its "fish story." Many Christians automatically connect the name Jonah with the word "whale." An old children's poem illustrates the message readers have traditionally derived from the book. Its final verse served up the message:

> Children, when you disobey, remember this tale.
> When you run from God's call, look out for the whale.
> There are animals to catch you on sea or land,
> And children are swallowed much easier than man.[1]

While the poem—in addition to bringing a laugh—may make valid theological points, the truth of the matter is that only three verses from Jonah, out of a total of eighty-four, deal with the fish. This should lead one to conclude that there must be much more to the book of Jonah than simply the story of the whale. Jonah's short prayer in 4:2 may be more appropriately regarded as the climax of the book, and it is certainly one of the most powerful statements of grace in the entire Bible. We will devote our attention to this prayer.

## JONAH—"THE PROPHECY OF ANTIRHETORIC"

Jonah is portrayed in the book that bears his name as a narrow-minded, fiercely zealous patriot: he is jealous for Yahweh and wants to see the enemies of his people destroyed. God's divine love for a heathen nation and His desire to spare it is magnified when shown in contrast to the spirit of the prophet.

Jonah's hate was directed toward the nation of Assyria, to whom he was being sent with a message of grace. Assyria was one of the most powerful and ruthless nations in the ancient world, and Nineveh was its capital. The Assyrians had brought incredible suffering to many people, and Jonah knew that in the future they would impose great suffering on Israel as well. It would seem that instead of sparing the Assyrians, Yahweh should take this great opportunity to destroy them.[2] This is a key part of what the entire book of Jonah is about. The fact should not be missed that God wants, more than anything, to be in a relationship with all people. Even repentance by the wicked Ninevites would result in forgiveness.[3]

Archaeologists have shown that during this time Assyria was torn with internal strife and by wars with revolting Assyrian towns. Not only were the revolts from within the empire, but the nation was also at war with one of its most powerful enemies.[4] No doubt the depressed state of the nation of Assyria contributed a great deal to the readiness of the people to hear Jonah as he began to preach to them.[5]

However, while the people of Nineveh may have been ready to hear Jonah's message, he was not ready to share it. In fact, Jonah was so unwilling to share his message of grace that his book has been called "a prophecy of antirhetoric." Yehoshua Gitay wrote,

> Unlike the classical prophets, who desire to appeal to their audience through the richness of their rhetorical utterances, Jonah's prophecy to Nineveh (3:4) is limited to only five words, thereby revealing a desire *to avoid a rhetorical speech that seeks to affect the audience's behavior.*[6]

In other words, while other prophets spoke as well as they could in the hopes of bringing their audience to repentance, Jonah spoke as ambiguously as he could in hopes of diminishing the chances that his audience would understand their need to respond to Yahweh. Gitay argues that "it is this specific antirhetorical tendency that lies behind the particular form of the book."[7]

## THE REPENTANCE OF NINEVEH

Jonah finally did obey God, went to Nineveh, and, according to the word of the Lord (3:3), delivered the Lord's message: "Forty days more, and Nineveh shall be overthrown!" (3:4). Interestingly, Jonah only described the *way* in which Nineveh would be destroyed. Jonah did not quote God as saying, "Forty days more and *I* will destroy Nineveh," nor did he use the traditional prophetic formula, "Thus saith the Lord." Instead, he deliberately hid God's role. Again, Gitay writes,

> Here is an intentional attempt to conceal God's role regarding Nineveh, employing instead a colorful word: the city will turn upside down! It is a bombastic and even ridiculing announcement (while it is just by itself and without the explicit stress on the performer). That is, Jonah expresses . . . the implied desire that his addressees, the people of Nineveh, will dismiss his announcement as nonsense. Thus, his mission to warn the Ninevites ("forty days more") will fail; they will continue in their wickedness and God will consequently destroy them.[8]

The people, nonetheless, "believed God; they proclaimed a fast, and everyone, great and small, put on sackcloth" (3:5). The king even came down from his throne and sat in the dust in a public place, setting an example of repentance among the people. The conclusion of the matter was this: "When God saw what they did, how they turned from their evil ways, God changed his mind about the calamity that he had said he would bring on them; and he did not do it" (3:10). The repentance of the Ninevites brings us to the climax of the book, which begins in chapter 4.

## JONAH'S ANGER AND GOD'S CHARACTER

The question that forms the climax of the book finally comes into full view: "Should Yahweh have pity on Nineveh?"[9] Jonah certainly did not think so, according to his reaction in 4:1: "But this was very displeasing to Jonah, and he became angry." Jonah knew God well enough to understand that the man who sincerely said, "God, be merciful to me, a sinner," would be justified in God's sight, like the man in Luke 18:14.[10] However, "this was very displeasing to Jonah" (v. 1). If this were translated literally, it might read, "But it was evil to Jonah with great evil." While this sounds awkward in English, the redundancy of the Hebrew is intended to emphasize. The term "evil" had been repeatedly applied to the Ninevites throughout the book, but here, ironically, it characterizes the prophet! By objecting to the character and actions of God, Jonah has effectively put himself out of fellowship with God as the evil and ignorant heathen.[11]

Jonah went on to tell Yahweh exactly why he was angry. He objected to God's having spared Nineveh. It was because Jonah knew for certain that God would spare Nineveh if it repented that he fled to Tarshish in the first place. Now that Nineveh had repented, Jonah knew the judgment he so desired for the evil nation would not fall, and he could not face this. He could not reconcile himself to what he knew to be the unchangeable character of God.

Many readers have the false conception that Jonah was angry because he had a misconception of who God was. The truth of the matter is that Jonah was angry exactly because he had such a good understanding of who God was. In 4:2, Jonah articulates his understanding of God for us in one of the most powerful statements of grace in the Old Testament:

> He prayed to the Lord and said, "O Lord! Is not this what I said while I was still in my own country? That is why I fled to Tarshish at the beginning; for I knew that you are a gracious God and merciful, slow to anger, and abounding in steadfast love, and ready to relent from punishing."

In this wonderful verse, Jonah uses a plethora of loaded theological words to describe the graciousness of God. He describes God, first of all, as "merciful" or "compassionate," a word related to the Hebrew word for "womb" and that can express the loving compassion of the mother to her child.

Next, Jonah describes God as abounding in "steadfast love," which is the NRSV's translation of the word *hesed*, a term always used to express God's behavior in the covenant relationship. No one English word can adequately express the wide and rich range of meaning of this kind of love that only God can show. *Hesed* was once understood to be the "love" of Yahweh required by the legal obligation of the covenant. However, scholars have come to recognize the extraordinary emphasis within the Old Testament on the element of divine mercy, grace, and forbearance. The kindness of *hesed* is expressed in Yahweh's endless, reconciling love and in the fact that He is always ready to forgive. *Hesed* has come to be understood as a unique word that expresses "the permanence of divine kindness."[12] Rather than having to do with reciprocation, whenever *hesed* is used it always "focuses on what Yahweh does for Israel and the individual worshiper."[13] *Hesed* is a special kind of love: it is a love motivated and expressed by grace. The *Theological Dictionary of the Old Testament* explains it thus:

> The history of Yahweh's people, past, present, and future, the life of the individual Israelite—in fact, the entire world—is the stage for the demonstration of Yahweh's kindness. Yahweh has decided in favor of Israel; he has promised life, care, alleviation of distress, and preservation—indeed, he has filled the whole earth with his kindness. He has thus granted fellowship with him to his people, to all mankind, to the whole world. And this act, like the promise and assurance of future help and fellowship, is characterized by permanence, constancy, and reliability.[14]

*Hesed* has been translated as "kindness," "mercy," "loyalty," "loving kindness," and "unfailing love,"[15] and, while none of these exhausts the rich meaning of the word, they all seek to show its graciousness.

The point here is that Jonah was not confused about the character of God. He was not finding fault with God as he imagined God to be. He was not critical of traits he imagined to be a part of Yahweh's character. Jonah was finding fault with God as God really is. Jonah prided himself on loyalty to Scripture, but he held doctrines that stood in plain contradiction to the revealed will of God. Jonah's statement on the nature of God almost seems to have been a confessional statement reflecting the orthodox Hebrew perception of God. In Exodus, when the Lord passed in front of Moses, the text reports, "The Lord, the Lord, the compassionate and gracious God, slow to anger, abounding in love and faithfulness, maintaining love to thousands, and forgiving wickedness, rebellion and sin" (Exod 34:6-7). A number of other passages include similar wording, supporting the idea that Jonah's description is basically a repetition of a central expression of God's character in the Old Testament.[16] As one commentator has written, "Jonah is here, however, highly critical of these divine attributes, and views them as regrettable weaknesses in the divine make-up."[17]

## INTERNATIONALISM IN THE OLD TESTAMENT

While Jonah wants to limit Yahweh's purview to a strict Israelite nationalism, the fact is that the nations are subjects of Yahweh's sovereignty and are a proper subject of His attention. The nations were, in fact, with Yahweh and under His sovereignty even before the existence of Israel. Even when reading oracles against the nations in the Old Testament, "Their assumption is that

Yahweh has created the nations, has given them life, authorized them to be, and placed in their midst the possibility of life and blessing."[18] Walter Brueggemann argues that "Yahweh is not, in principle, opposed to superpowers, but only to those that disregard the mandate of heaven and arrogate to themselves ultimate power and authority."[19]

Indeed, a number of Old Testament passages show Yahweh's prior involvement with the nations. Among the patriarchs, Job was not an Israelite but rather an Uzzite. Abraham was not indigenous to Canaan but was instead a Babylonian. When considering the exodus, Amos 9:7 reports multiple exoduses that Yahweh carried out:

> Are you not like the Ethiopians to me,
> O people of Israel? Says the Lord.
> Did I not bring Israel up
> from the land of Egypt,
> And the Philistines from Caphtor
>     And the Arameans from Kir?

Indeed, Israel's own exodus also served as an exodus for many foreigners who joined them as they left Egypt.[20] Rahab, an ancestor of Jesus, was a Canaanite encountered during the conquest. An early Israelite heroine following the settlement period was not an Israelite at all but a Moabite—Ruth. Throughout the Old Testament we can find examples like these of God working in, among, and even through the nations.

Some of the most dramatic cases are found in the prophets. In Isaiah 19:24-25, for example, Egypt and Assyria are described as Yahweh's people, with Israel as the mediator of the nations and bringing blessing upon them:

> In that day Israel will be the third with Egypt and Assyria,
>     A blessing in the midst of the earth,
>         Whom Yahweh of Hosts has blessed, saying:
> "Blessed be Egypt my people, Assyria the work of my hands,
>     and Israel my heritage."

Earlier in the same chapter, Isaiah apocalyptically envisions Egypt erecting an altar to Yahweh as a sign and witness of Yahweh's presence in the nation's midst. When Egypt is oppressed, they will turn to Yahweh and "he will send them a savior, and will defend and deliver them" (19:20). Duane Christenson writes,

The picture presented here is indeed remarkable: YHWH will one day send a new Moses to deliver Egypt from bondage! Moreover, YHWH will reveal himself to the Egyptians, who in turn will worship him (19:22). Then YHWH will build a highway from Egypt to Assyria, and both the Egyptians and the Assyrians will be one with Israel in their worship of YHWH in the restored land of promise (19:23-25).[21]

The new Israel envisioned by the prophets included the righteous from among all nations. This idea was intentionally propounded by the prophets to challenge the narrow nationalistic conception of Yahwism held by many Israelites. One of the most celebrated passages describing the Messianic kingdom is Isaiah 2:2-4, which envisions the nations streaming to Zion:

> It shall come to pass in the latter days
>     That the mountain of the house of Yahweh
> Shall be established as the highest of mountains,
>     And shall be raised up above the hills;
> And peoples shall flow to it,
>     And many nations shall come, and say:
> "Come, let us go up to the mountain of Yahweh,
>     to the house of the God of Jacob;
> That he may teach us his ways
>     and we may walk in his paths."
> For out of Zion shall go forth the Law,
>     And the word of Yahweh from Jerusalem.
> He shall judge between many peoples,
>     And shall decide for strong nations afar off;
> And they shall beat their swords into plowshares,
>     And their spears into pruning hooks;
> Nation shall not lift up sword against nation,
>     Neither shall they learn war any more.

Yahweh ultimately has "an inclusive propensity."[22] Israel's God wants to transcend a narrow nationalistic religion to become an international God. Israel's Lord has a universal interest in all peoples, and it may be possible for Him

> to accept Israel's ancient enemies as legitimate candidates for membership in the covenant. . . . That is, with the most recalcitrant of nation-partners, Yahweh acts in a characteristic rehabilitative way, moving beyond the harshness of rejecting sovereignty, in order to reembrace the established enemy.[23]

Indeed, we see in all of these texts "inchoate hints . . . that 'God so loved the world'—the world of the nations."[24]

These ideas "complement the universalistic message of the book of Jonah."[25] Christenson summarizes,

> YHWH's compassion for Nineveh will ultimately be extended to include all nations. . . . Even wicked Assyria is the work of YHWH's hands (Isa 19:24), and as such she enjoys the same potential relationship to YHWH as did Israel of old. As a light to the nations, servant Israel has a mission to the nations. Those who respond to YHWH's message, even among the Assyrians, will constitute YHWH's people—a new Israel.[26]

## GOD'S REBUKE OF THE NATION ISRAEL

Jonah is an unusual book in several ways.[27] First, and often overlooked, the book contains a strong rebuke of the nation of Israel. The man Jonah, in the book bearing his name, represents all Israelites. As a prophet, he should be the perfect example of spirituality. The prophets were the servants of the Lord. This servant, however, did everything he could to avoid fulfilling the divine command. When he finally did follow God's command and make the trip to Nineveh, he did it reluctantly. Then, when the people of Nineveh did repent and God spared them punishment, Jonah sank into a deep depression and felt great anger toward God.

The author of the book of Jonah wants to make the point that Jonah is out of touch with God. And if he, a so-called "perfect example of spirituality," is out of touch with God, then how much more is Israel as a nation out of touch with God! The area in which they are out of touch with God is one of the most striking characteristics of the book: their attitude toward those outside the covenant community. The idea that Yahweh shows concern for Gentiles certainly was not a new teaching—as we have seen.

## GOD'S COMPASSION TOWARD NON-ISRAELITES

The book of Jonah focuses on God's compassion for those outside of Israel in two ways. In the first place, the book contrasts spiritually sensitive pagans with the reluctant Israelite prophet in these ways:

• In chapter 1, the pagan sailors shake before Yahweh's wrathful storm while Jonah sleeps in the hold of the ship.

- The sailors are concerned that God not hold them accountable for Jonah's death when they throw him overboard.
- In the last half of the book, Jonah preaches to the people of Nineveh (3:4), but he never even mentions God's name or the possibility of repentance.

Nevertheless, the people do repent (3:5), and the king, who only hears of Jonah's message secondhand, calls for citywide repentance (3:7-9). The contrast between Jonah, the reluctant prophet, and spiritually sensitive pagans certainly impresses us with God's compassion for those outside Israel.

A second way the book of Jonah emphasizes Yahweh's compassion for those outside Israel is that it ends on a note that focuses on God's feelings toward Nineveh when He asks Jonah, "Should I not be concerned about that great city?" This is a rhetorical question, which means God is not asking it because He needs Jonah to tell Him before He will know the answer. Rather, it is a confrontational question, asked precisely to bring Jonah to discover the right answer for himself.

In ancient Judaism, the book of Jonah served as a defense against the narrow exclusivism that allowed Jews to think they alone were worthy of God's blessing while other peoples were not.[28] To more modern readers, the message may be seen in light of Jesus' own teaching about forgiveness: it is the sinners, not the righteous, who most often may recognize their need for forgiveness and do something about it.[29] No one should oppose God's mercy in receiving sinners into the kingdom.

## APPROACHING THE NEW TESTAMENT

How does the New Testament relate to this central message of the book of Jonah?

The New Testament, of course, proclaims clearly that Gentiles can come to God and be part of the covenant people. The last word is with God, whose character is always to have mercy. Jesus the Messiah was sent into the world, and not just to the nation of Israel.[30] The book of Jonah is another signpost to the full revelation of the salvation of God that, in His sovereign mercy and grace, was to be "a light for revelation to the Gentiles."[31] The evangelical message of the book of Jonah can be expressed in the words of Paul: "What shall we say then? Is there injustice on God's part? By no means! For he says to Moses, 'I will have mercy on whom I will have mercy, and I will have compassion on whom I will have compassion'" (Rom 9:14, 15). In fact, the book of Jonah would make a good commentary on John 3:16-17:

"For God so loved the world that he gave his only Son, so that everyone who believes in him may not perish but have eternal life. Indeed, God did not send the Son into the world to condemn the world, but in order that the world might be saved through him." Indeed, the book of Jonah is not nearly so much about a great big fish as it is about a great big God.

## CONNECTIONS: THE NEED FOR A RENEWAL OF EVANGELICALISM

Mainline churches have made a full retreat from evangelism over the last fifty years. Fifty years ago, mainline Protestant missionaries outnumbered those from evangelical churches by more than a factor of two. Today, however, evangelicals outnumber mainliners by more than a factor of ten.[32] As early as 1932, the Laymen's Foreign Mission Inquiry, a mainline organization, wrote that "missionaries should be ambassadors for Christ providing service, rather than witnesses for Christ seeking conversions."[33] As modernism began to predominate, belief in the absolute truth of Christianity gave way. Books began to appear with titles such as *Missions in Crisis*,[34] *The Ugly Missionary*,[35] *The Unpopular Missionary*,[36] and *Missionary, Go Home!*[37] Since the 1960s, mainline denominations have experienced a hemorrhage in membership, while their conservative counterparts have continued to grow.[38]

Must the mainline churches continue to decline? Christian sociologist David Moberg argues that the decline can be reversed by a recapturing of the values and mission the organization held in its formative period. In other words, declining mainline churches must "return to their first love" as the risen Christ called the drifting Ephesian church to do (Rev 2:4-5a, TEV). For the Ephesian church, this meant renewing their belief in and zeal for Jesus Christ. It meant experiencing a spiritual awakening.[39] There are signs that this has already begun to occur within many mainline denominations.[40]

## DISCUSSION QUESTIONS

1. Why was Jonah angry with God in Jonah 4:1? Was it because Jonah had a misconception about who God was? In what ways do we hold misconceptions of God today?

2. Discuss Jonah 4:2. What makes this one of the most powerful statements of grace in the entire Old Testament?

3. What is the central message of the book of Jonah? How does the New Testament relate to the message of Jonah? How does the message of Jonah relate to our lives today?

## CHAPTER 11

# A God Who Can Bring
# Good Out of Evil

*Habakkuk 3:1-19*

While the Book of Habakkuk may not be familiar to many modern believers, it has played an important role in both Judaism and Christianity. Marvin Sweeny, professor of Hebrew Bible at Claremont Graduate University, summarizes some of the importance of Habakkuk within the Judaeo-Christian heritage:[1]

- The Qumran sectarians, who produced the Dead Sea Scrolls, wrote a commentary on the first two chapters of Habakkuk in the first century BC. They interpreted these passages as having a bearing on their own origins.
- St. Paul used Habakkuk 2:4 as a key by which he unlocked the doctrine of "justification by faith" (Rom 1:17).
- Talmudic authors regarded Habakkuk 2:4 as a summary of all the 613 commandments of the Torah.
- Habakkuk 3 is regarded—within the Jewish tradition—as a description of the revelation of the Law at Mt. Sinai.

Habakkuk's identity is unknown. Some have suggested he was a Levite, which was a tribe associated with music.[2] Others have suggested that he was an official court or temple prophet.[3] However, while Habakkuk himself is a shadowy figure and his identity remains unknown, the prophet's character is clear. He is a devoted follower of Yahweh.

This devoted Yahwist, however, is deeply troubled by the rising power of the neo-Babylonians, whom he also refers to as the "Chaldeans." In fact, it seems that "the [entire] book evidently is a theological inquiry about the injustice of neo-Babylonian imperialism."[4] Habakkuk anticipates the impending invasion of the Babylonians, who would turn Israel into a vassal state in 586 BC. Jeremiah had been warning that this would happen and that when it did it would be God's punishment on the recalcitrant nation of Israel. The book of Habakkuk is about this prophet's difficulty with accepting a punishment from God by the hand of a wicked nation—Babylon. Initially, he protests against medicine that he perceives to be worse than the disease itself. However, he eventually draws some conclusions that he expresses in a powerful psalm or prayer in the final chapter of the book. The conclusions in Habakkuk's prayer will be the focus of our attention, but first we must work our way through Habakkuk's protest and Yahweh's response.

## HABAKKUK STRUGGLES WITH QUESTIONS ABOUT WICKEDNESS

The first major section of the book of Habakkuk (chs. 1–2) is a "pronouncement," a type of oracle that seeks to understand how God's will is being worked out in particular human affairs. The term "pronouncement" is sometimes translated as "burden" since the prophet is under the burden of trying to understand particular events. Habakkuk begins his pronouncement by complaining that the land of Israel is in chaos:

> O Lord, how long shall I cry for help,
> > And you will not listen?
> Or cry to you "Violence!"
> > And you will not save?
> Why do you make me see wrongdoing?
> > And look at trouble?
> Destruction and violence are before me;
> > Strife and contention arise.
> So the law becomes slack
> > And justice never prevails.

The wicked surround the righteous—
Therefore judgment comes forth perverted. (Hab 1:2-4)

Yahweh, however, denies that chaos is prevailing. Instead, He answers that what seems like turmoil is really the manifestation of His own plan to establish Chaldean dominance in the world:

Look at the nations, and see!
    Be astonished! Be astounded!
For a work is being done in your days
    That you would not believe if you were told.
For I am rousing the Chaldeans,
    That fierce and impetuous nation,
Who march through the breadth of the earth
    To seize dwellings not their own.
Dread and fearsome are they;
    Their justice and dignity proceed from themselves.
Their horses are swifter than leopards,
    More menacing than wolves at dusk;
Their horses charge.
    Their horsemen come from far away;
They fly like an eagle swift to devour.
    They all come for violence,
With faces pressing forward;
    They gather captives like sand.
At kings they scoff,
    And of rulers they make sport.
They laugh at every fortress,
    And heap up earth to take it.
Then they sweep by like the wind;
    They transgress and become guilty;
    Their own might is their god! (Hab 1:5-11)

Habakkuk's pronouncement is one of lament, or even protest. He is objecting to the great evil he sees God allowing to flourish in the world. The Chaldeans are increasing in power—to the extent that they are becoming a threat to Israel—and yet God seems to do nothing. The prophet goes on to complain about the extent of the Chaldeans' corruption: they have crossed the line of evil and refused to acknowledge Yahweh as the universal king:

Are you not from of old,
>O Lord my God, my Holy one?
>You shall not die.
O Lord, you have marked them for judgment;
>And you, O Rock, have established them for punishment.
Your eyes are too pure to behold evil,
>And you cannot look on wrongdoing;
Why do you look on the treacherous,
>And are silent when the wicked swallow
Those more righteous than they?
>You have made people like the fish of the sea,
Like crawling things that have no ruler.

The enemy brings all of them up with a hook;
>He drags them out with his net,
He gathers them in his seine;
>So he rejoices and exults.
Therefore he sacrifices to his net
>And makes offerings to the seine;
For by them his portion is lavish,
>And his food is rich.
Is he then to keep on emptying his net,
>And destroying the nations without mercy? (Hab 1:12-17)

As we can see clearly in Habakkuk's protest, the prophet is deeply troubled by what he perceives to be Yahweh's inactivity in the face of unrelenting evil. Why would a righteous God allow rampant sin to go unpunished continually? Why would a sovereign God allow it? The particular injustice that Habakkuk cannot understand is why the Chaldeans—or the neo-Babylonians—are being allowed to flourish unchecked and, worse, why they will be allowed to turn Israel into a vassal state. Babylon makes its own laws (v. 7), has a vicious military force (vv. 8-9), and ridicules the rulers of other nations (v. 10). As one commentator has written, "Given a theology that assumes God's goodness, holiness, and universal sovereignty, how does one explain God's standing aside while the wicked swallow the righteous (cf. v. 13)?"[5] Habakkuk understood that God had appointed the Chaldeans for judgment of Israel (v. 12), "but the judgment and the reproof seemed to be too harsh, too long, and from an undesirable agent. Instead of reproof it appears that the Babylonians aim at extinction of their victims."[6] The prophet compares the Chaldeans' treatment of their victims to the way fishermen treat their catch—dragging them in from the sea with hooks, pulling them out of the water with nets, and gathering them for future consumption (vv. 14-15). Habakkuk is deeply troubled by this because, in his mind,

> the "cure" of a Babylonian invasion in worse than the "illness" of Judean sin. The Babylonians were pagans and not worshipers of Yahweh at all, so how could God use them to punish his own people? Also their cruelty was proverbial and the punishment seemed to be greater than the crime could warrant (1:12-17).[7]

Why did God not do something?

God responds to Habakkuk's protests by granting him a vision, which reveals the basic principle that, in contrast to the wicked, the righteous will live by faith (2:4). Yahweh elaborates at length on this principle, and He reveals to Habakkuk a fivefold series of "woes" in which He explains how the Chaldeans will ultimately self-destruct as a result of their own insatiable avarice:

> Moreover, wealth is treacherous;
>> The arrogant do not endure.
> They open their throats wide to Sheol;
>> Like Death they never have enough.
> They gather all nations for themselves,
>> And collect all peoples as their own.
>
> Shall not everyone taunt such people
>> And, with mocking riddles, say about them,
> "Alas for you who heap up what is not your own!"
>> How long will you load yourselves
>>> With goods taken in pledge?
> Will not your own creditors suddenly rise,
>> And those who make you tremble wake up?
> Then you will be booty for them.
> Because you have plundered many nations,
>> All that survive of the peoples shall plunder you—
> Because of human bloodshed, and violence to the earth,
>> To cities and all who live in them.
>
> "Alas for you who get evil gain for your house,
>> Setting your nest on high

To be safe from the reach of harm!"
You have devised shame for your house
        By cutting off many peoples;
        You have forfeited your life.
The very stones will cry out from the wall,
        And the plaster will respond from the woodwork.

"Alas for you who build a town by bloodshed,
        and found a city on iniquity!"
Is it not from the Lord of hosts
        That people labor only to feed the flames,
And nations weary themselves for nothing?
But the earth will be filled
        With the knowledge of the glory of the Lord,
As the waters cover the sea.

"Alas for you who make your neighbors drink,
        pouring out your wrath until they are drunk,
in order to gaze on their nakedness."
You will be sated with contempt instead of glory.
Drink, you yourself, and stagger!
The cup in the Lord's right hand will come around to you,
        And shame will come upon your glory!
For the violence done to Lebanon will overwhelm you;
        The destruction of the animals will terrify you—
Because of human bloodshed and violence to the earth,
        To cities and all who live in them.

What use is an idol
        Once its maker has shaped it—
        A cast image, a teacher of lies?
For its maker trusts in what has been made,
        Though the product is only an idol that cannot speak!
Alas for you who say to the wood, "Wake up!"
        To silent stone, "Rouse yourself!"
        Can it teach?
See, it is gold and silver plated,
        And there is no breath in it at all.

But the Lord is in his holy temple;
        Let all the earth keep silence before him! (Hab 2:5-20)

God does not leave Habakkuk in despair. On the contrary, God assures His prophet that He will indeed hold Babylon responsible for their excesses.

The entire third chapter makes up the second major section of the book of Habakkuk and is often referred to as "the prayer of Habakkuk."[8] This prayer, or psalm, is Habakkuk's response to the "pronouncement" in chapters 1–2. It is the crescendo of the book of Habakkuk, for "Habakkuk's questions are answered in such a way that he can pronounce one of the most powerful statements of faith recorded in Scripture."[9]

O Lord, I have heard of your renown,
    And I stand in awe, O Lord, of your work.
In our own time revive it;
      In our own time make it known;
      In wrath may you remember mercy.
God came from Teman,
    The Holy One from Mount Paran.

His glory covered the heavens,
    And the earth was full of his praise.
The brightness was like the sun;
      Rays came forth from his hand,
      Where his power lay hidden.
Before him went pestilence,
    And plague followed close behind.
He stopped and shook the earth;
      He looked and made the nations tremble.
The eternal mountains were shattered;
      Along his ancient pathways
      The everlasting hills sank low.
I saw the tents of Cushan under affliction;
      The tent curtains of the land of Midian trembled.
Was your wrath against the rivers, O Lord?
      Or your anger against the rivers,
      Or your rage against the sea,
When you drove your horses,
      Your chariots to victory?
You brandished your naked bow,
      Sated were the arrows at your command.
You split the earth with rivers.
The mountains saw you, and writhed;
      A torrent of water swept by;

The deep gave forth its voice.
     The sun raised high its hands;
The moon stood still in its exalted place,
     At the light of your arrows speeding by,
At the gleam of your flashing spear.
In fury you trod the earth,
     In anger you trampled nations.
You came forth to save your people,
     To save your anointed.
You crushed the head of the wicked house,
     Laying it bare from foundation to roof.
You pierced with their own arrows
     The head of his warriors,
Who came like a whirlwind to scatter us,
     Gloating as if ready to devour the poor
Who were in hiding.
You trampled the sea with your horses,
     Churning the mighty waters.

I hear, and I tremble within;
     My lips quiver at the sound.
Rottenness enters into my bones,
     And my steps tremble beneath me.
I wait quietly for the day of calamity
     To come upon the people who attack us.

Though the fig tree does not blossom,
     And no fruit is on the vines;
Though the produce of the olive falls,
     And the fields yield no food;
Though the flock is cut off from the fold,
And there is no herd in the stalls,
Yet I will rejoice in the Lord;
     I will exult in the God of my salvation.
God, the Lord, is my strength;
     He makes my feet like the feet of a deer,
And makes me tread upon the heights. (Hab 3:2-19)

Verses 3-15 make up what is called a "theophany," or an appearance or manifestation of God. Yahweh's "glory" is manifested (v. 3), His "splendor" is
revealed (v. 4), and His "power" is revealed in judgment (v. 5). The earth

itself trembles at this judgment (vv. 6-7), and various people groups "quake" (v. 7). The Lord's "wrath" is given dramatic emphasis and is depicted as being directed against the sea (v. 8), which recalls the miraculous parting of the Red Sea, a focal point in Israel's history.[10] God's "horses and chariots" create martial imagery and also recall the exodus events,[11] as do the references to water in v. 10. The final verses of the prayer portray the presence of God as relative, depending on one's relationship with Him. Those who oppose God experience His wrath, whereas those who love and submit to God experience His salvation and deliverance (vv. 11-15). This is the real answer to Habakkuk's initial questions, and it conditions his response in vv. 16-19.

Following Yahweh's amazing theophany, Habakkuk's own reaction to the Lord of all is reverential fear (v. 16). His reaction, however, does not stop there. As we saw earlier in our discussion, Habakkuk felt close enough to God to be able to question Him. And here, at the close of his book, we find that he also feels close enough to Yahweh that he can put his faith in God and "wait" for Him to save Israel in His own time (v. 16). Habakkuk's reaction is personal, as he also comes to the conclusion that "his faith can safely be put in Yahweh's grace, not only in matters of national survival but also of personal well-being and even existence" (vv. 17-19a).[12] Habakkuk recognized that judgment was inevitable, as his vision of a devastated economy makes clear (v. 17). The prosperity of Israel's agricultural economy depended on the nation's obedience to the covenant, hence the natural disaster pictured is symptomatic of the national apostasy.[13] But even as the prophet faces his doubts and anticipates the possibility of oppression, he discovers that he wants to rejoice.[14] Indeed, the prophet's prayer closes on a celebratory note. Yahweh has made Habakkuk's feet "like the feet of a deer," enabling him to "tread upon the heights" (v. 19). When the writer of Deuteronomy reflected on the way Yahweh had chosen Israel, brought the nation out of Egypt, sustained them in the wilderness, and poised them on the brink of the promised land, he said Yahweh had "set him atop the heights of the land" (Deut 32:13).[15] Baker speculates as to the implications of this connection between Habakkuk's prayer and the themes of exodus and conquest:

> If this is the referent here, the entire chapter is united by its implicit and explicit references to the historical complex of Exodus-Sinai-Conquest. Habakkuk, who starts in depression, and doubt as to God's righteousness and justice, ends with a lively confidence in God's provision and sustaining power.[16]

Baker is surely correct, in light of the other correlations in theme between Habakkuk's psalm and the exodus events. Similarly, Habakkuk's reference to "strength" at the close of his song (v. 19) echoes the Song of Moses—again, a celebration of the exodus.[17] Like the deer, and like the armies of Israel, Habakkuk's faith in Yahweh takes him from despair and discouragement to the "high places." "In the very midst of disaster . . . Habakkuk himself stands as a noble example of the prophetic witness to a God who puts to death and who brings to life."[18]

## YAHWEH AND THE NATIONS

In the last chapter, we discussed internationalism in the Old Testament, discovering that Yahweh indeed has compassion on the unbelieving nations. At issue in Habakkuk, however, is the question raised by the prophet about how God can use an evil nation to punish Israel. While we have discussed some of the issues related to Habakkuk's question through looking at his prayer, the question warrants more attention.

As became clear in our study of Jonah, the horizon of Yahweh's governance went beyond the land of Israel. In fact, Israel's own theology recognized this. Psalm 96:10 instructs Israel, "Say among the nations, 'The Lord is king!'" Walter Brueggemann, in his magisterial *Theology of the Old Testament*, deals with these issues in a chapter titled "The Nations as Yahweh's Partner."[19] Commenting on Psalm 96:10's injunction that Israel proclaim Yahweh's kingly rule over the nations, he writes,

> This liturgical exclamation asserts the primary claim of this unsolicited testimony: that Yahweh holds sovereign authority over all the nations and that all the nations must come to accept that rule, which is characterized by equity (v. 10), righteousness, and truth (v. 13). This assertion, critically, is a rejection of any loyalty other nations may give to any other gods and a rejection of any imagined autonomy on the part of any political power.[20]

One of the immediate implications of this is that the nations are under the demands and sanctions of Yahweh's will for justice. Some of the most interesting passages in which this truth is demonstrated are in a group of texts commonly referred to as "the oracles against the nations," including passages from Isaiah, Jeremiah, Ezekiel, Amos, and Zephaniah, in which they indict foreign nations for rebelling against Yahweh. The oracles against the nations claim that Yahweh can call the nations to accountability.

Because of Yahweh's massive, overriding sovereignty, these oracles assert that the nations are subject to a governance, a requirement, and an expectation, no matter how secure and self-sufficient they seem to be or think they are. This governance, moreover, cannot be overcome, disregarded, or evaded.[21]

Some of the oracles against the nations include passages that may surprise some readers in that Yahweh, on occasion, is not reprimanding a particular country for a direct spite against Himself or His people but rather because they have abused a third party having nothing to do with Israel. The Ammonites, for example, were called to account for having killed pregnant women in Gilead, and the Moabites were condemned for an affront they had carried out against the Edomites.[22] Brueggemann suggests that, within the oracles against the nations, the Scriptures reveal a kind of standard by which God holds all the nations accountable.

> . . . under the aegis of Yahweh's sovereignty, there is a kind of international law or code of human standards that seems to anticipate the Helsinki Accords of 1975 in a rough way, a code that requires every nation to act in civility and humaneness toward others. Any affront of this standard is taken to be an act of autonomy, arrogance, and self-sufficiency, which flies in the face of Yahweh's governance. Thus Yahweh is the guarantor, not only of Israel, but also of the nations in their treatment of each other.[23]

Raw power and unrestrained might never go permanently unchecked. They are, according to this doctrine, ultimately subject to the will and restraint of Yahweh. Yahweh's impetus for justice cannot be stopped, although it may be delayed by terrorism, dictatorships, and brutality. But ultimately, the tyrant will fall.

Yahweh has the freedom to deal with the nations as He will. Brueggemann concludes that this freedom encompasses two dimensions. The first has to do with the way Yahweh operates behind the scenes—on an international level—to work His will. Brueggemann explains,

> Yahweh in freedom has the power and capacity to recruit nations for Yahweh's own purposes, even if those purposes are not the intention of the nations, or even if those purposes run against the expectation of Israel. Thus nations are pressed into Yahweh's service, both to punish Israel (Assyria, Babylon), and also to save Israel (Persia). That is, a large inten-

tionality operates in the geopolitical process that runs well beyond and perhaps counter to what the agents of the process themselves imagine.[24]

Yahweh's will, in other words, can and sometimes does supercede the will of the nations. And while it may appear that the nations are acting with sovereignty, their actions may ultimately work toward ends not their own.

> And while it may have been repulsive to have Nebuchadnezzar termed "my servant" (Jer 25:9, 27:6) in the process of nullifying Judah, it was no less abhorrent to have Cyrus termed "his messiah" (Isa 45:1) in support of Judah (cf. Isa 45:9-13). Yahweh's governing capacity is not derivative from or contingent on the intention of the nations, but operates in complete and commanding freedom.[25]

The second dimension Yahweh's freedom encompasses is His ability to terminate great nations. As stated in the chapter on Jonah, it does not appear that Yahweh is opposed to superpowers on principle, but he is opposed "to those that disregard the mandate of heaven and arrogate to themselves ultimate power and authority."[26]

As Baker noted, Habakkuk had felt that the "cure" of a Babylonian invasion was much worse than the "illness" of the sins of Judah.[27] And so, with great personal risk, Habakkuk had confronted Yahweh with the question of how God could use a wicked, cruel, and pagan nation to punish His own people. Yahweh's answer was that Babylon was morally responsible for its own actions and, indeed, it would not go unpunished (2:2-20). For the time being, however, they were carrying out the will of Yahweh—unbeknownst to themselves—in punishing Judah.

## September 11, 2001

On September 11, 2001, American freedom was assaulted when Islamic terrorists highjacked a number of airplanes, two of which they flew into the towers of the World Trade Center. The death toll was initially estimated at between 20,000 and 50,000, although now it is thought to be around 3,000. A third plane—flight 93—was downed outside Pittsburgh. A fourth plane was used in an attempt to destroy the Pentagon, resulting in between 100 and 800 deaths. Americans will never feel the same about their security in this country. A refrain we have heard repeatedly since the attacks is "I never thought it could happen here." People are wondering how this crisis will transform America and what impact this crisis will have on our nation as a free democracy. The answers to these questions remain unclear.

In some ways, the terrorist attacks on America are like the Babylonian invasion of Judah. Like Habakkuk, many Americans—especially people of faith—have asked how God could allow something this terrible to happen. Some have wondered why evil seems to have prevailed through this unprecedented attack. In the aftermath of the crisis, some religious leaders have pointed the finger of blame for the cause of America's national calamity. Abortionists, homosexuals, liberalism, the American Civil Liberties Union, and People for the American Way have been identified as the culprits who incited God's anger and brought about the terrorist attack. We must be cautious with this kind of reasoning for at least two reasons. First, America is not in a covenant relationship with God as ancient Israel was. To apply the paradigm of the covenantal blessings and curses to modern America cannot be justified from Scripture. Secondly, if the attacks represented God's judgment on America for national wrongdoings, then retaliation against the terrorists would be unjustifiable. If our attackers were indeed agents of God, then our response should be repentance rather than retaliation. Syndicated columnist Cal Thomas concludes that the terrorist attack of September 11 was simply an act of evil and that God is not the author of evil.[28]

We must be cautious, however, about these kinds of responses as well. Yes, the attacks were evil. But does that—in and of itself—preclude divine involvement in them? As discussed earlier in the chapter, surely Israel's first response to the Assyrian and later Babylonian invasions was that they were evil. When Israel was carried into captivity, surely they felt they were the victims of evil oppressors. Yet, Jeremiah urged Israel not to resist but to go willingly into captivity. Resistance would be futile, he counseled, because exile from the promised land was the punishment for flagrant violation of the covenant stipulations. It would be better, he said, to repent from within the land of their exile and then to pray for their future restoration to the land.

Again, I recognize that America is not in a covenant relationship with God, and I am not suggesting that God caused the September 11 attacks to occur. Yet, the religious leaders to whom Cal Thomas was responding are not the first in American history to question whether our nation's calamities might have been of its own making. After the Civil War, Abraham Lincoln asked whether the grisly war might have been due punishment for "the bondsman's two hundred and fifty years of unrequited toil." Lincoln suggested that America had "forgotten God" and was "intoxicated with unbroken success too proud to pray to the God who made us." Many years later, Alexander Solzhenitsyn said communism strangled the Soviet Union for seven decades because his people had "forgotten God." Certainly the least that could be said is that in times of travail, it is always healthy to examine our lives and ask ourselves to what extent we may have contributed to our own undoing. I think we can say that to the extent that disasters—whether natural or manmade—lead people to examine themselves and reorder their lives in ways that good comes from evil, then even horrible events can have redemptive effects.

On Friday, September 14, 2001, the day President Bush designated as a "National Day of Prayer and Remembrance," Billy Graham spoke at the National Cathedral in Washington, DC. The entire nation listened as Billy Graham sought to interpret the recent events through the lens of faith. Dr. Graham said,

> . . . [As] difficult as it may be for us to see right now—this event can give a message of hope—hope for the present, and hope for the future.
>
> Yes, there is hope. There is hope for the present because I believe the stage has already been set for a new spirit in our nation.
>
> One of the things we desperately need is a spiritual renewal in this country. We need a spiritual revival in America. And God has told us in His Word, time after time, that we are to repent of our sins and we're to turn to Him and He will bless us in a new way.[29]

In the days immediately following the September 11 attack on America, it seemed that Dr. Graham's message of hope might have been in the process of being realized. "Pray" became the rallying cry heard around the nation. Topics of religion and faith moved to the forefront of the news. Fox News reported, "We've seen a resurgence of public religion—Americans are rediscovering the power of faith." The public's renewed interest in faith was vividly symbolized when the members of Congress stood shoulder to shoulder on the Capitol steps and sang "God Bless America." Even secular newspapers were printing prayers, and USA Today featured a full-page ad titled "To help America speak to God with one voice: A Prayer by the Nation, For the Nation."

President Bush set the tone at the government level when he designated September 14 a "National Day of Prayer and Remembrance," asking Americans to attend religious services of their choice on their lunch hour and conduct candlelight prayer vigils in the evening. *The Washington Post* then reported that many people said they had taken "an unfamiliar step into a church to feel a solidarity with their fellow bereaved citizens," while others said they went for healing and to pray for the dead.[30] A spokesperson said the two morning services at the Washington National Cathedral drew about 7,000 people, with hundreds more listening to the service on loudspeakers in the plaza outside. Sunday services there normally draw about 1,500 people.[31]

## AN ANGEL EVEN HOLIER THAN PAIN

One of the great saints of modern times was a Lutheran pastor and theologian named Dietrich Bonhoeffer, who spent the final years of his life in a Nazi prison camp due to his refusal to join the "official" church sanctioned by the Third Reich and, ultimately, for becoming involved in a plot to assassinate Hitler. While languishing in a Tegel prison cell in the cold of November, Bonhoeffer wrote a letter to his fiancée in which he shared his thoughts about the impact of his struggles—indeed, the struggle of the world to survive Hitler—on his spiritual life. He first quoted another German writer, Adalbert Stifter, who had written these words: "Pain is the holiest angel, who reveals treasures that would otherwise have remained hidden in the depths forever. People have become greater through it than through all the world's joys."[32] Bonhoeffer then reflected on how difficult he found it to accept Stifter's ideas (he had to keep reminding himself of them):

> It is so, as I keep telling myself in my present predicament: the pain of deprivation, which is often physically perceptible, must exist, and we should not and need not argue it away. But it has to be overcome anew every time, so there is an even holier angel than pain, and that is joy in God.[33]

Pain, conflict, and suffering are surely difficult to bear. However, when and if we turn to God for help in the midst of pain, conflict, and suffering, then something holy has indeed occurred. On April 9, 1945, Bonhoeffer shared devotional thoughts with his fellow prisoners on Isaiah 53—"By his stripes we are healed." After he led the group in prayer, guards arrived, and Bonhoeffer was then escorted from a group cell at Flossenburg concentration camp to a gallows where he was hanged. As the guards led him from the cell, Bonhoeffer turned to one of his cellmates and said, "For me this is the end, but also the beginning of life." In what almost seemed like a cruel irony, on April 20, only eleven days after Bonhoeffer's predawn execution, American soldiers liberated Flossenburg Concentration Camp. Yet, Bonhoeffer walked unhesitatingly to the gallows because he had indeed found what he had called "an angel even holier than pain." That was joy in God, despite the difficult times.

As Dr. Graham said in his Washington Cathedral sermon following the September 11 attacks, there is a message of hope, and it is evident in *these* difficult times. The editor of *Religion Today* brought out this message of hope with these words:

> While the terrorists may have intended to bring America to its knees, perhaps they did not realize how fitting an analogy that would be. It has driven the nation to prayer. As Billy Graham said, "Those perpetrators who took this on to tear us apart, it has worked the other way."[34]

Evil will indeed continue to be a part of life in a world that is suffering from the effects of the fall, but we worship a God whose nature is to bring good out of evil. Believers today must pray that, out of these evil deeds that were sown, a greater harvest of goodness may be reaped.

## CONNECTIONS: DOES THE FALL STILL AFFECT US TODAY?

In the modern-day, post-Enlightenment world, we tend to explain things by naturalistic causes. Deviant behavior is seen as the result of economic poverty. Crime is regarded as the product of a deficient educational system. Seen through the lens of Darwinism, "evil was but a remnant of brute instinct in a world where emerging man gives content to the notions of good and evil. The possibility follows, then, of eradicating evil by mass education, bureaucratic socialization, and technological revision of human nature."[35] In this scheme, humanity is inherently good.

It has generally been thought that the perfectibility of humankind was a necessary implication of evolutionary philosophy—many present theologians have even adopted this approach.[36] The biblical idea, however, runs directly counter to this, teaching that "man's nature includes a radical defect which inevitably undercuts the realization of his ideals and distorts his moral insights."[37] Genesis 3:1-7 records the first sin—an occasion that has come to be referred to as "the fall." Genesis 3:16-19 records the consequences that follow, which include difficulty in pregnancy, conflict between parents and children, the battle of the sexes, and increased difficulty in raising crops in cursed ground.[38]

The New Testament elaborates on these consequences: the world is in darkness (John 1:5); it is ignorant of God in any sense of real understanding (John 17:25); the minds of men and women have been blinded by the "god of this world" (2 Cor 4:4). Donald Guthrie explains that "the whole of life, both individually and collectively, has been affected. It has even affected the family, the most closely knit of all social groups . . . . The environment in which man finds himself becomes infected by his own nature, biased towards self-centredness."[39] Carl Henry writes of the far-reaching effects of the fall:

> While the classic moral philosophers and founders of other world religions teach that man may and should achieve moral perfection by the gradual improvement of his present nature, Christianity teaches, to the contrary, that only through the atoning death of Christ and the regeneration and sanctification of the Holy Spirit is fallen man restored to fellowship with his righteous Creator and to holiness. The sinner's plight is such, says the Christian religion, that he needs supernatural rescue; in the terms of Scripture, he requires nothing less than justification, regeneration, and sanctification.[40]

## DISCUSSION QUESTIONS

1. What are the main concerns of the book of Habakkuk? In what ways do modern readers share the same kinds of concerns held by Habakkuk?

2. How is Habakkuk's despair resolved? How does his experience witness to the faithfulness of God?

3. Do you believe that God allows wickedness sometimes to go unpunished?

## CHAPTER 12

# A God Who Inspires Authentic Revolution

*Matthew 6:9-13*

The Lord's Prayer, or Our Father, has been a prominent piece of the church's liturgy for two millennia and has been recited in worship services, at weddings, baptisms, and funerals, and in peoples' homes. In every Roman Catholic Church and in many mainline Protestant denominations, the Lord's Prayer is recited every Sunday morning. Devotional books have been written about it and spiritual retreats organized around it. It has been a tool people have used in their private devotions in order to draw closer to their Lord. Yet, only in recent times has the Lord's Prayer begun to be studied and understood in relation to the context of first-century Judaism in which Jesus taught it. When we look at it in this way, we will see how radical Jesus' message was over against those of other first-century Jewish leaders. To set the stage for looking at the Our Father, we must first understand Jewish messianic expectations in the first century AD, Jewish revolutionary movements, and the Sermon on the Mount in which Jesus taught this prayer.

## MESSIANIC EXPECTATIONS IN THE FIRST CENTURY

The English word "messiah" comes from the Hebrew word *mashiach*. It literally means "anointed one." It comes into Greek as *Christos*, or Christ. When we say "Jesus Christ," we are literally saying "Jesus the anointed one." Israel's kings were anointed for their office,[1] but over time the monarchy became corrupt and kings were regarded as having gone hopelessly astray. Because of the corruption of the nation from the top down, Israel began to experience the consequences of covenant violation.[2] In 722 BC, the Assyrians destroyed northern Israel, and later, in 586 BC, the Babylonians attacked southern Israel—Judah. What was left of the nation was taken into exile and, even after the restoration to the land, Israel was essentially never a free people again.[3] It was in this milieu—often referred to as the period of "Second Temple Judaism"[4]—that the Messianic expectation as we encounter it in the New Testament was developed. Between 200 BC and AD 100, the term "anointed one," or messiah, came to be used to refer to an ideal Davidic king who would once again sit on Israel's throne, rule justly, restore Israel to its former glory, and represent Yahwism to the nations.[5] What the nature of this messiah was to be, however, was disagreed upon. It seems that, after the Roman conquest of Palestine, two ideas about the messiah had emerged: some longed for a political messiah and others expected a transcendental messiah, someone dissociated from any physical kingship. The idea of the political messiah was certainly the more popular and had supporters among the various sects of Judaism in the first century AD.

First-century Jewish historian Josephus mentions three different men as having "claimed the kingship" after the death of Herod in 4 BC. Judas in Galilee, Simon in Perea, and Ahtronges in Judea all led revolts in their respective areas, either claiming the throne or being proclaimed king by their followers. Simon's case is particularly interesting since he proclaimed "liberty for slaves and rewards for the free," echoing Jesus' inaugural sermon in Luke 4:16-30. When Jerusalem and the temple were destroyed in AD 70, Simon surrendered in a symbolically charged way: he stood at the spot where the temple had formerly stood, and he wore a white tunic with a royal purple mantle,[6] which was the attire a king would have worn on formal state occasions. Jesus was dressed this way when he was spitefully called "king of the Jews."[7] Simon of Perea was summarily executed.

Josephus mentions two other figures who appeared in the mid-first century AD who have been described as "messianic prophets" or "messianic pretenders." These were Theudas and an unknown man spoken of simply as "the Egyptian," both of whom led mass movements into the wilderness that were subsequently put down by Roman troops. Josephus relates the events surrounding the "imposter" Theudas as follows:

> During the period when Fadus was procurator of Judea, a certain imposter named Theudas persuaded the majority of the masses to take up their possessions and to follow him to the Jordan River. He stated that he was a prophet and that at his command the river would be parted and would provide them an easy passage.[8]

Theudas the revolutionary messiah was apparently attempting to inspire loyalty to himself by leading the Israelites in a reenactment of the exodus events, particularly the miraculous crossing of the Jordan in order to enter into the land victoriously. The case of Theudas is significant in that it is recognized by the New Testament in Acts 5:36. The story of the second messianic pretender, "the Egyptian," is told thus:

> There came to Jerusalem from Egypt a man who declared that he was a prophet and advised the masses of the common people to go out with him to the Mount of Olives . . . . For he asserted . . . that at his command Jerusalem's walls would fall down, through which he promised to provide them an entrance into the city.[9]

This Egyptian messiah was apparently also intent on reenacting one of the foundational events of Israel's formative period—in his case, the conquest of Jericho. The most clearly recognized case of messianism came in the early second century AD, when Bar Kokhba led a revolt against the Romans.[10] The aged and revered Rabbi Akiba publicly proclaimed that the leader of the revolt was none other than the fulfillment of the prophesy of Balaam in Numbers 24:17: "a star shall go forth from Jacob." The name "Bar Kokhba" itself means "son of the star."

Richard Horsley, in his survey of messianic movements in Judaism, summarizes, "The fundamental reality of all of these movements appears to be that the prophets were leading their followers into some great anticipated liberating action by God."[11] Apparently these leaders, through their actions, were hoping to incite God once again to break into history and act decisively on behalf of His people. These leaders were all political leaders who saw redemption for Israel as a national redemption from bondage to Rome.

These kinds of movements were popular in Jesus' day, and many Jews interpreted the role of the messiah to be that of a political leader. While many Jews among the Pharisees and Sadducees certainly held to these views, they held to them only theoretically. On the practical level, they cooperated with Rome and its governmental representatives who ruled over their people. There was another party of Jews, however, who took their political messianism beyond the realm of the theoretical and into the practical, believing they could pave the way for the messiah through violent insurrection. These people were called "Zealots" in Greek and "Sicarii" in Latin. The Greek word "zealot" refers to the "zeal" of these rebels and has been defined as "insurrectionist," while the Latin "sicarii" means "cutthroats" or "bandits." The Zealots were basically terrorists. They attempted to assassinate high priests who collaborated with Roman rule, and they carried out kidnappings of important leaders in order to gain leverage for freeing those of their number who had been taken captive.[12] In an attempt to eradicate the debts of the peasant classes by destroying the bonds of moneylenders, the Sicarii destroyed the public archives. Again, from the Roman point of view, the Zealots/Sicarii were anarchists or terrorists.

The casual reader of Scripture may wonder what all of this discussion of messianism has to do with understanding the ministry of Jesus and his teaching of the Our Father. It has everything to do with it, for although Jesus was not a Zealot, he had to come to terms with this movement at every turn. The Jews generally, and the Zealots particularly, had a theocratic ideal in which the kingdom of God was, to a large degree, equated with the state of Israel. This was one of the reasons the Romans persecuted those who practiced Judaism—because the religion had a genuinely theocratic program. There was no "separation of church and state" in ancient Judaism. During every step of Jesus' ministry, he had to explain his relationship to this conception of the kingdom of God. Not only were Zealots surely among the masses who followed Jesus, but there were even Zealots included in Jesus' inner circle of disciples.

## JESUS AND THE ZEALOTS

In the 1950s through the 1970s, Oscar Cullman, the famous New Testament theologian of Basel and Paris, built the case for Jesus' relationship to the Zealots in his book, *The State in the New Testament*. He argued that a number of those within Jesus' inner circle were Zealots.[13]

- In Luke 6 and Acts 1, Simon is explicitly listed as a Zealot.[14]
- Judas's last name, Iscariot, may not have been a last name at all. Cullman suggests that it is a transcription of the Latin word "sicarius," from which we get Sicarii, meaning Zealot.
- Peter may also have been a Zealot. Cullman gives three reasons for this suggestion. First, Peter objected to Jesus' proclamation of the messianic mission as one of suffering. Second, Peter had a sword with him in Gethsemane. Third, the name Simon "Bar Jona" given for this disciple in Matthew 16:17, traditionally rendered as Simon "son of John," may be a mistranslation. Cullman suggests that *barjona* is actually a word borrowed from Akkadian, meaning "terrorist."
- The sons of Zebedee may have exhibited behavior associated with Zealotism. They wanted to call down thunder on a town that refused Jesus[15] and also requested seats on Jesus' immediate right and left once he was enthroned.[16]

It is also clear that not only did some among Jesus' inner circle hold a political conception of messianism, but many of those in his broader circle of followers—the masses—held this conception as well. One of the clearest examples of this is the triumphal entry, an event recorded in all four Gospels.[17] On that occasion, the masses waved palm branches and laid them on the ground in front of Jesus as he rode toward Jerusalem on a donkey. William Heinrich has recently explored the usage of palm branches in political contexts,[18] and he points to the Maccabean recapture of the temple from the Syrians in 164 BC as one of the first recorded occasions of such. The celebration that followed, recorded in the book of 2 Maccabees, is similar to the triumphal entry: "Therefore, carrying ivy-wreathed wands and beautiful branches and also fronds of palm, they offered hymns of thanksgiving to him who had given success to the purifying of his own holy place" (2 Macc 10:6a, 7).

The palm branches became symbols of victory that the victors then minted on their coins. Bar Kochba minted a similar coin following his revolt of AD 132–135, picturing a palm branch within a wreath on one side. In light of these and other usages of the palm branch, Heinrich concludes that the use of the palm branch at the triumphal entry was a deliberate political statement. He writes,

> The people were proclaiming nationalistic pride and their desire to be free of Roman rule. As Jesus rode by the crowd they shouted "Blessed is the

King of Israel." The message was clear. They were looking for deliverance from Roman tyranny and they tied that hope to Jesus, whose miraculous powers made Him a powerful foe to the Romans. By presenting the palm branches to Him, the people were declaring their loyalty to Him as a victorious general or king might expect.[19]

The people proceeded to shout "Hosanna" which, in the Bible, was simply a term of praise to God.

But since the Maccabean Revolt it had been redefined with a nationalistic meaning—"deliver us," "save us," "give us our freedom." The religious leaders feared such shouting would bring the Roman guards, and they told Jesus to keep his disciples quiet. They would not have requested silence if the people were merely praising God.[20]

What was taking place at the triumphal entry was more akin to a political rally than a worship service. And it was a political rally of Jews who were at least sympathetic to the Zealot cause, if not Zealots themselves.[21]

## THE TEMPTATIONS OF CHRIST

All of Jesus' ministry must be seen in relation to the Zealot movement to liberate Israel from bondage to Rome. Oscar Cullman argued that it was the Zealot ideal that constituted the greatest temptation for Jesus during his earthly ministry. From the beginning of his ministry, the devil offered Jesus world dominion via a path that did not involve the suffering of the cross. This is initially seen in the temptation stories, which are struggles over the nature of the messianic office, as has long been recognized.

Jesus detaches the nationalistic idea of revenge from the hope of redemption. . . . this [is] implied in the temptation-stories; for in all three versions of the narrative the rejection of the nationalistic Messianic expectation appears as the central issue. Jesus is not the Messiah of Israel's expectation; it is not his business to set up the kingdom of Israel, but the Kingdom of God; he has not come to deliver his people from the yoke of Rome, but from Satan's bondage.[22]

Following the three temptations, the devil "departed from him until another occasion" (Luke 4:13). Later, Jesus certainly faced other occasions when he was tempted by the Zealot ideal of political power: the masses tried to make him king by force,[23] Peter insisted that the true messiah could never suffer,[24] the masses hailed him as king at the triumphal entry,[25] Jesus contemplated shrinking back from death as he prayed in the garden,[26] and Jesus realized during his arrest that he could call twelve legions of angels.[27]

In the controversial film *The Last Temptation of Christ*, Jesus is depicted on the cross as passing out for a brief moment, and, in that brief moment, he imagines he has succumbed to the temptation to come down from the cross and live a normal life. He imagines that an angel stands before the cross and offers to free him. Jesus accepts the invitation and is led, stupefied but grateful, back to his home. He marries, has children, and lives out a fairly normal life. The years pass and, ultimately, he lies on his death bed, where he begins to have pangs of conscience as to whether or not he should have left his work on the cross unfinished. Jesus then awakens with a start to find himself still on the cross; he had only dozed off for a moment. He gives a pained half-smile and mutters, "It is accomplished," after which he is able to die victorious, not having been deterred from his mission.

While Jesus surely struggled with the desire to live a normal life, I believe Cullman is correct in his argument that Jesus' last temptations were toward political messianism. Cullman suggests that Jesus' final temptation came in the garden of Gethsemane, where Jesus' disciples waited while he prayed. Some of the disciples were armed. As the Roman cohort approached, Cullman speculates that Jesus may have then considered the Zealot path once again—this time as his "last temptation":

> The Roman cohort approaches. Would it not be possible to kindle a popular revolt? Has the moment not come when the Zealot ideal, the holy war, is to become a reality? And would not God assist him with "more than twelve legions" (Matt 26:53)? Jesus resists this decisive temptation. "Put your sword back into its place" (Matt 26:52). The Romans arrest him and his disciples flee.[28]

I believe there remained yet another temptation to the Zealot path that Jesus had yet to face, and it actually came while Jesus hung on the cross. Luke tells us Jesus was crucified between two thieves—probably Zealots[29]—and one of them "kept deriding him and saying, 'Are you not the Messiah? Save yourself and us!'" (Luke 23:39). While the thief was likely speaking sarcastically, he was taunting Jesus because he believed the true Messiah would not suffer. If Jesus were really the Messiah, he was saying, then he should be able to free himself, those crucified next to him, and indeed all of Israel.

Surely this provoking and taunting from the Zealot crucified next to him must have been a final temptation to Jesus.

## THE RADICAL SERMON ON THE MOUNT

Only when we put Jesus into this context can we realize how striking and dramatic his own vocation and agenda were. In every case, Jesus spoke *against* the political idea of the kingdom of the son of David. As one commentator has written, "He wanted to be some kind of spiritual king, not a physical and political one."[30] On first appearances, when Jesus went with his disciples and the masses up into the hills above the Sea of Galilee, it may have appeared he was about to do something similar to what Theudas or "the Egyptian" had attempted to do. The hills above the Sea of Galilee had indeed been hideouts for "holy revolutionaries," for outlaws who wanted to defeat the pagan Romans and to bring in the kingdom of God—by force if necessary. Instead of inciting a revolution, however, Jesus delivered the Sermon on the Mount.

Many believers think of the Sermon on the Mount as simply an occasion on which Jesus taught people to be nice to each other. The popular image of the sermon is of a gentle, quietly romantic view of the religious life, somewhat detached from the rest of the world. Some think Jesus was talking about how to go to heaven when one dies, something that in reality was practically absent from the entire sermon. Instead, Jesus was staging something that would look to us much more like a political rally. He had led his followers—many of whom were Zealots—into the mountains in order to call them to a new way of being God's people for the world. God had chosen Abraham and his family, the ancestors of Israel, as his means of addressing and solving the problems of the whole world. Israel was called to be the light of the world and the salt of the earth. Israel was to be the city on the hill, where it would function for the benefit of the whole world. In the Sermon on the Mount, Jesus confronted his contemporaries and their revolutionary ideals. Had the prophets looked forward to violent revolution? Was that the way the Old Testament taught that the kingdom would come? Was it through violent revolution that Israel was to be the light of the world? Jesus' answer was an unequivocal "no."

The Sermon on the Mount was not a private message aimed at leading individuals to salvation, nor is it simply a great moral code. British New Testament scholar N. T. Wright explains,

The Sermon is a challenge, in particular, to find a way of being Israel other than the normal revolutionary way. "Do not resist evil"; "turn the other cheek"; "go the second mile"; these are not invitations to be a doormat for Jesus but constitute a warning not to get involved in the ever-present resistance movement. Instead, Jesus' hearers are to discover the true vocation of Israel—to be the light of the world, the salt of the earth.[31]

Jesus did indeed found a revolution when he gave his Sermon on the Mount. But it was a revolution with a difference: he called on Israel to become the real light of the world. If Israel renewed its vocation to be the means by which all nations could be blessed, then Jesus' revolution would be much more far reaching than a simple military insurrection, which would likely result in failure and death.

## THE OUR FATHER

Jesus taught the Lord's Prayer, or the Our Father, in the context of this hilltop gathering in which he redefined Israel's mission. Following his presentation of the Beatitudes and a discussion on how to live in the world, Jesus taught his disciples to pray as follows:

> Our Father in heaven,
> Hallowed be your name.
> Your kingdom come.
> Your will be done,
>     On earth as it is in heaven.
> Give us this day our daily bread.
> And forgive us our sins,
>     As we also forgive those who sin against us.
> And do not bring us to the time of trial,
>     But rescue us from the evil one. (Matt 6:9-13)

Bible scholars have continued to debate the origin of the Lord's Prayer,[32] but we assume here that Jesus taught his disciples about prayer on a number of occasions. One can think of various occasions in the Gospels when Jesus addressed issues with his disciples, such as God's name, reign, and provision of bread, the importance of forgiveness, and the need for divine help in resisting temptation. The variety of teaching occasions would certainly account for the slight differences between the Lord's Prayer as recorded in Matthew and Luke. While we assume that Jesus certainly spoke these words to his disciples, it is possible that the Our Father (or various forms of it) was already known and revered among the Jews and that Jesus was here, as in the rest of the Sermon on the Mount, changing its meaning.

Recently, Bernhard Lang, a professor of New Testament in Germany, wrote an article on the Our Father in which he made radical proposals.[33] While I do not agree with all of his arguments, I think he presents lucid arguments about the background of the Lord's Prayer. He suggests that political expectations of Israel serve as the background for the prayer. I think he may be right, but I also think that, just as he did in his Sermon on the Mount, Jesus shifted the meaning from political to spiritual as he taught the Our Father. Let us look at each of the seven requests of the prayer to see what our Lord has to teach us.

(1) *Our Father in heaven, hallowed be your name.* The first petition is for the "hallowing" of God's name, which means the realizing of God's power in the world, "that is for the coming of the End."[34] In technical language, the study of "the End" is called *eschatology*, and things that concern the end are *eschatological*. Jesus' prayer that God's power be realized plainly in the world is, therefore, an eschatological prayer. While modern believers often think of the End as referring to the end of time, however, ancient Jews often thought of it as referring to the great, climactic day when God would break into history and restore the chosen people to national independence. That "Great Day of the Lord" would be a preview of what the final, eschatological end would be like. What this means is that, here in the Lord's Prayer, the eschatological request for God's name to be hallowed is not a prayer for the end-time to come, but for God's power to be realized plainly in the world in the here and now. "The implication is that God himself is asked to hallow his name, to bring his rule, and to do his will."[35]

In the first part of the first request, Jesus instructs his disciples to speak to God as "Father," which, while more familiar than "Holy Master" or "God in Heaven," may still sound somewhat formal. How many young children do you hear address their biological fathers as "Father"? The New Testament scholar Joachim Jeremias, who was a leading New Testament scholar in the last century, pioneered the idea that behind the Aramaic word *abba* lies the Greek word we translate as "father." Jeremias explained the significance of Jesus' use of the word *abba* in reference to God:

> This is . . . of fundamental importance. Jewish prayers on the one hand do not contain a single example of *abba* as an address for God; Jesus on the other hand always used it when he prayed (with the exception of the cry

from the cross, Mark 15:34). This means that we here have an unequivocal characteristic of the unique way in which Jesus expressed himself.[36]

One can understand why the Jews did not address God as *abba*, Jeremias claimed, when one looks at the background of the word, which basically means "daddy." Jeremias points to a Talmudic passage to support his case: "When a child experiences the taste of wheat (that is, when it is weaned) it learns to say *abba* and *imma*."[37] In other words, the first words it learns are "Daddy" and "Mommy." We even find grown up children calling their fathers *abba* in the New Testament.[38] Jeremias concludes,

> We are now in a position to say why *abba* is not used in Jewish prayers as an address to God: to a Jewish mind, it would have been irreverent and therefore unthinkable to call God by this familiar word. It was something new, something unique and unheard of, that Jesus dared to take this step and to speak with God as a child speaks with his father, simply, intimately, securely. There is no doubt then that the *Abba* which Jesus uses to address God reveals the very basis of his communion with God.[39]

In Jeremias's view, then, the instruction to call God "Father" in the first request of the Lord's Prayer has to do with teaching the disciples about the intimate relationship they are to have with God.

Bernhard Lang, however, sees a different meaning to this reference to God as "Father." He notes that in urgent supplications, particularly when one's life is at stake, God is often addressed as Father. In the intertestamental period, Eleazar the priest urgently prayed to God as "Father" as Ptolemy's elephant brigade advanced against the Jews.[40] Lang suggests that the prayer we know as the "Lord's Prayer" had been a political prayer in which those addressing God saw their situation as desperate: Israel had been in bondage for hundreds of years and longed for God to intervene, hence their use of the term "Father." Lang explains,

> In situations of extreme distress, God is addressed with a kinship term. In a society in which kinship implies solidarity, we can understand why this should be the case: in times of need, people would ask the help of their kinsfolk. . . . A prayer for Israel's national deliverance actually calls God both Father and Redeemer and refers to the Jews as people called by the divine name: "You, O Yahweh, are our father; our Redeemer of old is your name . . . . We have long been like those not called by your name." (Isa 63:6, 19)[41]

Addressing God as Father, therefore, "aims at giving the plea for national liberation a new urgency."[42]

I think Lang may be right that the Our Father (or some form of it) existed previously as a primarily political prayer. But if Jesus is using a preexisting political prayer, then, in light of his other teaching, I believe he is altering its meaning. Jesus is teaching the Lord's Prayer as an eschatological prayer—a prayer concerned with the future. When the disciples begin to pray this prayer by addressing God as *abba*, they are sharing in the eschatological revelation of God as Father. Ultimately, every knee will bow when God reveals Himself to be the Father Almighty, the Creator of Heaven and Earth. However, as Jeremias has explained,

> This address, Abba, when spoken by the disciples, is a sharing in the revelation, it is actualized eschatology. It is the presence of the kingdom even here, even now. It is a fulfillment, granted in advance, of the promise:
>
> *I shall be their father*
> *And they my children.*
> *They shall all be called children of the living God.* (Jub 1:24f.)[43]

Jesus is teaching his disciples to pray for something far more dramatic than mere political revolution. He is teaching them to pray for spiritual revolution. He is teaching them to realize now what all will realize ultimately—God as Father.

(2) *Your kingdom come.* This could be paraphrased "Bring in your kingdom." Lang interprets it to mean "Restore the independent Jewish kingdom!" While modern believers may think of this as a prayer for Christ to return or for the consummation of history to arrive, Lang is likely right in seeing it as a petition for God's restoration of Israel. He explains that "For them, the kingdom of God was a rather small, this-worldly state in the Near East."[44] Indeed, many such prayers for Jewish liberation survive from the intertestamental period, one of which may serve as an elaboration of the prayer that "your kingdom come":

> Have mercy upon us, O God of all, and put all the nations in fear of you. Lift up your hand against foreign nations and let them see your might. Destroy the adversary and wipe out the enemy . . . . Gather all the tribes of

Jacob, and give them their inheritance, as in the beginning. (Sir 36:1-3, 9, 13, 16)[45]

Lang sees the petition as purely political.

If a major object of his prayer is the petition that God come to rule as king, then "this naturally means that in some sense, according to Jesus, God is not yet fully ruling as king."[46] Jesus left his disciples with the instruction to continue praying that God's kingdom would fully come. The purpose of Israel's election in the first place was that the Gentiles might ultimately share in Israel's knowledge of the one true God.[47] I believe that in this second petition of the Lord's Prayer Jesus is teaching his disciples not to pray for the restoration of the independent Jewish state, but that the eschatological realization of Israel's true purposes would be realized; that is, that all people would allow God to reign in their lives. John Paul Meier explains, "Measureless divine might, about to explode in the final act of human history, is accessible even now in prayer by those who enjoy intimacy with the divine king, who is also their loving father."[48]

(3) *Your will be done, on earth as it is in heaven.* Lang again relates the petition to Jewish autonomy, paraphrasing the petition this way:

Cause us to do your will, which is the only law of your kingdom! In the restored divine kingdom, the faithful will of course do God's will, as Ezekiel clearly indicated: "I will put my spirit within you, and cause you to walk in my statutes and be careful to observe my ordinances" (Ezek 36:27; cf. 37:24).[49]

Again, I believe Jesus is going beyond simply local political concerns. He is teaching his disciples to pray that God's ultimate purposes be realized. He teaches them to pray that those purposes be realized to the extent that they are in heaven. In heaven, God's will is already observed perfectly by angels (Matt 26:53). Disciples are to pray that God's will be observed throughout the earth, even among people who do not currently acknowledge Him as Lord. Again, this is a prayer that eschatological realities will be realized in the here and now. In the end, all people will acknowledge God as Lord. The Our Father petitions God to make those eschatological realities contemporary realities.

(4) *Give us this day our daily bread.* One of the curses of covenant violation was famine. As a result of their covenant violations, Israel had been exiled from the land for many years. Even after their restoration, Israel

existed primarily as a subject people and never regained its former economic prosperity. Lang sees the petition for bread as, once again, a prayer for the restoration of Israel's independence and affluence within their own state. He points to Ezekiel's prophetic vision of what it would be like if Israel were to be restored to its land:

> I will summon the grain [says Yahweh] and make it abundant and lay no famine upon you. I will make the fruit of the tree and the increase of the field abundant, that you may never again suffer the disgrace of famine (Ezek 36:29-30). The land will indeed become "like the garden of Eden" (v. 35).[50]

That Israel would "never again suffer the disgrace of famine" is the same as praying that, once Israel was restored to independent nationhood, it would never again violate the covenant and have to live in exile under Yahweh's curse.

The petition for "daily bread" has been notoriously difficult to interpret, for reasons we will not explore here.[51] Many interpreters argue that Jesus is teaching his disciples to rely on God for their literal, daily bread. One commentator defends this interpretation, saying that although this might not sound relevant to affluent, Western readers, "it is a precious and urgent petition from those who live from hand to mouth."[52] While I would not suggest that this petition completely excludes literal requests for daily provision, I think its first and foremost concern is eschatological. Roman Catholic priest and New Testament scholar Raymond Brown has explained the petition this way: "The coming of the kingdom will involve the heavenly banquet, and so they [are taught to] ask for a share of its food (bread)."[53] Jesus was certainly concerned with the heavenly banquet, which he anticipated in some of his miracles,[54] taught about in his parables, and especially anticipated in his table fellowship with tax collectors and sinners.[55] Although his disciples did not know it at the time when Jesus taught this prayer to them, their Lord would establish a meal in which they could regularly be fed in a way that anticipated the heavenly banquet—the Eucharist, or Holy Communion. Each time believers share the Eucharist together, they can give thanks that they are being given a share of the food of the heavenly banquet.[56]

(5) *And forgive us our sins, as we also forgive those who sin against us.* Lang argues here that if we think of the Our Father as a national prayer, then "the sin to be forgiven can only be a national sin." Lang explains, "The sins to be forgiven can only be those that led to punishment with the destruction of

the monarchy and with the Babylonian exile. As soon as God forgives, he will also restore the exiles to their home country."[57]

If the repentance is national, Lang suggests, then the statement that the Jews are also forgiving those who sin against them must also be national.

> A condition for God's forgiving seems to be that the faithful also forgive their oppressors—the Babylonians, Greeks, Romans, and so on. If this is the correct understanding, it has an important implication. [The] message is essentially pacifist. Although he expects an independent Jewish kingdom to emerge shortly, he does not encourage hostile, let alone military, action against the Romans.[58]

Indeed, in the Sermon on the Mount, just prior to teaching the Our Father, Jesus had said, "You have heard that it was said, 'An eye for an eye and a tooth for a tooth.' But I say unto you, 'Do not resist an evildoer. But if anyone strikes you on the right cheek, turn the other also'" (Matt 5:38-39). In other words, resist the temptation to join the Jewish resistance movement. Again, Jesus was initiating a revolution, but it went far beyond the political realm. Through extending the peace of Christ, the disciples were to work toward transforming the entire world.

(6) *And do not bring us to the time of trial.* In the Old Testament, God had often tested His people as a nation. They were tempted to commit acts of disloyalty, such as returning to Egypt after God had liberated them, making pacts with the Canaanites once they had entered the promised land, and worshiping other gods. Ultimately, due to their disloyalty to the covenant, they were sent into exile. "Viewed in this light, the petition can only mean: Do not bring us to another time of trial, for we went through enough national trials."[59] While this petition likely has other, eschatological dimensions, Lang is probably correct in suggesting that it does not refer to resisting everyday "temptations" to individual sin.[60] It is a petition that God will help His people remain faithful to Him, to His will, and to the tasks to which He has called them.

(7) *Deliver us from evil.* This petition echoes the Israelites' second-century belief that God would deliver them from domination, as they expressed in the intertestamental literature: "You deliver us from every evil."[61] Many passages can be found in the Psalms in which the writers prayed for national protection from misfortunes, political foibles, and foreign domination.[62] "These misfortunes [about which the psalmists pray] are of course political

ones, and so the last petition of the Our Father is for delivery from foreign domination."[63]

While Lang limits his interpretation to Israel's national interests, I think Jesus had more eschatological interests in mind. Believers await the perfection of the kingdom of God, which has already been inaugurated.[64] Yet, while they await that perfection, Christians must maintain a tenuous balance, living in the world but not of it. In this vein, D. A. Carson suggests broadening our interpretation of this petition:

> It . . . . may be that we are forcing this sixth petition into too rigid a mold. The NT tells us that this age will be characterized by wars and rumors of wars but does not find it incongruous to urge us to pray for those in authority so "that we may live peaceful and quiet lives" (1 Tim 2:2). While Jesus told his disciples to rejoice when persecuted (5:10-12) he nevertheless exhorted them to flee from it (10:23) and even to pray that their flight should not be too severe (24:20).[65]

What we see here is that, although the kingdom of God has been inaugurated, there will be an interim period bereft with challenges before the kingdom is perfected. During that time Christians will have to struggle to maintain a balance between the kingdom of God and the ruler of this world. The coming of the kingdom will involve a dangerous struggle with Satan, and so the disciples are taught constantly to be petitioning God for help in resisting the Evil One.

## CONCLUSIONS

I am suggesting here that when Jesus taught the Our Father, he may have been appropriating a prayer that already existed in whole or in part in Jewish tradition. We saw many of the same themes of the prayer in Old Testament prayers and, in particular, in intertestamental prayers. If the Our Father was a prayer the Jews had been using, then it was likely a highly political prayer, as Bernhard Lang suggested. However, in teaching it to his disciples in the context we have described, Jesus depoliticized it and gave it an even more profound message. "The thrust of all the petitions is arguably the same: the realization of God's ultimate purpose for the world and for his people. The thrust is firmly eschatological."[66] The transformation of the disciples would culminate in the transformation of Israel and ultimately the world, until every knee would bow and every tongue confess that Jesus Christ is Lord.

## Not by Politics Alone

What we have seen is that Jesus the Messiah did indeed start a revolution. In transforming the political messianism of the first century into an even more revolutionary messianism—a world-transforming messianism—he teaches modern believers where they are to place their priorities. To quote Anglican bishop and theologian N. T. Wright, "What Jesus was to Israel, the church must now be for the world. Everything we discover about what Jesus did and said within the Judaism of his day must be thought through in terms of what it would look like for the church to do and be this for the world."[67] So how does what we have learned about Jesus' mission and message to Israel in the first century apply to the church today? We have seen that his mission was not primarily political. Does this mean Christians are to withdraw from political activism of any kind and pursue a strictly spiritual agenda? What does it mean for us to "implement [Jesus'] work today"?[68]

The Christian church has been divided over the extent to which its mission overlaps into the political arena. The liberal left has criticized the "Christian Right" for the way it has taken "increasingly conservative positions on all types of issues."[69] In the early 1990s, Clyde Wilcox, professor in the Department of Government at Georgetown University, predicted that the survival of the Christian Right "is unlikely, in this century or the next."[70] The "Moral Majority" did undergo hard times and has, for a variety of reasons, lost some of its influence. However, toward the end of the decade, other liberals were noting "the enduring influence of the Christian Right." Despite her disdain for their "regressive" positions, Sara Diamond, writing from Berkeley, California, admired the Christian Right's "power to keep a movement base in motion even during times of apparent political setbacks."[71]

While some of the liberal criticisms of conservative political involvement are certainly legitimate,[72] the involvement of religious liberals in politics seems to have been equally detrimental. Ralph Reed, the onetime executive director of Christian Coalition, has written,

> The sad truth is that involvement in politics has corrupted the religious faith of liberals. Today, mainstream churches and liberal religious lobbies like the National Council of Churches are mere shells of their former greatness. Since World War II, membership in these denominations has hemorrhaged, and their share of total membership has declined by 50 percent. Why? Because they confused their liberal politics with the gospel, causing a mass exodus from the pews.[73]

Indeed, the mainline denominations have primarily seen their role in society as one of "social ministry" rather than one of "evangelical witness."[74] Until mainline denominations recover the message of salvation by grace through faith in Christ as an equal agenda, they will continue to decline.[75]

So where is the balance? Are believing people to abandon politics altogether? Certainly not. But it must be recognized that

> . . . our deepest hopes for restoring and renewing America do not rest solely on our political involvement. In fact, though it may come as a surprise to some, I believe there are strict limits to what politics can accomplish. In many cases our best agenda may not be a political agenda at all. . . . What America needs is not political revolution but spiritual renewal.[76]

Alexis de Tocqueville, French observer of American culture, insightfully observed, "In forming an alliance with a political power, religion augments its authority over a few and forfeits the hope of reigning over all."[77] Christ does not want to reign over a few. He wants to reign within every heart. And so, while Christians must always seek to have an influence within the political sphere, they must never relegate to government what can only be accomplished by the church: the salvation of the soul and the moral renewal of society.

This is why the message Jesus wanted to communicate with the Lord's Prayer is so significant. It is not the sword that empowers real revolution in society and in the world, but faith. The early church connected the Lord's Prayer to societal revolution through conversion and baptism. In the Lord's Prayer, believers pray continually for the coming of the kingdom. For the early church, baptism was the point at which a convert submitted to the reign of God in his or her life.[78] Prospective Christians, then, were not allowed to say the Lord's Prayer with the congregation. Instead, prior to their baptism, they were required to undergo an extensive period of instruction, followed by baptism, after which they would join the assembly in receiving Holy Communion and reciting the Lord's Prayer.[79] After baptism, the new believer was then enjoined to recite the Lord's Prayer three times every day, praying constantly for the coming of the kingdom.[80] In this way, Christians were distinguished from hypocrites, or non-Christians, who obviously would not have been praying constantly for the coming of God's kingdom.[81]

The Lord's Prayer is not a prayer for revolution or armed revolt. It is, rather, a prayer for God's action. It is a prayer that, by allowing God to reign in our lives and in the life of His church, we might play a part in God's perfection of His kingdom. By praying that God might revolutionize His creation, Christians open themselves up to much greater possibilities than could ever be available through violent revolution. In the midst of World War II, the great theologian Reinhold Niebuhr reflected on humankind's inability to effect world transformation and acknowledged that the kingdom of God could only be realized by faith. His words make a fitting conclusion to our study:

> The world community, toward which all historical forces seem to be driving us, is mankind's final possibility and impossibility. The task of achieving it must be interpreted from the standpoint of a faith which understands the fragmentary and broken character of all historic achievements and yet has confidence in their meaning because it knows their completion to be in the hands of a Divine Power, whose resources are greater than those of men, and whose suffering love can overcome the corruptions of man's achievements, without negating the significance of our striving.[82]

## CONNECTIONS: WHO IS JESUS CHRIST FOR US TODAY?

Beginning with the Enlightenment in the late eighteenth century, an effort was begun to understand Jesus in strictly rationalistic terms. This approach to studying Jesus has continued into the present, and it has produced a dizzying array of reconstructions of "the historical Jesus." Jesus has been styled as an early example of the Hasidim,[83] a wandering Cynic,[84] an all-accepting universalist,[85] a "spirit person,"[86] and a peasant Jewish Cynic whose main concern was religious and economic egalitarianism.[87]

Many modern critics have argued that the idea of Jesus' divine nature and all that went along with it—his miraculous knowledge, power, and resurrection—were invented by the early church.[88] This rationale says the Jesus of the first quarter of the first century had only been a man, but his followers in the latter half of that century and beyond built him up into a cult figure. They projected all kinds of legends back onto this simple man, some of which they even copied from the Hellenistic mystery religions.[89] While these kinds of arguments have been common through the nineteenth and twentieth centuries, they no longer stand up in the light of new understandings of Second Temple Judaism that have emerged with the discoveries of new texts.[90] In the Dead Sea Scrolls, for example, the titles "Son of God"[91] and "suffering servant"[92] have been found to have been applied to the Messiah, who was also described as raising the dead at the end of time.[93]

What we see from these and other Second Temple texts is that Christianity did not borrow its ideas from Greco-Roman religion at all, nor did it invent them. Instead, the ideas it held were consistent with the common messianic expectations of at least some other groups of Second Temple Jews.[94] The earliest followers of Jesus were among these Jews who were able to speak about the divinity of the Messiah in the same breath that they spoke about the God of Jewish monotheism.[95] One of them, Rabbi Paul, explained who Jesus the Messiah was and is with these words:

> He is the image of the invisible God, the firstborn of all creation; for in him all things in heaven and on earth were created, things visible and invisible, whether thrones or dominions or rulers or powers—all things have been created through him and for him. He himself is before all things, and in him all things hold together. He is the head of the body, the church; he is the beginning, the firstborn from the dead, so that he might come to have first place in everything. For in him all the fullness of God was pleased to dwell, and through him God was pleased to reconcile to himself all things, whether on earth or in heaven, by making peace through the blood of his cross (Col 1:15-20).[96]

## DISCUSSION QUESTIONS

1. What were some of the common messianic expectations circulating within Judaism during the first century AD? How did these movements contribute to the way in which Jesus defined himself and articulated his mission for others?

2. Go through the Lord's Prayer line by line, discussing the meaning of each. Why do you believe this prayer came to hold such importance in the Christian faith?

3. Does the portrayal of Jesus in this chapter affect how we understand the church and its mission in the world today?

# POSTSCRIPT

The God of the Bible has not fared well in today's "post-Christian" world. Popular culture has argued that Christian believers have no basis on which to claim any uniqueness for their God. Within secular universities, and sometimes even in seminaries, professors of religion teach that the religion of the Old Testament simply evolved out of prior systems of thought and is therefore not superior to other religions that developed in other times and in other places. William G. Dever, for example, one of America's foremost biblical archaeologists, has recently written that "today few biblical scholars and no archaeologists would dare to characterize early Israelite religion as rigidly monotheistic, much less unique."[1]

Statements like this one by Dr. Dever, however, are broad generalizations and only represent one approach to interpreting the data we have available.[2] They also fail to acknowledge the work of more conservative scholars, many of whom have argued that there is substantial evidence for the integrity of the Old Testament and a certain degree of uniqueness in the religion it describes. In 1960, famous Israeli scholar Yehezkel Kaufmann wrote a massive, seven-volume series called *The Religion of Israel, from Its Beginnings to the Babylonian Exile*.[3] Kaufmann believed that Israelite religion did not evolve, but that it originated within Israel and "was absolutely different from anything the pagan world ever knew."[4] William F. Albright, dean of American archaeology during the 1960s and '70s, while somewhat critical of Kaufmann's approach, agreed that Canaanite influences did not seriously distort Israelite religion.[5]

Sharp distinctions can be drawn between the Hebrew heritage and Canaanite culture. Canaanite religions believed the gods were capricious, unpredictable, and essentially unconcerned with the affairs of men. Pagan participation in the divine was mainly through the ultimate processes of nature. The religion portrayed in the Old Testament, on the other hand, stresses the themes of election, covenant, divine action in history, and the personal involvement of God in the affairs of humankind. In a 1967 article titled "The Biblical Idea of History," professor David Noel Freedman of the University of California wrote this about the uniqueness of Israel's understanding of their God and the ways in which their God had been involved with them as a people:

> The biblical idea is summed up in the statement that God is lord of history. He is the creator of the world and master of the destiny of men and nations. The relationship between God and man is defined in moral terms, with a fundamental obligation to obey the will of God devolving upon the human party. The covenant pattern with its detailed stipulations is largely limited to the relationship with Israel, but the implications can be generalized: the response to the divine demand will determine the course and conclusion of human history. Every nation and all people will be judged according to their deeds and rewarded as they deserve.[6]

In *While I Was Praying*, we have explored a number of distinctive ideas about God held by the ancient Israelites—ideas that set their religion apart from the religions of their neighbors. We have done this by looking at several prayers of Old Testament believers in which we have seen that they perceived their God, Yahweh, as unique, just, trustworthy, forgiving, and involved in the affairs of humankind.

The Old Testament saints discovered most of these truths about Yahweh while they were praying.

## Introduction

[1] For a review of the history of the study of ancient Israelite religion, see Bill T. Arnold, "Religion in Ancient Israel," in David W. Baker and Bill T. Arnold, *The Face of Old Testament Studies: A Survey of Contemporary Approaches* (Grand Rapids MI: Baker Book House, 1999), 391-420.

[2] E.g., Mark S. Smith, *The Early History of God: Yahweh and the Other Deities in Ancient Israel* (San Francisco: Harper and Row, 1990), 145-60.

[3] Rudolf Smend, "Tradition and History: A Complex Relation," in Douglas A. Knight, ed., *Tradition and Theology in the Old Testament* (Sheffield England: JSOT Press, 1990), 49-68.

[4] Baruch Levine, *Numbers 21–36: A New Translation with Introduction and Commentary* (New York: Doubleday, 2000), 226.

[5] Giovanni Garbini, *History and Ideology in Ancient Israel* (New York: Crossroad Publishing Co., 1988), 132.

[6] Peter Machinist, "Distinctiveness in Ancient Israel," in Mordechai Cogan and Israel Eph'al, eds., *Ah, Assyria: Studies in Assyrian History and Ancient Near Eastern Historiography Presented to Hayim Tadmor* (Jerusalem: The Magnes Press, 1991), 196-212.

[7] Douglas A. Knight, *Tradition and Theology in the Old Testament* (Sheffield England: JSOT Press, 1990), 3.

[8] Ibid., 5.

[9] Norman H. Snaith, *The Distinctive Ideas of the Old Testament*, reprint (Great Britain: Paternoster Press, 1997), 11, 14.

## Chapter 1

[1] The most likely date for Abraham is probably what archaeologists call the Middle Bronze II, which dates from 1800–1650 BC.

[2] The divine name, "Yahweh" or "Jehovah," is revealed in Exod 3:14.

[3] Gordon J. Wenham, *Genesis 16–50* (Dallas: Word, 1994), 62.

[4] Ibid.

[5] For example, R. N. Whybray, "Shall Not the Judge of All the Earth Do What Is Just?," in David Penchansky and Paul L. Redditt, eds., *Shall Not the Judge of All the Earth Do What Is Right? Studies on the Nature of God in Tribute to James L. Crenshaw* (Winona Lake IN: Eisenbrauns, 2000), 5-7.

[6] Walter C. Kaiser, Jr., "Genesis," in Frank E. Gaebelein, ed., *The Expositor's Bible Commentary*, vol. 2 (Grand Rapids MI: Zondervan, 1990), 150.

[7] Bill T. Arnold, *Encountering the Book of Genesis* (Grand Rapids MI: Baker Book House, 1998), 102.

[8] Ibid.

[9] Wenham, *Genesis 16–50*, 63.

[10] Arnold, *Encountering the Book of Genesis*, 102.

[11] Modern-day Iraq.

[12] Arnold, *Encountering the Book of Genesis*, 102.

[13] Dr. James Dobson, *When God Doesn't Make Sense* (Wheaton IL: Tyndale House Publishers, Inc., 1993), 23-42.

[14] Charles Colson and Nancy Pearcey, *How Now Shall We Live?* (Wheaton IL: Tyndale House Publishers, Inc., 1999), 14.

[15] Cf. George Barna, *Think Like Jesus: Make the Right Decision Every Time* (Nashville: Integrity Publishers, 2004), 19-43.

[16] George Barna and Mark Hatch, *Boiling Point: It Only Takes One Degree* (Venture CA: Regal, 2001), 191-94.

[17] Ibid.

[18] Colson and Pearcey, *How Now Shall We Live?*, 15.

[19] Ibid.

**Chapter 2**

[1] Bill T. Arnold, *Encountering the Book of Genesis* (Grand Rapids MI: Baker Books, 1998), 133.

[2] Chullin 91a, cited in Rabbi Meir Zlotowitz and Rabbi Nosson Scherman, *Bereishis* (Brooklyn: Mesorah Publications, 1989), 185.

[3] Gordan J. Wenham, *Genesis 16–50* (Dallas: Word Books, 1994), 295.

[4] Joyce G. Baldwin, *The Message of Genesis 12–50*, The Bible Speaks Today (Downers Grove IL: InterVarsity, 1986), 137.

[5] Zlotowitz and Scherman, *Bereishis*, 185.

[6] Claus Westermann, *Genesis: A Practical Commentary* (Grand Rapids MI: Eerdmans, 1987), 228-30.

[7] Robert Alter, *Genesis: Translation and Commentary* (New York: W. W. Norton and Co., 1996), 181.

[8] David F. Pennant, "Gen. 32: Lighten Our Darkness, Lord, We Pray," in R. S. Hess, G. J. Wenham, and P. E. Satterthwaite, eds., *He Swore an Oath: Biblical Themes from Genesis 12–50* (Grand Rapids MI: Baker Book House, 1994), 176.

[9] Wenham, *Genesis 16–50*, 295.

[10] Ibid.

[11] Ibid., 296.

[12] Alter, *Genesis: Translation and Commentary*, 181.

[13] John J. Sailhamer, "Genesis," in Frank E. Gaebelein, ed., *The Expositor's Bible Commentary*, vol. 2 (Grand Rapids MI: Zondervan, 1990), 210.

[14] Arnold, *Encountering the Book of Genesis*, 134.

[15] To Abraham, Genesis 17:5.

[16] To Jerubbaal, Judges 6:32.

[17] To Peter, John 1:42.

[18] Derek Kidner, *Genesis*, Tyndale Old Testament Commentaries, 4th reprint (London: Tyndale Press, 1973), 169.

[19] Arnold, *Encountering the Book of Genesis*, 133.

[20] Rabbi Burton L. Visotzky, in Bill Moyers, *Genesis: A Living Conversation* (New York: Doubleday, 1996), 278.

[21] Roberta Hestenes, in Moyers, *Genesis*, 280.

[22] E. A. Speiser, *Genesis*, 3rd ed. (New York: Doubleday and Co., Inc., 1987), 257.

[23] Hestenes, in Moyers, *Genesis*, 286.

[24] John Kselman, in Moyers, *Genesis*, 291.

[25] Zlotowitz and Scherman, *Bereishis*, 186.

[26] Pennant, "Gen. 32: Lighten Our Darkness, Lord, We Pray," 180.

[27] Ibid., 180-81.

[28] Kselman, in Moyers, *Genesis*, 305.

[29] Robert M. Alter, with Jane Alter, *The Transformative Power of Crisis: Our Journey to Psychological Healing and Spiritual Awakening* (New York: Regan, 2000).

[30] Ibid., 110.

[31] As told in Brennan Manning, *The Rabbi's Heartbeat* (Colorado Springs: NavPress, 2003), 25.

[32] Henri J. M. Nouwen, *The Wounded Healer* (New York: Continuum, 2000), 156.

[33] Henri J. M. Nouwen, *The Path of Power* (New York: Crossroad, 1995), 33.

## Chapter 3

[1] Cf. Exod 12:12; 15:11; 18:11.

[2] John I. Durham, *Exodus* (Waco TX: Word, 1987), 419.

³ John O. Oswalt, "Golden Calves and the 'Bull of Jacob': The Impact on Israel of Its Religious Environment," in Abraham Gileadi, ed., *Israel's Apostasy and Restoration: Essays in Honor of Roland K. Harrison* (Grand Rapids MI: Baker Book House, 1988), 12.

⁴ P. Kyle McCarter, Jr., "Exodus," in James L. Mays, ed., *The HarperCollins Bible Commentary* (New York: HarperCollins, 2000), 142.

⁵ Ibid. McCarter also states that "scholars disagree whether the bull was understood as an image of Yahweh himself or as a pedestal upon which he was believed to be invisibly present."

⁶ T. D. Alexander, "Exodus," in D. A. Carson, R. T. France, J. A. Motyer, and G. J. Wenham, eds., *New Bible Commentary: 21st Century Edition* (Downers Grove IL: InterVarsity Press, 1997), 116.

⁷ Oswalt, "Golden Calves," 12.

⁸ Ibid., 14.

⁹ Bill T. Arnold, *Encountering the Book of Genesis* (Grand Rapids MI: Baker Books, 1998), 50.

¹⁰ Oswalt, "Golden Calves," 15.

¹¹ Durham, *Exodus*, 422.

¹² McCarter, "Exodus," 142.

¹³ Cf. Gen 26:8; 39:14, 17.

¹⁴ Durham, *Exodus*, 422.

¹⁵ One could certainly argue that an atheist or a Buddhist might adhere to these same ethical standards, but the biblical view is that they are real, objective standards built into the very fiber of the universe and reflecting the character of a real, objective God. For the atheist or the Buddhist (who is non-theistic), ethical demands are subjective postulants. The Hebrew Bible sees all commands regarding human ethics as hinging on an acceptance of the commands regarding monotheism, idolatry, and graven images. Objective ethics, according to this view, cannot be built on a subjective foundation. Instead, they must be built on the objective foundation of Yahweh and His character.

¹⁶ Walter C. Kaiser, Jr., "Exodus," in Frank E. Gaebelein, ed., *The Expositor's Bible Commentary*, vol. 2 (Grand Rapids MI: Zondervan, 1990), 478.

¹⁷ Goran Larsson, *Bound for Freedom: The Book of Exodus in Jewish and Christian Traditions* (Peabody MA: Hendrickson, 1999), 251.

¹⁸ Ibid., 251-52. Larsson is quoting from Everett Fox, *Now These Are the Names: A New English Rendition of the Book of Exodus* (New York: Schocken Books, 1986), 181.

¹⁹ Edward P. Myers, "Mercy," in David Noel Freedman, ed., *Eerdmans Dictionary of the Bible* (Grand Rapids MI: Eerdmans, 2000), 885.

²⁰ Christoph Barth, *God with Us: A Theological Introduction to the Old Testament*, ed. Geoffrey W. Bromiley (Grand Rapids MI: Eerdmans, 1991), 51.

²¹ Nahum M. Sarna, "Israel in Egypt: The Egyptian Sojourn and the Exodus," in Hershel Shanks, ed., *Ancient Israel: A Short History from Abraham to the Roman Destruction of the Temple* (Washington DC: Biblical Archaeological Society, 1988), 45.

²² For a detailed description of the covenant form, cf. G. E. Mendenhall's *Law and Covenant in Israel and the Ancient Near East* (Pittsburgh: Bible Colloquium, 1955). For a readable

summary of these forms and their meaning, cf. Charles F. Pfeiffer, *The Biblical World* (Grand Rapids MI: Baker Book House, 1966), 175-177.

[23] Barth, *God with Us*, 51.

[24] Andrew E. Hill and John H. Walton, *A Survey of the Old Testament* (Grand Rapids MI: Zondervan, 1991), 198.

[25] Contra. Michael D. Guinan, "Davidic Covenant," in David Noel Freedman, ed., *Anchor Bible Dictionary*, vol. 2 (New York: Doubleday, 1992), 69-70.

[26] Walter C. Kaiser, in W. Kaiser, P. Davids, F. F. Bruce, and M. T. Brauch, *Hard Sayings of the Bible* (Downers Grove IL: InterVarsity, 1996), 209.

[27] Cf. Gleason L. Archer, *Encyclopedia of Bible Difficulties* (Grand Rapids MI: Zondervan, 1982), 174.

[28] Larsson, *Bound for Freedom*, 249.

[29] Ibid.

[30] C. Leonard Allen, *The Cruciform Church: Becoming a Cross-Shaped People in a Secular World* (Abilene TX: Abilene Christian University Press, 1990), 88.


## Chapter 4

[1] Walter Brueggemann, *First and Second Samuel* (Louisville KY: John Knox Press, 1990), 10.

[2] Cf. Gen 11:30; 26:22; 29:31; Luke 1:36.

[3] 1 Chr 6:22-27.

[4] Cf. Gen 11:30; 15:2-4; 16:1-2; 17:15-16; 21:1-2; 25:5.

[5] Exod 34:23; Deut 12:5-7; Luke 2:41.

[6] 1 Sam 4:3-4; Josh 18:1; Judg 18:31.

[7] Cf. Exod 29:26; Lev 7:33; 8:29.

[8] Cf. Deut 12:17-18; 16:13-14.

[9] Vv. 5-6; cf. Gen 15:3; 16:2; 20:18; 30:2.

[10] Cf. the actions of Sarai, Gen 16:2; Rachel, 30:3; and Leah, 30:9.

[11] The Hebrew word *tsarah*, in v. 6, can mean "adversary" or "enemy."

[12] Cf. Deut 32:35. See also David's statement in 2 Sam 3:39.

[13] The only other precise OT parallel for this phrase is Deut 15:10: "Do so without a grudging heart." Literally, "May your heart not be bad when you do so" (i.e., when you give generously to the Lord).

[14] Ten, like seven, represents completeness or fullness, as in the Ten Commandments.

[15] Num 6:2.

[16] In a broader sense, every Israelite mother was expected to dedicate her children to the Lord (Exod 22:29).

[17] Num 6:3-7.

[18] The Mishnah argues that Samuel was indeed a Nazirite (*Nazir* 9.5).

[19] Judg 13:5; 16:17; see also Num 6:5.

[20] Cf. Pss 3:4; 4:1; 6:9; Dan 6:10-11.

[21] Roland de Vaux, *Ancient Israel*, 496.

[22] Cf. Pss 42:4; 62:8; Lam 2:19.

[23] Cf. Ruth 4:13.

[24] Cf. Ps 115:14; Isa 48:19; 54:1-3.

[25] Cf. 2 Macc 7:27.

[26] Brueggeman, *First and Second Samuel*, 16.

[27] Ronald F. Youngblood, "1–2 Samuel," in Frank E. Gaebelein, ed., *The Expositor's Bible Commentary*, vol. 3 (Grand Rapids MI: Zondervan, 1992), 579.

[28] See John T. Willis, "The Song of Hannah and Psalm 113," *Catholic Biblical Quarterly* 25/2 (1973): 139-54.

[29] See especially Pss 89:17; 92:10.

[30] Bruce C. Birch, "1 and 2 Samuel," in Leander E. Keck et al., eds., *New Interpreter's Bible*, vol. 2 (Nashville: Abingdon Press, 1998), 981.

[31] D. F. Payne, "1 and 2 Samuel," in D. A. Carson, R. T. France, J. A. Motyer, and G. J. Wenham, *New Bible Commentary: 21st Century Edition* (Downers Grove IL: InterVarsity Press, 1997), 299.

[32] Robert L. Cohn, "1 and 2 Samuel," in James L. Mays, ed., *The HarperCollins Bible Commentary* (New York: Harper SanFrancisco, 2000), 247.

[33] William Foxwell Albright, *Yahweh and the Gods of Canaan* (London: Athlone Press, 1968), 18.

[34] For application of this to Christian thought, see Hugh J. Blair, "Kingship in Israel and Its Implications for the Lordship of Christ Today," *Evangelical Quarterly* 47/2 (1975): 71.

[35] As in Exod 15:11; Ps 99:3, 5, 9; Isa 5:16.

[36] Cf. Gen 49:24; Deut 32:4; Isa 26:4; Hab 1:12; and frequently in the Psalms.

[37] Pss 31:18; 75:4; 138:6; Isa 5:15-16.

[38] Ralph W. Klein, *1 Samuel* (Waco TX: Word Books, 1983), 16.

[39] Joyce Baldwin, *1 and 2 Samuel* (Downers Grove IL: InterVarsity Press, 1988), 57.

[40] Ibid.

[41] Cf. Prov 21:30-31.

[42] Cf. Judg 13:2-3.

[43] Cf. Ruth 4:15.

[44] 1 Sam 2:21.

[45] Baldwin, *1 and 2 Samuel*, 57.

[46] Deut 32:39 and 2 Kgs 5:7 have the same two sets of contrasts.

[47] Zech 9:3-4.

[48] Job 5:11; Ps 75:7; and esp. 2 Sam 22:28.

[49] Baldwin, *1 and 2 Samuel*, 57.

[50] Birch, "1 and 2 Samuel," 982.

[51] Baldwin, *1 and 2 Samuel*, 59.

[52] Norman K. Gottwald, *The Tribes of Yahweh, A Sociology of the Religion of Liberated Israel, 120–1050 BCE* (London: SCM Press, 1980), 540.

[53] Cf. Ps 72:1-4, 12-14.

[54] Brevard S. Childs, *Introduction to the Old Testament as Scripture* (Philadelphia: Fortress Press, 1979), 272-73.

[55] Brueggemann, *First and Second Samuel*, 21.

[56] Birch, "1 and 2 Samuel," 983.

[57] Ibid. Cf. Ps 72:1-4, 12-14.

[58] Luke 1:46-55.

[59] Dan Brown, *The DaVinci Code* (New York: Doubleday, 2003), 309.

[60] Priscilla (Rom 16:3); Mary (v. 6); probably Junia (v. 7); Tryphena and Tryphosa, who may have been twin sisters, and Persis (v. 12); Rufus's mother (v. 13); Julia and Nereus's sister (v. 15).

[61] See the interpretation of these passages in Ralph K. Hawkins, "'I Permit Not a Woman to Teach': Women's Roles as a Test Case for Biblical Authority," in *Quarterly Review* 24/3 (Fall 2004): 289-99.

[62] Cf. Jan Faver Hailey, "Neither Male and Female" (Gal 3:28), in Carroll D. Osburn, *Essays on Women in Earliest Christianity*, vol. 1 (Joplin MO: College Press, 1993), 131-66.

## Chapter 5

[1] See 2 Sam 21:15-17.

[2] 2 Sam 23:9.

[3] See 1 Sam 21:4-5.

[4] Eugene H. Peterson, *Leap over a Wall: Earthy Spirituality for Everyday Christians* (New York: HarperSanFrancisco, 1997), 183.

[5] Ibid., 187.

[6] Eugene Peterson, *The Message: The Bible in Contemporary Language* (Colorado Springs: Navpress, 2002), 975-76.

[7] Carroll Stuhlmueller, "Psalms," in James L. Mays, ed., *The HarperCollins Bible Commentary* (New York: HarperSanFrancisco, 2000), 414.

[8] Iain S. Maclean, "Descent into Hell," in David Noel Freedman, ed., *Eerdmans Dictionary of the Bible* (Grand Rapids MI: Eerdmans, 2000), 338.

[9] Quoted in Peter Gorday, ed., *Colossians, 1-2 Thessalonians, 1-2 Timothy, Titus, Philemon*, Ancient Christian Commentary, vol. 9, ed. Thomas C. Oden (Downers Grove IL: InterVarsity, 2000), 20.

[10] For detailed references, see Richard Bauckham, "Descent to the Underworld," in David Noel Freedman, ed., *The Anchor Bible Dictionary*, vol. 2 (New York: Doubleday, 1992), 156-59.

[11] For a recent review of the history of the doctrine of Christ's descent into hell, see Heidi J. Hornik and Mikeal C. Parsons, "The Harrowing of Hell," in *Bible Review* 3 (June 2003): 18-26, 50.

[12] Cf. Num 19:13, 20. See also Num 15:32-36 and Josh 7.

[13] See Heb 9:22.

[14] Andrew E. Hill and John H. Walton, *A Survey of the Old Testament* (Grand Rapids MI: Zondervan, 1991), 124. "Salvific" simply means to bring about salvation.

[15] See 1 Sam 15:22-23; Ps 51:16-17; Prov 21:3; Isa 1:12-17; Jer 7:21-23; Hos 6:6; Amos 5:21-24; Mic 6:6-8.

[16] Hill and Walton, *Survey of the Old Testament*, 126.

[17] Hendrik L. Bosman, "Adultery," in Freedman, ed., *Eerdmans Dictionary of the Bible*, 24. See Lev 19:20-21 for cases in which adultery could be atoned by a sin offering.

[18] Gerald M. Bilkes, "Murder," in Freedman, ed., *Eerdmans Dictionary of the Bible*, 926.

[19] Marvin E. Tate, *Psalms 51–100* (Dallas: Word, 1990), 13.

[20] Ibid.

[21] Gregory Mobley, "Loving-Kindness," in Freedman, ed., *Eerdmans Dictionary of the Bible*, 826.

[22] Hos 1:2.

[23] Ibid., 14.

[24] Prov 30:20; Isa 25:8; Deut 9:14; et al.

[25] Exod 19:10, 14; Lev 13:6; et al.

[26] As in Lev 11:32; et al.

[27] E. R. Dalglish, *Psalm Fifty-One in the Light of Ancient Near Eastern Patternism* (Leiden: Brill, 1962), 88.

[28] L. H. Kohler, *Old Testament Theology*, trans. A. S. Todd (Philadelphia: Westminster Press, 1957), 170.

[29] Tate, *Psalms 51–100*, 16.

[30] Stuhlmueller, "Psalms," 414.

[31] Lev 14; Num 19.

[32] Exod 12:22.

[33] Willem A. VanGemeren, "Psalms," in Frank E. Gaebelein, ed., *The Expositor's Bible Commentary*, vol. 5 (Grand Rapids MI: Zondervan, 1991), 382.

[34] J. A. Motyer, "Psalms," in D. A. Carson, R. T. France, J. A. Motyer, and G. J. Wenham, eds., *New Bible Commentary: 21st Century Edition* (Downers Grove IL: InterVarsity Press, 1997), 519.

[35] Tate, *Psalms 51–100*, 26.

[36] Stuhlmueller, "Psalms," 414.

[37] Motyer, "Psalms," 518.

[38] Ibid., 519.

[39] Tate, *Psalms 51–100*, 31.

[40] Peterson, *Leap over a Wall*, 189-90.

[41] John Powell, *Why Am I Afraid to Love* (Allen TX: Tabor Publishing, 1982), 12.

[42] Robert Bolt, *The Mission* (New York: Jove Books, 1986). The story Bolt tells is based on actual events.

[43] Powell, *Why Am I Afraid to Love*, 12, (emphasis mine).


**Chapter 6**

[1] 1 Kgs 3:28; ch. 4; 4:29-34.

[2] 1 Kgs 4:29-34

[3] Cf. 1 Kgs 5:3-4.

[4] Gary N. Knoppers, "Solomon," in David Noel Freedman, ed., *Eerdmans Dictionary of the Bible* (Grand Rapids MI: Eerdmans, 2000), 1236. The term "Deuteronomistic history" is a theoretical construct used by biblical scholars to refer to the history contained in the books of Deuteronomy, Joshua, Judges, Samuel, and Kings.

[5] Knoppers, "Solomon," 1236.

[6] Howard F. Vos, *1, 2 Kings* (Grand Rapids MI: Lamplighter Books, 1989), 68.

[7] The temple lay in ruins, of course, for seventy-one years after its destruction by Nebuchadnezzar in 587 BC before it was rededicated by Zerubbabel in 516 BC.

[8] Carol Meyers, "Temple, Jerusalem," in David Noel Freedman, ed., *The Anchor Bible Dictionary*, vol. 6 (New York: Doubleday, 1992), 350-51.

[9] Most of these references deal with either the Second Temple or the later Herodian Temple.

[10] John M. Lundquist, "Temple," in Freedman, ed., *Eerdmans Dictionary of the Bible*, 1280.

[11] J. Edward Wright, *The Early History of Heaven* (New York: Oxford University Press, 2000), 75.

[12] W. F. Albright, "What Were the Cherubim?" in *Biblical Archaeologist* 1/1 (February 1938): 1-3.

[13] Wright, *Early History of Heaven*, 76-80.

[14] Ibid., 76-78.

[15] Choon-Leong Seow, "1 and 2 Kings," in Leander E. Keck, ed., *The New Interpreter's Bible*, vol. 3 (Nashville: Abingdon Press, 1999), 70.

[16] Seow, "1 and 2 Kings," 70.

[17] Ibid.

[18] Ibid.

[19] Ibid., 72.

[20] Ibid.

[21] Deut 31:9-13.

[22] Seow, "1 and 2 Kings," 75.

[23] Vos, *1, 2 Kings*, 69.

[24] Ibid.

[25] Seow, "1 and 2 Kings," 75.

[26] Ibid.

[27] John J. Bimson, "1 and 2 Kings," in D. A. Carson, R. T. France, J. A. Motyer, and G. J. Wenham, eds., *New Bible Commentary: 21st Century Edition* (Downers Grove IL: InterVarsity Press, 1997), 348.

[28] Richard D. Nelson, "1 and 2 Kings," in James L. Mays, ed., *The HarperCollins Bible Commentary* (New York: HarperCollins, 2000), 285.

[29] Simon J. DeVries, *1 Kings* (Waco TX: Word, 1985), 125.

[30] Bimson, "1 and 2 Kings," 348.

[31] Vos, *1, 2 Kings*, 70.

[32] Ibid.

[33] DeVries, *1 Kings*, 126.

[34] Seow, "1 and 2 Kings," 78.

[35] John Thompson and Randy Scruggs, "Sanctuary," in *The Faith We Sing* (Nashville: Abingdon, 2000), 2164.

[36] Though I have heard this anecdote told in various ways, I give credit to H. B. London, who gave a recent variation of it in "A Passion for Unity," in *Focus on the Family* 26/8 (August 2002): 9.

## Chapter 7

[1] 1 Sam 8:4-9.

[2] 1 Sam 8:10-18.

[3] This would become Saul's policy (1 Sam 14:52).

[4] 1 Sam 8:12.

[5] 1 Sam 8:12.

[6] 1 Sam 8:11. Cf. the practice of Absalom in 2 Sam 15:1 and of Adonijah in 1 Kgs 1:5.

[7] 1 Sam 8:13.

[8] Amos 7:1.

[9] I. Mendelsohn, "Samuel's Denunciation of Kingship in the Light of the Akkadian Documents from Ugarit," BASOR 143 (1956): 17-22.

[10] 1 Sam 22:6-19.

[11] 2 Sam 15:1-6.

[12] Joseph Blenkinsopp, *Sage, Priest, Prophet: Religious and Intellectual Leadership in Ancient Israel* (Louisville KY: Westminster John Knox Press, 1995), 120.

[13] Ibid., 121.

[14] Thomas W. Overholt, "Prophet, Prophecy," in David Noel Freedman, ed., *Eerdmans Dictionary of the Bible* (Grand Rapids MI: Eerdmans, 2000), 1086.

[15] Ibid.

[16] 1 Kgs 16:30, 33; 21:25; Mic 6:16.

[17] Cf. Paul K. Hooker, "Omri," in Freedman, ed., *Eerdmans Dictionary of the Bible*, 986-87.

[18] 1 Kgs 16:32.

[19] 1 Kgs 16:33.

[20] Winfried Thiel, "Ahab," in David Noel Freedman, ed., *The Anchor Bible Dictionary*, vol. 1 (New York: Doubleday, 1992), 102.

[21] 1 Kgs 20, 22.

[22] The name Obadiah means "servant of Yahweh."

[23] 1 Kgs 22.

[24] Deborah A. Appler, "Ahab," in Freedman, ed., *Eerdmans Dictionary of the Bible*, 31.

[25] 1 Kgs 16:29–22:40; 2 Chr 18, 21.

[26] Mark Anthony Phelps, "Baal, Deity," in Freedman, ed., *Eerdmans Dictionary of the Bible*, 134.

[27] Ibid.

[28] See the discussion on the worship of Yahweh as a bull in chapter 3.

[29] Ziony Zevit, *The Religions of Israel: A Synthesis of Parallactic Approaches* (London and New York: Continuum, 2001), 648-49.

[30] See Zevit, *Religions of Israel*, for a discussion of Baal names and their significance.

[31] 1 Chr 5:5 and 8:30. However, it is not clear whether the element *ba'al* refers to the divinity or whether it should be understood to mean "master," which could be an appellation for Yahweh. Cf. the discussion by Marc Z. Brettler, "Baal," in Freedman, ed., *Anchor Bible Dictionary*, vol. 1, 549-50.

[32] Zevit, *Religions of Israel*, 650.

[33] John Day, "Baal (Deity)," in Freedman, ed., *Anchor Bible Dictionary*, vol. 1, 548.

[34] Judg 2:11, 13; 3:7; 10:6, 10; 1 Sam 7:4; 12:10.

[35] Jer 2:8.

[36] 1 Kgs 16:31-33.

[37] Joseph Blenkinsopp, *A History of Prophecy in Israel* (Philadelphia: Westminster Press, 1983), 72.

[38] Susan Ackerman, "The Prayer of Nabonidus, Elijah on Mount Carmel, and the Development of Monotheism in Israel," in William G. Dever and J. Edward Wright, eds., *The Echoes of Many Texts: Reflections of Jewish and Christian Traditions, Essays in Honor of Lou H. Silberman* (Atlanta: Scholars Press, 1997), 63-64.

[39] James R. Battenfield, "YHWH's Refutation of the Baal Myth through the Actions of Elijah and Elisha," in Avraham Gileadi, ed., *Israel's Apostasy and Restoration: Essays in Honor of Roland K. Harrison* (Grand Rapids MI: Baker Book House, 1988), 20.

[40] Ibid.

[41] John J. Bimson, "1 and 2 Kings," in D. A. Carson, R. T. France, J. A. Motyer, and G. J. Wenham, eds., *New Bible Commentary: 21st Century Edition* (Leicester, England, and Downers Grove IL: InterVarsity Press, 1997), 359.

[42] Donald J. Wiseman, *1 and 2 Kings: An Introduction and Commentary* (Downers Grove IL: InterVarsity Press, 1993), 169.

[43] See A. R. Millard, "Abraham, Akhenaten, Moses, and Monotheism," in R. S. Hess, G. J. Wenham, and P. E. Satterthwaite, eds., *He Swore an Oath: Biblical Themes from Genesis 12–50* (Cambridge: Tyndale House, 1993), 119-29.

[44] Norman K. Gottwald, *All the Kingdoms of the Earth: Israelite Prophecy and International Relations in the Ancient Near East* (New York: Harper and Row, 1964).

[45] Ibid.

[46] Mordechai Cogan, *1 Kings* (New York: Doubleday, 2001), 440.

[47] Cf. Thomas Jemielity, *Satire and the Hebrew Prophets* (Louisville KY: Westminster John Knox Press, 1992).

[48] Deut 14:1 and Lev 19:28; 21:5.

[49] Moshe Weinfeld, "Ancient Near Eastern Patterns in Prophetic Literature," in *Vetus Testamentum* 27 (1977): 182. The classic example of an individual Canaanite who goes into a frenzy upon possession while carrying out a sacrifice is contained in the late-7th century BC Egyptian text of Wen-Amon. See ANET, 26b.

[50] Louis Ginzberg, *Legends of the Bible* (Old Saybrook CT: Konecky and Konecky, 1956), 587.

[51] Cogan, *1 Kings*, 442.

[52] Ibid., 443. Cf. Exod 3:2; 19:18; 24:17.

[53] Richard D. Nelson, "1 and 2 Kings," in James L. Mays, ed., *The HarperCollins Bible Commentary* (New York: HarperSanFrancisco, 2000), 293.

[54] Terence E. Fretheim, *First and Second Kings*, Westminster Bible Companion (Louisville KY: Westminster John Knox Press, 1999), 106-107.

[55] Bimson, "1 and 2 Kings," 359.

[56] Cogan, *1 Kings*, 444.

[57] Gordon McConville, "Deuteronomy," in D. A. Carson et al., eds., *New Bible Commentary*, 213.

[58] Ibid.

[59] Bernard M. Levinson, "Deuteronomy," in Michael D. Coogan, ed., *The New Oxford Annotated Bible* (New York: Oxford University Press, 2001), 265.

[60] Fretheim, 106.

[61] Nelson, ibid.

[62] Howard F. Vos, *1, 2 Kings* (Grand Rapids, MI: Lamplighter Books, 1989), 119.

[63] Cogan, 445.

[64] As suggested by Robert R. Cohn, in "The Literary Logic of 1 Kings 17-19," *Journal of Biblical Literature* 101 (1982): 341.

[65] Fretheim, *First and Second Kings*, 105.

[66] Ibid.

[67] Ibid.

[68] Ibid.

[69] R. T. France, *Matthew* (Grand Rapids MI: Eerdmans, 1985), 133.

[70] Anonymous, "Incomplete Work of Matthew, Homily 13," cited in Manlio Simonetti, ed., *Matthew 1–13: Ancient Christian Commentary on Scripture* (Downers Grove IL: InterVarsity Press, 2001), 129.

[71] This is just a sample of the heresies that existed during the early centuries of the church. See chs. 3, 5, 8 and 9 in Hershel Shanks, ed., *Christianity and Rabbinic Judaism: A Parallel History of Their Origins and Early Development* (Washington DC: Biblical Archaeology Society, 1992).

[72] "Fallout Escalates over Goddess Sophia Worship," *Christianity Today* (4 April 1994): 72.

[73] John Shelby Spong, *Why Christianity Must Change or Die: A Bishop Speaks to Believers in Exile* (New York: HarperCollins, 1998). Chapter 3 is titled "In Search for God: Is Atheism the Only Alternative to Theism?"

[74] Robert W. Funk, "The Coming Radical Reformation: Twenty-one Theses," *The Fourth R* 11/4 (July/Aug 1998).

[75] While this final, standard version dates to the 7th century AD, variations of the Apostles' Creed appear as early as about AD 215.

[76] Robert W. Funk, Roy W. Hoover, and the Jesus Seminar, *The Five Gospels* (New York: Macmillan, 1993), 7-8.

[77] Luke Timothy Johnson, *The Creed: What Christians Believe and Why It Matters* (New York: Doubleday, 2003), 7.

## Chapter 8

[1] F. Rachel Magdalene explains that the word "bless" is "most often a relational marker, signifying the existence of some sacral, legal, or social relationship," in David Noel Freedman, ed., *Eerdmans Dictionary of the Bible* (Grand Rapids MI: Eerdmans, 2000), s.v. "Bless, Blessing."

[2] Magdalene, "Bless, Blessing," in Freedman, ed., *Eerdmans Dictionary of the Bible*.

[3] Bruce H. Wilkinson, *The Prayer of Jabez* (Sisters OR: Multnomah, 2000), 24-25.

[4] Ibid., 25.

[5] Ibid.

[6] Ibid., 27.

[7] Ibid., 27 and 29.

[8] From the Greek word for "mind," *noeo*.

[9] For example, Jonah 1:3.

[10] For example, 1 Kgs 19:4; Jonah 4:3.

[11] For example, Gen 15:13-16; Num 22–24.

[12] Wilkinson, *Prayer of Jabez*, 13.

[13] Ibid.

[14] The books of Chronicles come at the end of the Hebrew Bible.

[15] Roddey Braun, *1 Chronicles* (Waco TX: Word, 1985) 3.

[16] *Atzav.*

[17] Wilkinson, *Prayer of Jabez*, 20.

[18] Prov 6:10-11; 13:18; 21:17.

[19] In Hebrew this word refers to a foreigner.

[20] For more in-depth study of the poor in the Bible, see "Poor, Poverty," in the *Anchor Bible Dictionary*, vol. 5, ed. David Noel Freedman (New York: Doubleday, 1992), 402-24.

[21] These resources can be ordered from the Family Research Council at 801 G Street, N.W., Washington DC, 20001, or by calling 1.800.225.4008.

## Chapter 9

[1] Jer 25:11-14.

[2] This chapter approaches the book of Daniel as having been written by the prophet himself, or a close associate, during the exilic period. It is commonplace to date the composition of Daniel to the 2nd century BC. Cf. John J. Collins, *Daniel*, Hermeneia (Minneapolis: Fortress, 1993), 60-66. The traditional view is that Daniel was written in the late 6th or early 5th century in Babylon, as argued by E. J. Young, *A Commentary on Daniel* (Grand Rapids MI: Eerdmans, 1949), 19-20; also, Ernest Lucas, *Daniel*, Apollos Old Testament Commentary, vol. 20 (Leicester England: Apollos, 2002), 312-15, briefly but cogently suggests that the traditional view still has merit. For a detailed treatment of the traditional dating of Daniel, see Bruce K. Waltke, "The Date of the Book of Daniel," BSac 133 (1976): 329ff. Future discussions of the date of Daniel will have to consider the Daniel tradition at Qumran, where at least eleven manuscripts featuring Daniel have been discovered, eight of which are manuscripts of the book of Daniel. This is important since the large number of preserved copies is a clear indication of its authoritative status. This would seem unlikely to have been the case if the book had just been published.

[3] Isa 58:5; Jer 6:26; Jonah 3:6; Jdt 4:11; Esth 4:3; Matt 11:21.

[4] Cf. Dan 1:1-2.

[5] Walter Brueggemann, *Theology of the Old Testament: Testimony, Dispute, Advocacy* (Minneapolis: Fortress Press, 1997), 435.

[6] Daniel I. Block, *The Gods of the Nations: Studies in Ancient Near Eastern National Theology*, 2nd ed. (Grand Rapids MI: Baker Books, 2000), 134-35.

[7] Ibid., 140-43.

[8] Ezek 8:3-18.

[9] Ezek 10:1-22 and 11:22-25.

[10] Ezek 11:7-11.

[11] Ezek 11:16.

[12] Ezek 11:18-21.

[13] Ezek 11:22-23.

[14] Block, *Gods of the Nations*, 138.

[15] Lev 26:14-39; Deut 27:14-26; 28:15-68.

[16] Block, *Gods of the Nations*, 104; see also 101-109, a section titled "The Effects of Feudal Infidelity."

[17] Cf. Ps 145:17.

[18] Exod 13:3, 9, 14, 16; Deut 5:15; 6:21; 7:8; 9:26; 26:8; Jer 32:21.

[19] Cf. Pss 25:11; 79:9; 109:21; 143:11.

[20] John E. Goldingay, *Daniel* (Dallas: Word, 1989), 246.

[21] 2 Kgs 22:13; Jer 3:25; 14:20; Ezra 9:7; Neh 1:6; 9:2, 16.

[22] Goldingay, *Daniel*, 248.

[23] Ibid.

[24] Gleason L. Archer, Jr., "Daniel," in Frank E. Gaebelein, ed., *The Expositor's Bible Commentary*, vol. 7 (Grand Rapids MI: Zondervan, 1985), 110.

[25] Mark 15:38.

[26] W. Sibley Towner, "Daniel," in James L. Mays, ed., *The HarperCollins Bible Commentary* (New York: HarperSanFrancisco, 2000), 631.

[27] Ibid.

[28] ANET, 316.

[29] Edwin M. Yamauchi, "Persians," in Alfred J. Hoerth, Gerald L. Mattingly, and Edwin M. Yamauchi, *Peoples of the Old Testament World* (Grand Rapids MI: Baker Books, 1994), 112.

[30] Norman K. Gottwald, *All the Kingdoms of the Earth: Israelite Prophecy and International Relations in the Ancient Near East* (New York: Harper and Row, 1964), 335.

[31] Cf. Dan 6:1-2.

[32] Leon J. Wood, *A Survey of Israel's History*, rev. (Grand Rapids MI: Zondervan, 1986), 327.

[33] Exod 13:3.

[34] Gal 5:1; 1 Pet 2:16.

[35] Lev 26:14-39; Deut 28:15-68.

[36] Calvin Miller, *The Table of Inwardness: Nurturing Our Inner Life in Christ* (Downers Grove IL: InterVarsity Press, 1984), 66.

[37] Ibid., 67.


## Chapter 10

[1] Author unknown.

[2] Homer Hailey, *A Commentary on the Minor Prophets* (Grand Rapids MI: Baker Book House, 1972), 62.

[3] James L. Crenshaw, "Jonah, the Book of," in Bruce M. Metzger and Michael D. Coogan, eds., *The Oxford Companion to the Bible* (Oxford: Oxford University Press, 1993), 381.

[4] Urartu, near the Caspian Sea.

[5] For more on Assyria, see William C. Gwaltney, Jr., "Assyrians," in Alfred J. Hoerth, Gerald L. Mattingly, and Edwin M. Yamauchi, eds., *Peoples of the Old Testament World* (Grand Rapids MI: Baker Books, 1994), 77-106.

[6] Yehoshua Gitay, "Jonah: The Prophecy of Antirhetoric," in Astrid B. Beck, Andrew H. Bartelt, Paul R. Raabe, and Chris A. Franke, eds., *Fortunate the Eyes that See: Essays in Honor of David Noel Freedman in Celebration of His Seventieth Birthday* (Grand Rapids MI: Eerdmans, 1995), 197, my emphasis.

[7] Ibid.

[8] Gitay, "Jonah: The Prophecy of Antirhetoric," 203.

[9] D. W. B. Robinson, "Jonah," in Donald Guthrie and J. A. Motyer, eds., *The New Bible Commentary* (Grand Rapids MI: Eerdmans, 1970), 751.

[10] H. L. Ellison, "Jonah," in Frank E. Gaebelein, ed., *The Expositor's Bible Commentary*, vol. 7 (Grand Rapids MI: Zondervan, 1985), 384.

[11] Cf. Rom 2:1.

[12] H.-J. Zobel, "hesed," in *Theological Dictionary of the Old Testament*, vol. 5, ed. G. Johannes Botterweck and Helmer Ringgren (Grand Rapids MI: Eerdmans, 1986), 62.

[13] Ibid.

[14] Ibid.

[15] TWOT, 1:305.

[16] Num 14:18; Neh 9:17; Pss 86:15; 103:8; 145:8; Joel 2:13.

[17] T. Desmond Alexander, "Jonah," in David W. Baker, Bruce Waltke, and T. Desmond Alexander, *Obadiah, Jonah and Micah* (Downers Grove IL: InterVarsity Press, 1988), 127.

[18] Walter Brueggemann, *Theology of the Old Testament: Testimony, Dispute, Advocacy* (Minneapolis: Fortress Press, 1997), 502.

[19] Ibid., 513.

[20] Exod 12:38.

[21] Duane L. Christenson, "A New Israel: The Righteous from among All Nations," in Avraham Gileadi, ed., *Israel's Apostasy and Restoration: Essays in Honor of Roland K. Harrison* (Grand Rapids MI: Baker Book House, 1988), 253.

[22] Brueggemann, *Theology of the Old Testament*, 524.

[23] Ibid.

[24] Ibid., 523.

[25] Christenson, "A New Israel," 255.

[26] Ibid.

[27] The comments made here regarding the theological message of Jonah are adapted primarily from Raymond B. Dillard and Tremper Longman III, *An Introduction to the Old Testament* (Grand Rapids, MI: Zondervan, 1994), 394-95.

[28] Douglas Stuart, *Hosea-Jonah*, WBC 31 (Waco TX: Word, 1987), 434.

[29] Matt 12:41; cf. Luke 15:10.

[30] John 1:6-14.

[31] Luke 2:32.

[32] Mark Toolery, "Missions Expert Laments Decline of Mainline Missions," *Good News* 35/1 (July/August 2001): 37.

[33] John R. Fitzmier and Randall Balmer, "A Poultice for the Bite of the Cobra: The Hocking Report and Presbyterian Missions in the Middle Decades of the Twentieth Century," in *Reimagining Denominationalism*, ed. Robert Bruce Mullin and Russell E. Richey (New York: Oxford University Press, 1994), 105-109, as cited in Milton J. Coalter, John M. Mulder, and Louis B. Weeks, *Vital Signs: The Promise of Mainstream Protestantism* (Grand Rapids MI: Eerdmans, 1996), 92.

[34] Eric S. Fife and Arthur F. Glasser (Downers Grove IL: InterVarsity Press, 1961).

[35] John Carden (London: Highway Press, 1964).

[36] Ralph Dodge (New York: Revell, 1964).

[37] James T. Sherer (New York: Prentice Hall, 1964).

[38] Dean M. Kelley, *Why Conservative Churches Are Growing: A Study in Sociology of Religion* (New York: Harper and Row, 1972).

[39] See also Ralph K. Hawkins, "Is the Church Moving into a Postdenominational Age?" in *Simul Iustus et Peccator: Essays in Honor of Donald S. Armentrout*, ed. Ralph K. Hawkins (Sewanee TN: School of Theology, 2003), 239-61.

[40] Thomas C. Oden, *The Rebirth of Orthodoxy: Signs of New Life in Christianity* (New York: HarperSanFrancisco, 2003), 139-55.

## Chapter 11

[1] Marvin A. Sweeney, "Habakkuk," in James L. Mays, ed., *The HarperCollins Bible Commentary* (New York: HarperSanFrancisco, 2000), 669.

[2] Because of the musical notations within Habakkuk and the form of the psalm in chapter 3. Cf. Ezra 3:10; Neh 12:27.

[3] Sweeney, "Habakkuk," 668.

[4] Norman K. Gottwald, *All the Kingdoms of the Earth: Israelite Prophecy and International Relations in the Ancient Near East* (New York: Harper and Row Publishers, 1964), 233.

[5] Ralph L. Smith, *Micah-Malachi* (Waco TX: Word Books, 1984), 103.

[6] Ibid., 104.

[7] David W. Baker, *Nahum, Habakkuk and Zephaniah* (Downers Grove IL: InterVarsity Press, 1988), 47.

[8] As the superscription in 3:1 titles the section.

[9] Baker, *Nahum, Habakkuk and Zephaniah*, 76.

[10] E.g., Exod 14:2–15.22; Deut 11:4.

[11] Cf. vv. 9-11, 15; Exod 14:21; 15:8, 10.

[12] Baker, *Nahum, Habakkuk and Zephaniah*, 76.

[13] Carl E. Amerding, "Habakkuk," in Frank E. Gaebelein, ed., *The Expositor's Bible Commentary*, vol. 7 (Grand Rapids MI: Zondervan, 1985), 533.

[14] Cf. Ps 32:11; Isa 25:9; Joel 2:23 et al.

[15] The expression is also used in anticipation of the conquest. Cf. Deut 33:29.

[16] Baker, *Nahum, Habakkuk and Zephaniah*, 77.

[17] Exod 15:2, 13.

[18] Amerding, "Habakkuk," 534.

[19] Walter Brueggemann, *Theology of the Old Testament: Testimony, Dispute, Advocacy* (Minneapolis: Fortress Press, 1997), 492-527.

[20] Ibid., 493.

[21] Ibid., 503.

[22] Amos 1:13; 2:1.

[23] Brueggemann, *Theology of the Old Testament*, 503.

[24] Ibid., 522-23.

[25] Ibid., 523.

[26] Ibid., 513.

[27] Baker, *Nahum, Habakkuk and Zephaniah*, 47.

[28] Cal Thomas, "Was God Behind the Terrorist Attacks? A Reply to Religious Broadcasters," in *Human Events* 57/35 (24 September 2001): 14.

[29] Billy Graham, "When Life Seems at Its Darkest," reprinted in *Human Events* 57/35 (24 September 2001): 12.

[30] Janet Chismar, "God Returns to America's Public Square," *Religion Today* (17 September 17 2001); online at <Featurestory@lists.crosswalk.com>.

[31] Ibid.

[32] Ruth-Alice von Bismarck and Ulrich Kabitz, eds., *Love Letters from Cell 92: The Correspondance between Dietrich Bonhoeffer and Maria von Wedemeyer, 1943–1945* (Nashville: Abingdon Press, 1992), 118.

[33] Ibid.

[34] Ibid.

[35] Carl F. H. Henry, *God, Revelation and Authority* 6 (Waco TX: Word, 1983), 259.

[36] See especially Matthew Fox, *Original Blessing: A Primer in Creation Spirituality* (Santa Fe NM: Bear & Company, 1983) and, more recently, *Sins of the Spirit, Blessings of the Flesh: Lessons for Transforming Evil in Soul and Society* (New York: Harmony Books, 1999).

[37] Carl F. H. Henry, *The Protestant Dilemma* (Grand Rapids MI: Eerdmans, 1949), 19.

[38] It is not clear whether returning to the ground from which they were made (v. 19) is one of the consequences of the fall. John H. Sailhamer argues that it is here that the verdict of death, warned of before the fall (2:17), is enacted ("Genesis," in *The Expositor's Bible Commentary*, vol. 2, ed. Frank E. Gaebelein [Grand Rapids MI: Zondervan, 1990], 57). James Barr, on the other hand, argues that death appears to have been part of the original human condition established at creation (James Barr, *The Garden of Eden and the Hope of Immortality* [Minneapolis: Fortress Press, 1992], esp. 21-56).

[39] Donald Guthrie, *New Testament Theology* (Downers Grove IL: InterVarsity Press, 1981), 936-37.

[40] Carl F. H. Henry, *The God Who Shows Himself* (Waco TX: Word, 1966), 78-79.

## Chapter 12

[1] Cf. e.g., 2 Sam 2:4-7, when David is anointed king over the house of Judah.

[2] This concept is discussed in chapters 9–11.

[3] They did experience a short period of freedom in the intertestamental period, under the Maccabeans.

[4] The term "Second Temple Judaism" refers to Judaism from 515 BC, when the second temple was completed, to AD 70, when it was destroyed. For an overview of this period and its literature, see Anthony J. Tomasino, *Judaism before Jesus: The Ideas and Events that Shaped the New Testament World* (Downers Grove IL: InterVarsity Press, 2003).

[5] For a detailed review of the background of the term "messiah," see Marinus De Jonge, "Messiah," in David Noel Freedman, ed., *The Anchor Bible Dictionary*, vol. 4 (New York: Doubleday, 1992), 777-88.

[6] *JW* 7.2.2, par. 29.

[7] Mark 15:16-20.

[8] *Ant.* 20.5.1, par. 97.

[9] *Ant.* 20.8.6, par. 169-170. Cf. *JW* 2.13.5, par. 261-62.

[10] The dates for the revolt are AD 132–135.

[11] Richard A. Horsley, "Messianic Movements in Judaism," in Freedman, ed., *Anchor Bible Dictionary*, vol. 4, 796.

[12] *Ant.* 20.8.10, par. 186-87; 20.9.3, par. 208; *JW* 2.13.3, par. 254-57.

[13] Oscar Cullman, *The State in the New Testament* (New York: Charles Scribner's Sons, 1956), 14-17.

[14] This Simon is listed in Mark 3:18 and Matt 10:4 as "Simon the Canaanite." Cullman argues that the Greek word traditionally translated "Canaanite," however, is really a transliteration of the Aramaic word for Zealots, which is *Kenana*. If Cullman is correct, then both of these passages should be translated "Simon the Zealot."

[15] Luke 9:54.

[16] Mark 10:37.

[17] Matt 21:7-9; Mark 11:7-10; Luke 19:35-40; John 12:12-15.

[18] William H. Heinrich, "The Enigma of the Palm Branch," in *Bible and Spade* 14/2 (Spring 2001): 55-57.

[19] Ibid., 56.

[20] Ibid.

[21] For a comprehensive study of the Zealots, see Martin Hengel, *The Zealots: Investigations into the Jewish Freedom Movement in the Period from Herod I until 70 A.D.*, trans. David Smith (Edinburgh: T & T Clark, 1989).

[22] Joachim Jeremias, *Jesus' Promise to the Nations* (London: SCM Press, 1958), 43-44.

[23] John 6:15.

[24] Mark 8:32.

[25] Matt 21:7-9.

[26] Matt 26:39-44.

[27] Matt 26:53.

[28] Oscar Cullman, *Jesus and the Revolutionaries* (New York: Harper and Row, 1970), 40-41.

[29] The Greek word traditionally translated "thieves" here is *lestes*, which means "insurrectionist."

[30] Doron Mendels, *The Rise and Fall of Jewish Nationalism* (New York: Doubleday, 1992), 229.

[31] N. T. Wright, *The Challenge of Jesus: Rediscovering Who Jesus Was and Is* (Downers Grove IL: InterVarsity Press, 1999), 46.

[32] For a brief survey of theories, see Warren Carter, "Lord's Prayer," in David Noel Freedman, ed., *Eerdmans Dictionary of the Bible* (Grand Rapids MI: Eerdmans, 2000), 821.

[33] Bernhard Lang, "The 'Our Father' as John the Baptist's Political Prayer: A Ritual Response to the Absence of God's Kingdom," in David Penchansky and Paul L. Redditt, eds., *Shall Not the Judge of All the Earth Do What Is Right? Studies on the Nature of God in Tribute to James L. Crenshaw* (Winona Lake IN: Eisenbrauns, 2000), 239-54.

[34] J. L. Houlden, "Lord's Prayer," in Freedman, ed., *Anchor Bible Dictionary*, vol. 4, 360.

[35] Lang, "The 'Our Father' as John the Baptist's Political Prayer," 244.

[36] Joachim Jeremias, *The Central Message of the New Testament* (New York: Charles Scribner's Sons, 1965), 20.

[37] Babylonian Talmud, Tractate Berachoth, 40a (Bar.) par. Tractate Sanhedrin, 70b (Bar.), quoted by Jeremias, *Central Message of the New Testament*, 20.

[38] Cf. Luke 15:21.

[39] Jeremias, *Central Message of the New Testament*, 21.

[40] 3 Macc 6:3.

[41] Lang, "The 'Our Father' as John the Baptist's Political Prayer," 244.

[42] Ibid., 245.

[43] Jeremias, *Central Message of the New Testament*, 29.

[44] Lang, "The 'Our Father' as John the Baptist's Political Prayer," 245.

[45] Cited by Lang, "The 'Our Father' as John the Baptist's Political Prayer," 246.

[46] John Paul Meier, *A Marginal Jew: Rethinking the Historical Jesus* (New York: Doubleday, 1994), 299.

[47] Gen 12:1-3; 15; 17.

[48] Meier, *A Marginal Jew*, 300.

[49] Lang, "The 'Our Father' as John the Baptist's Political Prayer," 246.

[50] Ibid., 247.

[51] For a detailed review of the difficulties and proposals for interpretation, see Arland J. Hultgren, "The Bread Petition of the Lord's Prayer," in Arland J. Hultgren and Barbara Hall, eds., *Christ and His Communities: Essays in Honor of Reginald H. Fuller* (Cincinnati: Forward Movement Publications, 1990), 41-54.

[52] D. A. Carson, "Matthew," in Frank E. Gaebelein, ed., *The Expositor's Bible Commentary*, vol. 8 (Grand Rapids MI: Zondervan, 1984), 171.

[53] Raymond E. Brown, *An Introduction to the New Testament* (New York: Doubleday, 1997), 180.

[54] The wedding at Cana in John 2:1-11.

[55] Meier, *A Marginal Jew*, 301.

[56] This is acknowledged in the prayer of thanks recited by the congregation after having received the bread and wine, as included in the liturgy of Roman Catholic and mainline Protestant liturgical books.

[57] Lang, "The 'Our Father' as John the Baptist's Political Prayer," 247.

[58] Ibid., 248.

[59] Ibid., 250.

[60] Meier, *A Marginal Jew*, 301.

[61] 2 Macc 1:25.

[62] Lang refers to Pss 25:22; 28:9; 53:6; 80:20.

[63] Lang, "The 'Our Father' as John the Baptist's Political Prayer," 250.

[64] Jesus announced the inauguration of the kingdom of God in Mark 1:15 and Luke 4:16-30.

[65] Carson, "Matthew," 173.

[66] Houlden, "Lord's Prayer," 359.

[67] Wright, *The Challenge of Jesus*, 53.

[68] Ibid.

[69] Clyde Wilcox, *God's Warriors: The Christian Right in Twentieth-Century America* (Baltimore MD: Johns Hopkins University Press, 1992), 232.

[70] Ibid.

[71] Sara Diamond, *Not By Politics Alone: The Enduring Influence of the Christian Right* (New York: Guilford Press, 1998), ix.

[72] See the interesting discussion of Cal Thomas and Ed Dobson, *Blinded by Might: Can the Religious Right Save America?* (Grand Rapids MI: Zondervan, 1999).

[73] Ralph Reed, *Active Faith: How Christians are Changing the Soul of American Politics* (New York: Free Press, 1996), 279.

[74] See, for example, the new report by David Devlin-Foltz, ed., *Finding a New Voice: The Public Role of Mainline Protestantism* (Washington, DC: Aspen Institute, 2001).

[75] I have made a lengthy case for this in my article, "Are We Living in a Postdenominational Age?" in Ralph K. Hawkins, ed., *Simul Iustus et Peccator: Essays in Honor of Donald S. Armentrout* (Sewanee TN: University of the South Press, forthcoming).

[76] Reed, *Active Faith*, 267.

[77] Quoted in Reed, *Active Faith*, 267.

[78] Laurence Hull Stookey, *Baptism: Christ's Act in the Church* (Nashville: Abingdon Press, 1982), 17.

[79] Ibid., 103-104.

[80] J. B. Lightfoot and J. R. Harmer, eds., *The Apostolic Fathers*, 2nd ed. (Grand Rapids MI: Baker Book House, 1989), 153.

[81] Justo L. Gonzalez, *A History of Christian Thought*, vol. 1, rev. (Nashville: Abingdon Press, 1987), 69-70.

[82] Reinhold Niebuhr, *The Children of Light and the Children of Darkness: A Vindication of Democracy and a Critique of Its Traditional Defence* (New York: Charles Scribner's Sons, 1949), 189-90.

[83] Geza Vermes, *Jesus the Jew* (Philadelphia: Fortress, 1974).

[84] Burton Mack, *A Myth of Innocence* (Philadelphia: Fortress Press, 1988).

[85] Elisabeth Schüssler Fiorenza, *In Memory of Her* (New York: Crossroad, 1983).

[86] Marcus J. Borg, *Meeting Jesus Again for the First Time: The Historical Jesus and the Heart of Contemporary Faith* (New York: HarperCollins, 1995), 31-32.

[87] John Dominic Crossan, *The Historical Jesus: The Life of a Mediterranean Jewish Peasant* (San Francisco: Harper San Francisco, 1991).

[88] Norman Perrin and Dennis C. Duling, *The New Testament: An Introduction*, 2nd ed. (San Diego: Harcourt Brace Jovanovich, 1982), 398.

[89] Robert W. Funk, Roy W. Hoover, and the Jesus Seminar, *The Five Gospels: The Search for the Authentic Words of Jesus* (New York: Macmillan, 1993), 4.

[90] For a review of the Second Temple texts, see Tomasino, *Judaism before Jesus*, 17-47.

[91] Cf. the "Son of God" text, 4Q246, in Geza Vermes, *The Complete Dead Sea Scrolls in English* (New York: The Penguin Press, 1997), 576-77.

[92] Israel Knohl, *The Messiah Before Jesus: The Suffering Servant of the Dead Sea Scrolls* (Berkeley: University of California Press, 2000).

[93] Cf. 4Q521, titled "A Messianic Apocalypse," in Vermes, *Complete Dead Sea Scrolls*, 391-92.

[94] See Richard S. Hess and M. Daniel Carroll R., eds., *Israel's Messiah in the Bible and the Dead Sea Scrolls* (Grand Rapids MI: Baker Academic, 2003).

[95] E.g., 1 Cor 8:1-6; Phil 2:5-11; Gal 4:1-7 et al. See N. T. Wright, *The Challenge of Jesus: Rediscovering Who Jesus Was and Is* (Downers Grove IL: InterVarsity Press, 1999), 96-125.

[96] While Colossians is sometimes considered to be "post-Pauline," this particular passage is often regarded as an earlier poem incorporated by the author of the epistle.

## Postscript

[1] William G. Dever, *Who Were the Early Israelites and Where Did They Come From?* (Grand Rapids MI: Eerdmans, 2003), 128.

[2] See Ralph K. Hawkins, review of *Who Were the Early Israelites and Where Did They Come From?* by Wiliam G. Dever, *Biblical Theology Bulletin* 33/3 (Fall 2003): 118-19.

[3] Yehezkel Kaufmann, *The Religion of Israel, from Its Beginnings to the Babylonian Exile*, translated and abridged by Moshe Greenburg (Chicago: University of Chicago Press, 1960).

[4] Ibid., 2.

[5] William Foxwell Albright, *Yahweh and the Gods of Canaan* (University of London: School of Oriental and African Studies, 1968; reprint, Winona Lake IN: Eisenbrauns, 1990), 206-207.

[6] *Divine Commitment and Human Obligation: Selected Writings of David Noel Freedman*, ed. John R. Huddlestun, vol. 1, *History and Religion* (Grand Rapids MI: Eerdmans, 1997), 231.